Dear Friends:

    Price Chopper Supermarkets is pleased to provide this book for your reading enjoyment.

    It gives us great pleasure to be part of the Tri-Centennial and the publication of this volume.

    Experiencing Albany: Perspectives on a Grand City's Past is an outstanding contribution to recording the proud history of the city of Albany.

Neil M. Golub
President & Chief Operating Officer
Price Chopper Supermarkets

EXPERIENCING A·L·B·A·N·Y

PERSPECTIVES ON A GRAND CITY'S PAST

Edited by
Anne F. Roberts
and
Judith A. VanDyk

The
Nelson A.
Rockefeller
Institute
of
Government

State University
of New York

The
Nelson A.
Rockefeller
Institute
of
Government

State University
of New York

Clifton R. Wharton, Jr.
    Chairman, Board of Overseers

Warren F. Ilchman
    Director

James K. Morrell
    Deputy Director

Alison M. Chandler
    Publications Director

Barbara A. Plocharczyk
    Marketing Director

Susan C. Lenz, Susan B. Campbell,
Veronica Evangelista, Diane Naughton, Elaine Y. Phillips
    Staff Assistants

B. Michael Kantrowitz
    Special Editorial Consultant

Cover Design: The Type & Design Center, Inc.
Cover Illustrations: Jonathan P. Slocum
Printing: The Saratoga Printing Co., Inc.

The Nelson A. Rockefeller Institute of Government
State University of New York
411 State Street, Albany, New York 12203
(518) 472-1300

Price $15.00

ISBN 0-914341-04-9

April 1986

EXPERIENCING ALBANY

A·L·B·A·N·Y

TABLE OF CONTENTS

THE PEOPLE AND HISTORY OF ALBANY

INDUSTRY AND TRANSPORTATION

ALBANY POLITICS

ARCHITECTURE

ALBANY ART

POPULAR CULTURE

FINAL RESTING PLACES

FURTHER WORD ON ALBANY   226

Welcome to Albany

This grand city of Albany is 300 years old. Albany has operated under its city charter continuously since 1686, longer than any other city in the United States. And throughout this history, it has acquired a rich and fascinating heritage.

The following collection is the culmination of a series presented at historic sites throughout the city during 1985. Participants included some of our city's best informed and most colorful experts on the region's heritage.

The *Experiencing Albany* series has been preserved for us in the pages of this book. Tap this well of knowledge for yourself and learn more about this wonderful city of ours.

Thomas M. Whalen, III
mayor of Albany

The publication of this volume was made possible through
the generous support of the following institutions:

Albany Academy for Girls
Albany International Corporation
Allied Business Equipment
Americana Inn
Capital District Dermatology Association
Capital Newspapers
Certified Allergy Consultants
Cheese Connection
College of Saint Rose
First American Bank of New York
Golub Foundation
Bob Howard Realty, Inc.
Hudson Valley Paper Company
New York Telephone Company
Norstar Bancorp, Inc.
Roberts Real Estate
Siena College
SUNYA Research Foundation
SUNYA Friends of the Libraries
L.A. Swyer Company, Inc.
Zubres, D'Agostino, & Hoblock

Also thanks to the following individuals for their support:

Virginia Abele
Dorice Brickman
Carol Bullard
Betty Crummey
Estelle Freedman
Harold Hanson
Dr. and Mrs. James Hoehn
Richard H. Kendall
William Kennedy
Anne LaFalce
Thompson Littlefield
William McEwan
Florence Milano
K. L. Rabinoff-Goldman
Warren E. Roberts
John Smircich

Introduction

Herein lies a portrait gallery of the historic city of Albany in its 300th year. This collection of essays offers visions of our grand city through a variety of disciplines: Through the eyes of the anthropologist, archaeologist, historian, economist, sociologist, artist, architect, and politician, we can gain new appreciation for its unique, even extraordinary heritage.

Operating under the nation's oldest city charter, Albany is replete with anecdotes and records of a rich and vital past. Those forces which first shaped the city and its environs still influence the lives of Albanians.

Experiencing Albany was conceived as a series of investigations into Albany's past which would bring a new understanding to present audiences. Indeed, the essays in this collection bring new insights into the city's local, urban, and oral history.

It is my hope that this collection will be a model for other American cities as they celebrate their own anniversaries.

This project was funded by the National Endowment for the Humanities and made possible through the cooperation of SUNYA University Libraries, New York State Museum and Library, Albany Public Library, the Albany Institute of History and Art, and the city of Albany.

Anne F. Roberts
project director

THE PEOPLE AND HISTORY OF ALBANY

Anthropology is the study of human culture and, as a discipline, is broadly defined. Anthropologists most often focus their work in one of the subdisciplines of anthropology. One of these is archaeology. While archaeology is sometimes taught in classics departments, classical archaeology has traditionally been aligned with history and art. Anthropological archaeology concerns the processes of human activity over time. Many of the important processes that have produced human culture are known to us only through archaeology. After all, most of our history, which extends back millions of years, is prehistoric. Thus, most of the extinct processes that made us what we are came and went before recorded history. Archaeology is our only access.

Archaeological research is fraught with traps and deceptions. It is easy to interpret evidence in light of one's own prejudices rather than scientific reasoning. It is difficult to construct hypotheses that do not defy testing. This paper points out some of the ways we can find a path through this minefield.

The Europeans and American Indians deeply affected each other during the sixteenth century. There was rapid technological change as the Indians adopted guns, glass, and brass; the Europeans adopted the pelting of beaver fur and Indian crops. But the most catastrophic aspect of this cultural collision was the introduction of European "crowd infections" into the Western Hemisphere. The Europeans had experienced their own epidemic catastrophes in the fourteenth century, when perhaps a third of them died of the Black Death. But they had also generated strains of smallpox and measles, epidemics that were only possible in dense populations. The American Indians had not been living in dense concentrations long enough to have developed their own crowd infections, and they had no experience with these European diseases. The Mohawk Valley offers a rare laboratory in which to measure the effects of the epidemic catastrophes of the sixteenth and seventeenth centuries. Albany was the point of first contact, and the port of entry for those epidemics.

THE FIRST DUTCH SETTLERS MEET THE NATIVE AMERICANS

Dean Snow

The goal of the Mohawk Valley Project is to locate, map, and test Mohawk village sites occupied from the last centuries before Europeans came to America until 1800. Hundreds of sites have already been discovered, and nearly 100 of them are known to date to the critical period (1500-1800). Major excavations have been carried out on a dozen sites in this and earlier projects. Sites which are large, historically significant, or in danger of destruction are being nominated for inclusion on the National Register of Historic Places. Although some sites have been destroyed in the past, public awareness of the importance of Mohawk Indian heritage has drastically slowed the trend.

Local residents have long known the sites. This helps the archaeologist's search. As a result, project crews are able to move quickly to the solution of specific problems. In each case, the first step is to determine when and for how long each village was occupied by a Mohawk community. Ultimately, the investigators expect to have a nearly complete list of Mohawk villages and towns

and to be able to trace the movements of communities over time.

Like the Iroquois, the Mohawk periodically moved their villages. A single community could leave behind several village sites in the course of a single century. This is an advantage rather than a disadvantage for archaeologists. While sites in other parts of North America are often confused by long periods of occupation, Mohawk sites tend to be snapshots of past village life unconfused by earlier or later remains. Just as important, Mohawk villages tend to be tight clusters of long houses, each of which was built according to a fairly regular plan. The mapping of such sites is relatively quick and easy; it can be accomplished with little destructive excavation.

When the Mohawk Valley Project ends, perhaps as much as ten years from now, Mohawk cultural history may be the best documented of any American Indian nation. Moreover, the project will yield important scientific results unavailable elsewhere in North America. Mohawk villages and towns can be almost completely inventoried. They are so clear and consistent in form that archaeologists are able to estimate their original population sizes with unusual accuracy. Because of this, scientists will eventually be able to make an accurate estimate of the total Mohawk population for any point in time before, during, and after the epidemics and wars which brought such hardship to them.

The Indian populations of the New World experienced at least one abrupt, major, demographic shift--the catastrophic population decline resulting from the introduction of European diseases during and after the sixteenth century. There may have been other major shifts during the course of prehistory. Many archaeologists infer that there were major population increases in eastern North America accompanying the adoption of full-scale maize agriculture around the end of the first millenium A.D. Some archaeologists infer declines in some areas after 10,000 B.C., and some infer population peaks about 4,000 years ago. While some efforts have been made to explore prehistoric demography archaeologically, many have suffered from inadequately developed theory, and all have been denied the benefit of comparison with estimates based on documented historic population levels. The latter problem stems from inadequate assessments of the impact of epidemics and a consequent uncertainty about what fractions of original populations the known post-epidemic remnants represent. The principal difficulty lies in the extreme mortality rates; even when we have accurate data on remnant populations, small differences in assumed mortality rates yield very different results.

Thus, although the seriousness of historic epidemics has long been understood, accurate measurements have not been made. Death rates above 90 percent were not uncommon in the seventeenth century. The epidemics began in Mexico shortly after 1520, but current evidence indicates that they did not reach the Mohawk until over a century later. An account of Mohawk villages written in 1634 describes communities just after the first severe epidemic, which struck in 1633. The total Mohawk population prior to the epidemic is estimated at 10,600. In the decades which followed, it crashed to a fraction of that, and only came back up to the 1633 level in the twentieth century.

A Thermonuclear Analogy

The effects of direct contact between Europeans and Americans were certainly devastating for the latter. Crowd epidemics which had already ravaged the Eastern Hemisphere in previous centuries, and to which European populations were already accustomed, ravaged some American Indian communities within a few years of Columbus' voyages. Smallpox was introduced into Santo Domingo and Mexico with the Spanish conquest. The first severe epidemic, the exact nature of which has not been established, wiped out Indian communities in southeastern New England beginning in 1616, clearing the way for the pilgrims of 1620. Contact between the Dutch and Mohawk around Albany did not lead to an immediate epidemic, but smallpox and perhaps measles did their grim work along the Mohawk beginning in 1633.

It is difficult to grasp the magnitude of these epidemics. The only analogy familiar to modern Americans is the probable outcome of a thermonuclear war. In the 1960s, the Department of Defense decided that 20 to 25 percent mortality rates and a minimum of 50 percent loss of industry was unacceptably high for any modern nation, and that the ability to inflict at least that much damage was a sufficient deterrent. A more specific example might be the explosion of ten relatively small nuclear devices over Boston, resulting in nearly 100 percent prompt casualties in Boston, and (assuming a northeast wind) 80 percent mortality as far as the Rhode Island line. Beyond that, there would be 50 percent mortality in Providence and 20 percent in Newport. As appalling as these figures are, it is not an exaggeration to conclude similar percentages in the same area for the 1616 epidemic. The overall mortality at that time was probably about 85 percent. My analysis of New England population indicates that the Mohegan-Pequot, who lived in the eastern portion of what is now Connecticut, had a population of 16,000 and a population density of 266 per 100 square kilometers. The combined effects of the 1616 and 1633 epidemics on the Mohegan-Pequot amounted to the death of 81 percent of their population. The Mohawk, who were less numerous and less dense, escaped the 1616 epidemic. Still, the 1633 epidemic probably killed about 55 percent of all Mohawk. Van der Donck, a contemporary observer, estimates that by 1656, the Mohawk were at only 10 percent of their previous number.

The Mohawk in 1634

The Mohawk nation was not significantly affected by epidemics prior to 1633. Demographic readjustments in the Mohawk Valley occurred largely in the 45 years between 1633 and 1678. We can use documentary evidence to specify conditions in 1633 and later and archaeological data to test and refine our conclusions.

The first step is to establish a base line for 1633, something which, fortunately, we are able to do on the basis of a journal written in 1634-35 by Harmen Myndertsz Van den Bogaert. Van den Bogaert was sent from Albany with two other men, to visit the Mohawk and Oneida in an attempt to discover why the fur trade had fallen off. They left late in 1634 and returned early the following year. Van den Bogaert's description of eight Mohawk villages is the earliest providing a relatively detailed assessment of settlement pattern. He clearly states that an epidemic had been recently active in the villages, and, in the case of the largest village (Tenotoge), he indicates that the palisade was in disrepair. He describes long houses in several villages as having lengths as great as 80, 90, or 100 "steps" (as opposed to paces or strides). In one village he implies that houses 100 steps long were average, but at another village (Canagere) he counted 16 houses that were 50, 60, 70, or 80 steps long, and another only 16 steps long. The average length of the houses he observed, in all eight villages, appears to have been 80 steps. Greater lengths are cited as extremes.

Mohawk long houses were composed of a center aisle with parallel rows of compartments, each compartment occupied by a nuclear family. The ends of the houses tended to be storage areas rather than residential compartments. Families in facing compartments shared cooking hearths strung along the center line of the house. These features have been archaeologically documented many times. Van den Bogaert gives us measurements in increments of 10 steps, suggesting a standard compartment length of the same. We should also allow for storage compartments of 10 steps at both ends of all houses. Thus, an 80-step house is assumed to have had only six facing pairs of compartments, enough to accommodate 12 families.

Van den Bogaert mentions, in his journal, that each house had four, five, or six cooking hearths, numbers which we know to be too low for houses up to 100 steps in length. However, an average of six hearths is appropriate for houses averaging 80 steps in length. Moreover, epidemics had begun to reduce the population, and many Mohawks were probably living in houses designed to accommodate a larger population. That is, the houses and villages described by Van den Bogaert were built to accommodate the pre-epidemic populations of 1633 and earlier.

Table 1 lists the eight villages with the numbers of houses Van den Bogaert counted in each. Because an 80-step house probably contained six hearths, we can derive the number of hearths for seven of the villages simply by multiplying this number by the house counts. In the case of Canagere, Van den Bogaert provides more precise figures allowing us to calculate 73 hearths.

Van den Bogaert's figures generate a total of 1,057 hearths. If each hearth was shared by two families, we need only estimate the number of persons per family to derive village populations. Isaack de Rasieres observes that in 1628, Indian families were small, "so that it is a wonder when a woman has three or four children." In three well-documented 1730s long house villages outside Detroit, there were actually two or three families per hearth, apparently depending upon family size. Smaller nuclear families probably joined to make more efficient use of long house compartments. When analyzed, the Detroit data yield 9.3 people per hearth, or 4.7 per compartment. Although the figures are based on estimates, they are strong enough to justify adopting a standard of five individuals per compartment. Thus, Table 1 shows population figures based on a standard of 10 individuals per hearth.

Table 1

Mohawk Villages in 1634

Villages	Houses	Hearths	Inhabitants
Onekagoncka	36	216	2,160
Canawarode	6	36	360
Schatsyerosy	12	72	720
Canagere	16	73	730
Schanidisse	32	192	1,920
Osquage	9	54	540
Cawaoge	14	84	840
Tenotoge	55	330	3,300
Totals	180	1,057	10,570

Earlier and Later Evidence

Having established a population base line of 10,570 for the Mohawk in 1633 on the basis of documentary sources, we turn to archaeological tests of our hypotheses. The Mohawk Valley is an ideal region in which to measure demographic changes by archaeological means. Late prehistoric and early historic sites tend to be single component sites occupied for about two decades each. Most are located on good soils which are currently cultivated, and few appear to have been lost to modern construction. Professional and amateur interest in the sites has been high for over a century. Therefore, few sites are complicated by earlier or later occupations, few have been destroyed prior to detection, and it is likely that most have been discovered.

One test involves the investigation of a site visited by Van den Bogaert in 1633 in order to obtain a count of houses and hearths. We have the site of Canagere, the village for which Van den Bogaert provides the most detailed information. The trade goods date to the appropriate decade (1630-1640). The Canagere site appears not to have had a palisade, which, according to Van den Bogaert, was the only large village or "castle" lacking a palisade. The site is properly located in terms of Van den Bogaert's description of the valley and the locations of neighboring villages. Further, the two long houses we excavated conform to Van den Bogaert's measurements (as specified above). The site contains at least 10,800 square meters of village area, and might be as large as 22,100 square meters. Analysis of excavated sites in the Mohawk Valley and elsewhere allows us to calculate the average number of square meters of Mohawk village area per inhabitant. The derived figures are 18 for Caughnawaga and 22 for Nodwell, both well-known sites. For the time being, I am using 20 as an average figure, but will probably refine it in the future. The importance of this ratio is that it allows us to derive village population size directly from village area without complex intervening assumptions. The ratio generates a probable population range of 500 to 1,100 for Canagere. Van den Bogaert gives figures generating a population of 730, so our findings provide further support both for the identification of the site as Canagere and for the area/population ratio. The discovery anchors both the spatial relationships of circa 1635 villages and a crucial occupation in the sequence of village sites occupied by the Canagere community.

A second test is to demonstrate archaeologically that the pre-epidemic population level suggested in Table 1 for 1633 holds true for the preceding two centuries. This cannot be accomplished through a simple tally of sites by age and distribution because evidence from a sequence of securely dated sites indicates that earlier smaller villages were fusing into larger villages over time. Twelve sites may well have accommodated as many people in 1550 as 6 times that number of smaller villages held 100 years earlier. Sites circa 1450 were relatively small palisaded villages in relatively open locations. Our excavations on the Elwood site in 1982 supported this generalization, and other known sites of the same general age appear to be similarly small. I know of no villages in 1450 that were as large as the smallest of the 1634-35 villages. Assuming a constant population size, we predict we will eventually identify as many as 50 sites occupied in the year 1450.

A third test has been to locate and excavate a successor site to one of the 1634-35 Van den Bogaert villages and compare the resulting data with the appropriate village in Table 1. We found such a site in 1983. Our excavations on the little site were technically difficult because of the hard clay soil and the open character of the hilltop site location. We were unable to define long house dimensions in a convincing way, and the nearly flat topography did not define the site boundary. Air photos and surveys with metal detectors and a magnetometer helped, however, and we were eventually able to determine primary dimensions for the site. The village could have been no more than 60 meters wide on its southeast-northwest axis. It could have been no less than 140 meters and no more than 225 meters long in its northwest-southeast dimension. These dimensions produce an elliptical village of 6,600-10,600 square meters for a population of 330-530 people when the standard ratio is applied. This is currently supposed to be the immediate post-epidemic successor village to the village of Tenotoge, which Van den Bogaert's figures allow us to conclude had a population of 3,300. This implies a catastrophic mortality of 84 to 90 percent for this village during the 1633 epidemic. It is possible, however, that the Tenotoge community experienced some emigration or that our measurements on the little site could be too conservative. Future work will probably clarify the matter.

The Dutch and the Mohawk

We have begun to detect the extraordinary changes the Dutch and Mohawk cultures imposed on one another through and after the seventeenth century. First, there is the obvious. The Mohawk eagerly traded for glass beads, which the Dutch regarded as worthless trinkets. The Dutch just as eagerly traded for beaver pelts, preferably those the Indians regarded as worn out. Both parties thought they were getting a bargain, and the trade system became a vehicle for many pervasive changes.

Then there are the less obvious changes. The Dutch acquired and learned to use corn, beans, and squash--principal Mohawk domestics. The Mohawk acquired brass kettles and guns. The Dutch learned to work wood and bark into snowshoes and canoes, while the Mohawk learned to work worn-out brass kettles into arrow points and personal adornment. The Mohawk shifted their traditional chert-chipping technology from the production of arrow points to the production of gunflints. They traded for lead and learned to cast their own musket balls. More than that, however, they used the new material to make animal effigies and other decorative items from molten lead. The Dutch, in turn, adopted Indian shell bead technology, improved it with the use of iron drills, and produced their own shell wampum. Because coinage was in short supply, wampum quickly became an important medium of commercial exchange, in addition to its traditional use in treaties and other political interaction. Although we found almost no wampum at all at the 1634 site of Canagere, there were many wampum beads at the 1645 site excavated in 1983. Our fine-tuned site sequences are clearly yielding detailed information regarding the rapid changes which affected the residents of the region during the seventeenth century.

The Mohawk persisted through both depopulation and rapid culture change, and are still with us today. The Mohawk language is alive and well, and there are now more than twice as many Mohawk as there were just before the 1633 epidemic. Regrettably, few of them live in the Mohawk Valley today, primarily because of their alliance with the British during the American Revolution. Given the quick and complete disappearance of so many other Indian nations, the survival of the Mohawk has been remarkable. Their importance in colonial history up to and through the American Revolution is even more remarkable. The Mohawk Valley Project has as one of its aims the study of this long-term cultural survival. A major reason for the success of the Mohawk over time appears to be their traditional practice of taking in refugees and war captives, both individually and in groups. In one case, late in the seventeenth century, the Mohawk absorbed an entire village of Huron. After joining the other Iroquois nations in defeating the Huron, the Mohawk brought a refugee community from Quebec to the Mohawk Valley and established a separate village for them. Students from SUNY Albany tested the suspected site of that village in 1983 and found it contained predominantly Huron (not Mohawk) pottery, a discovery which confirmed the identification. By absorbing refugees and allowing them to become ethnically Mohawk, the Mohawk nation escaped the extinction suffered by so many other Northeast Indian nations.

Many problems remain unsolved. Not least amongst these is the dating of the emergence of the league of the Iroquois, which has escaped archaeologists to date. Tradition suggests this occurred about the beginning of the sixteenth century. Indeed, there is a specific tradition stating that when the Seneca joined the league, there was an eclipse at about the time of the second hoeing of the corn. The more remarkable candidate is an eclipse which occurred on 18 June 1526 (Julian). However, the emergence of the league was a long process rather than a single event, and the Seneca decision to join may not have coincided with the Mohawk decision. So far as the Mohawk are concerned, we are likely to detect the emergence of the League in the westward shift of Mohawk village relocations during the critical period. Preliminary indications are that in the face of hostile relations with the Mahican on the Hudson, the growth of the league encouraged a westward shift of Mohawk villages in the direction of their Oneida and Onondaga allies.

Circumstances have made Albany and the Mohawk a region extraordinarily rich in both prehistoric and historic archaeological resources. We have only begun to tap these resources and to understand the processes which powered the cultural evolution of our region. Circumstance have also allowed archaeologists to investigate scientific issues in the context of these resources which, for various reasons, are unapproachable in many other parts of the world. I hope that in experiencing Albany this year, its residents will rediscover it, and come to realize more fully just how much the remarkable past of our region has to give to its future.

Dean Snow, professor of anthropology at SUNYA, is an expert in the field of early Dutch settlers and Indians in New York State. He holds degrees from the Universities of Oregon and Minnesota in anthropology, archaeology, and ethnohistory of the northeast. He has written books, articles, and critical reviews in his discipline and currently edits an anthropological journal.

Further Readings

Grassman, Thomas, ed. *The Mohawk Indians and Their Valley, Being a Chronological Documentary Record to the End of 1693.* Schenectady: Eric Hugo Photography and Printing Company, 1969.

Norton, Thomas E. *The Fur Trade in Colonial New York 1686-1776.* Madison: The University of Wisconsin Press, 1974.

Ritchie, William A. *The Archaeology of New York State.* Rev. ed. Garden City: New York. Published for the American Museum of Natural History by the Natural History Press, 1969. Focuses primarily upon prehistoric Iroquoian culture, ending with the seventeenth century.

Trelease, Allen W. *Indian Affairs in Colonial New York: The Seventeenth Century.* Ithaca: Cornell University Press, 1960.

Trigger, Bruce, ed. *Handbook of North American Indians.* Volume 15: *Northeast.* Washington: Smithsonian Institution, 1978.

Weinman, Paul L. *A Bibliography of the Iroquoian Literature.* New York State Museum and Science Service *Bulletin* Number 411. Albany: The University of the State of New York, The State Education Department, December 1969. This bibliography is arranged by subject and is an important source for anyone interested in further study of the Iroquoian culture.

Wilcoxen, Charlotte. *Seventeenth Century Albany: A Dutch Profile.* 2nd ed. Albany: Education Department, Albany Institute of History and Art, 1984. Chapter 7 examines the Dutch relations with the Iroquois.

The native American and early Dutch settlers did not always have a harmonious relationship, for example, the Schenectady massacre (above); Joseph Brant (right), a prominent Indian, was known as "Captain of the Six Nations."

In the 1780s, Abraham Yates, Jr., a prominent Albany politician, wrote in his unpublished *History of Albany* that from the time the Albany town charter was granted in 1686, the associates of the Van Rensselaer patroons pursued "the plan to get such a number of members in the Albany town corporation as were sufficient to frustrate" the Albany town interest and to get the city into "such measures as to humor the patroon's interest."

This paper tests this thesis in the light of historical evidence and looks at whether the patroons were successful in their attempt: How did Albany maintain its identity and independence and manage relations with the landlords that controlled such vast resources? Was the story of Albany's relations with the patroonship always a stormy one? Indeed, this relationship led to much of what is Albany today.

THE VAN RENSSELAER PATROONSHIP: ONE DUTCH LANDOWNER'S INFLUENCE

Sung Bok Kim

As part of the 1886 bicentennial celebration of Albany's colonial town charter, the town marked the sites of 47 significant events in its history. One of the markers honored Kiliaen Van Rensselaer, the first patroon and one of the founders of Rensselaerswyck. The patroons, of course, were Dutch landowners in the American colonies. His marker is still intact on the face of Albany City Hall. From the point of view of the town residents of the day, the patroon and his domain had a great deal to do with the town history. One hundred years later, it is unclear just how many townsmen are aware of this important historical fact.

The relationship between the town of Albany and the patroonship can be traced back to two events, the first being the construction of Fort Orange by the Dutch West India Company in the spring of 1624. A wooden stockade with a few small guns, this fort was more like a "pound to impound cattle and pigs" than a military post. Nevertheless, it was to serve as a fur trading center and company headquarters for the management of Indian affairs on the northern frontier. This "miserable little fort," as one visitor called it, was actually the beginning of this town. The second event was the establishment of a patroonship above and below Fort Orange, in 1629, under the leadership of Kiliaen Van Rensselaer. The patroon was entitled to twelve miles of land along both banks of the Hudson River, over which he had supreme judicial and administrative authority ("high, middle, and low" jurisdiction). From August 1630 to May 1631, the Van Rensselaers made several land purchases from Indian proprietors, including Barren Island and extending to the Mohawk River. One of the purchases comprehended the land on which the fort was erected. Additional purchases were made and later confirmed by the Dutch government in 1640.

The patroon and the people of Fort Orange were on good terms until 1639, when the Dutch West India Company relinquished its monopoly on the fur trade, and opened the lucrative trade to all. The company also gave up its policy of restricting fort residency to company officials, employees, and traders. Now permits were issued indiscriminately, permitting anyone to build houses and huts within the fort for a fee. In 1644, the company abandoned the maintenance of its trading house there and fur trading for its own account. Neither the people of Fort Orange nor the Van Rensselaers wanted free trade, though. Rather, each wanted to monopolize the trade of furs and other goods on the northern frontier at the expense of the other. From 1639, their relationship soured and they competed for control of area resources-- initially furs, later tax revenue, lumber, and even political power.

As long as the company held a monopoly in the fur trade, Kiliaen Van Rensselaer (who never came to his American domain) and his agents were content to reap windfall trade benefits. They never challenged the company's monopoly. Once the company opened the trade to the public, the patroon was determined to corner the trade for himself and his tenants. He went about this in several ways. First, for a fee of 16 to 20 guilders, he rented out a lot just north of the fort stockade, creating a village called Fuyck. Second, he set up a customs office (the Steyn) on Barren Island to control Hudson River shipping from that point to Fort Orange. Third, he prohibited outsiders--free traders--from using his domain to contact Indians. Fourth, he required traders to sell their furs to his agents. Fifth, his trader-tenants were prohibited from having any dealings with any traders of the fort. Sixth, he issued an ordinance to fort residents preventing them from securing timber and firewood from his domain without permission. In sum, Van Rensselaer intercepted furs and made access to the visiting Indians difficult. The fort villagers, whose livelihood had revolved around the fur trade under the auspices of the Dutch and West Indian Company, simply could not tolerate this. To worsen their lot, fort residents were not issued titles to the lands they lived on, as the company had no land-ownership there.

The patroon's aggressive attempts to turn his domain into a trade center made his land very attractive to people who wanted a lion's share of the trade. After all, as David De Vries said in 1639, everyone, whether "boor" or peasant, is a "merchant" at heart. The Van Rensselaer's land, particularly that in the vicinity of Fort Orange, was taken up very fast. While in 1640 there were only 4 farms in cultivation under Van Rensselaer, in 1643 there were 25-30 farms along the river for 2 or 3 leagues (about 100 persons). By 1651, there were 18 farms with 128 horses and 151 head of cattle. Since the land on which the fort stood belonged to him, Kiliaen Van Rensselaer believed the residents in the fort had no claim to the fort, except at his pleasure. He may have been right, considering the fact that his deed with the Indians, dated 13 May 1631, included the land. On the other hand, his claim was flawed, as evidenced by his initial registration and description of 1629, according to which the domain boundary "(began) above and below Fort Orange." It is clear that he had no right to buy the fort land in the first place.

But the Van Rensselaer patroon's effort to gobble up Fort Orange and establish a trade monopoly was met with a rebuff from Governor Peter Stuyvesant of New Netherland. On 23 July 1648, the governor ordered Van Rensselaer's agent, Brant A. Van Slichtenhorst, not to grant any more lots or approve any construction on land within a cannon shot of Fort Orange until further order from the company or the States General. In March 1651, the company rejected Van Rensselaer's claim to the fort land, as well as the right of staple on Barren Island to obstruct navigation on the river. In January 1652, he also issued orders declaring void all grants or leases of lands in the immediate vicinity of Fort Orange (i.e., houses and lots granted at Fuyck), and annulling Rensselaerswyck's ordinance against securing timber and firewood in the domain. On 6 March 1652, the governor issued an order forbidding the construction of any buildings within 600 "geometrical paces" of 5 feet each. This limitation embraced a radius of 3,000 feet from the river bank, including all of what is now capitol hill. It is worth noting that this newly fixed boundary included the whole of Fuyck, (the village developed by Slichtenhorst). Finally, on 8 April 1652, the governor provisionally created Beverwyck, the area comprehending the fort and Fuyck, and gave it an inferior "court of justice." This court jurisdiction covered the patroon's hamlet, the house of Slichtenhorst, and the patroon's commercial building.

Interestingly, even the patroon's tenants at Fuyck joined the residents of Fort Orange in their resistance against the patroon's efforts to take over the fort and establish a monopoly on the fur trade. Needless to say, Stuyvesant's creation of Beverwyck shattered the patroon's long cherished dream for a monopoly. Paradoxically, it was now Beverwyck's government of traders that tried to set up a monopoly in the trade for themselves. At any rate, when the Dutch period was coming to an end, many ambiguities and uncertainties existed with respect to domain boundaries, the relationship between the patroon's court and Beverwyck's court, and even the very existence of the Beverwyck government.

A new chapter of conflict between the town and the patroonship opened soon after the British took over the Dutch colony in 1664. When the Van Rensselaers, particularly Kiliaen's son, Jeremiah, tried to persuade British governors to recognize their claim to Beverwyck's land (by then renamed Albany), a claim based on the Indian deed of 1631 and a confirmatory patent given to the family by the State General in 1631, the governors were more attentive to the Albanians' desire for independence and a monopoly in the fur trade, and to Albany's governmental status in relation to the patroonship. It would appear these governors were convinced that it was not advantageous for the proprietary government of New York to let Albany, the second major town of the province and the hub of one of its primary revenue producing areas, slip out of their control, even if the family's pretension was legally valid. In 1665, Richard Nicolls, the first British governor, abolished the patroon's court. In its place, he established a six member court with two representatives from Albany, Rensselaerswyck, and Schenectady, respectively. This means,

in effect, that Van Rensselaer could influence only two votes in the court. Jeremiah Van Rensselaer, director of the domain, complained that "there is nothing left of our high, middle and low jurisdiction." Nicholas Van Rensselaer, younger brother of Jeremiah, hoped to annex Albany from King Charles II. In November 1666, Governor Nicholls severely chastised Jeremiah Van Rensselaer:

> I perceive that you conclude the Town of Albany to be part of Renzelaerwick; I give you friendly advice not to grasp at too much authority . . . If you imagine there is a pleasure in titles of Government I wish that I could serve your appetite . . . Sett your hearth therefore at rest to bee contented with the profitt not the government of a Colony, till we heare from His Royal Highness.

Like his predecessor Nicolls, Francis Lovelace pursued a policy intended to reduce the privileges of Rensselaerswyck and enhance Albany's position. On 2 August 1671, he upgraded the town by assigning a third commissioner to the court of Albany, Rensselaerswyck and Schenectady. To this the governor added a directive that any four of the magistrates would constitute a quorum to conduct judicial business. The governor's explanation for this action was the inconvenience caused by the absence of the Rensselaerswyck members. Whatever the reason, the outcome was that Albany could now dominate the court and therefore influence, often decisively, local affairs. This order regularized the organization until its replacement by new forms.

Once the town of Albany had advanced in political standing and influence, it was granted a monopoly on the fur trade, by Governor Edmund Andros in 1676. But the Van Rensselaers continued to annex Albany to their domain. In 1678, they managed to persuade the Duke of York, proprietor of the colony, to accept most of their basic claims, namely, their right to Albany (except the fort) and the restoration of ancient privileges enjoyed by the patroonship prior to

1652. That year the Duke dispatched an order to Andros to issue a royal patent for the domain. One of the stipulations in the order stated that Albanians should pay rent for their homes and land for a period of 31 years. But the governor decided to serve the best interests of his master by ignoring the proprietor's order. With this, the Van Rensselaers finally gave up on Albany. In 1685, the new governor, Thomas Dongan, required that the Van Rensselaers relinquish all claims on Albany and an additional tract of land called "Albany Liberty," which extended 16 miles toward Schenectady, for the benefit of Albany and its expansion.

When Dongan granted a charter to Albany on 22 July 1686, giving the town independent corporate status, it was a corollary to the long historic process. More important, the charter gave the town the authority and power base necessary to manage the administrative, judicial, and financial affairs of Albany County, under whose jurisdiction the Rensselaerswyck patroonship fell. County administration was conducted by a court of general sessions, composed of justices of the peace. Such town officials as mayor, recorder, and alderman, who were also justices, constituted a majority of the administrative machinery of the county and were, therefore, in a position to promote the interests of the town over those of the county. More often than not, they forced county residents to serve the town's needs and interests. Even court juries deciding both criminal and civil cases tended to be dominated by town members, when impaneled.

To illustrate, in 1721, Rensselaerswyck Assemblyman Andrew Coeymans expressed disgust with the town's custom of bending everything, and every other town in Albany County, to its advantage. Referring specifically to the tax assessment of the county, Coeymans wrote, "If any precinct brings in their estimate, the town justices out vote them and make that precinct pay as they please, taking off one less and putting so much as they please the other. Some precincts they have raised above half in two years and threaten next time to make them pay more." As owner of the manor, Kiliaen Van Rensselaer informed Albany magis-

trates in 1721 that the privilege of cutting timber or firewood on the manor, a privilege granted to town residents by the charter for 21 years, had long since expired; he urged them to negotiate with him for renewal. Henceforth, he said, he would prosecute anyone cutting the wood without a license. The magistrates were outraged. They resolved to defend any city inhabitant prosecuted by Van Rensselaer. This resolution reflected their unshakable confidence that they would try the case and pronounce the verdict in favor of the accused at the court of sessions, which, in fact, they controlled. When Philip Livingston, an Albany town official, referred to Albany County as "oppressive," he must have had in mind the magistrates of Albany Town, who were closely identified with the county they dominated.

By virtue of its charter, the town also had authority over two major businesses-- the fur trade and tavern-keeping. Before 1722, Albany had a monopoly on the Indian trade; one had to be a town freeman in order to trade with the natives. For that matter, freemanship was prerequisite to any business within the town before and after that date. Besides, the town had authority to license tavern businesses in the county. Thus, associating with and befriending the town's powerful officials was the golden path to economic advantage.

The preponderance of the town of Albany was due to the town's important economic and social functions. Albany was the "central-place" in the frontier county, to use the terminology of historical geography. Because of Albany's fur trade monopoly (often infringed upon by interlopers), its superior fortifications, and its common use as an embarkation point for military expeditions against enemy Indians and French Canada, those seeking lucrative trade with the Indians and the garrisons at the fort gravitated toward it. Along with these commercial interests came service industries and associated craftsmen, such as blacksmiths, carpenters, bricklayers, masons, brewers, and inn holders. The growth of farming villages in neighboring areas, encouraged in the early decades of the eighteenth century by a great demand for wheat and flour, further contributed to the town's growing wealth. Farmers sold their produce to shopkeepers in exchange for merchandise and borrowed money from merchants. Wheat and flour were certified and packed in the city, then frequently exported directly to overseas markets. For most county inhabitants, Albany was the entrepôt for goods and the main link with the outside world. Farmers also came to town to settle litigation at court each spring and fall and to register their deeds with the county clerk. This enviable political and economic position continued even after the Indian trade monopoly was partially broken in 1722, and completely broken in 1826. For, once started, the growth of the town became self-generating, even after the primary stimulus for growth had disappeared.

Aside from economic and political advantages, Albany offered certain other attractions. Though dusty in the dry season and muddy in the rainy--for its streets, unlike the city of New York, were not paved, and the low-lying area near the river was regularly flooded in the early spring--it had a certain glamour for most country folks. It was a place where society gathered. Lawyers, merchants, and other men of means lived there, and nicely dressed, perfumed ladies were seen in its narrow streets. It was a town where one enjoyed lively entertainment and small talk, or celebrated a friend's birthday at one of its several taverns. At least one manor landlord defined a trip to Albany as "to go a pleasuring." Until the large influx of New Englanders in the 1750s, this small, homogeneous, Dutch community consisted of about 300 families where everyone knew everyone else and relationships were personal. Albany enjoyed a social setting in which the Van Rensselaers were just as concerned with their social standing and acceptance as with their economic position and the pursuit of profit. Defiance of accepted norms, or an addiction to excess in any form, could have meant social ostracism.

Albany town was dominant in relation to the Van Rensselaers and others in Albany county, despite the fact that many of the city residents were tenants of the patroon.

Since 1699, the town had a satellite colony named Schaghticooke, measuring six square miles in area and located 20 miles north on the east side of the Hudson River. But the colony remained too dangerous a place for many Albanians, since it was badly exposed to the threats of French and Indian incursions. As grains and lumber began to play a dominant role in the economy of the northern frontier of New York in the first two decades of the century, many Albanians naturally coveted the Rensselaerswyck land along the river; it was available only for rental. As of 1720, 32 of Albany's 149 freemen also had manor leaseholds, and in 1763, at least 87 of 242 town freemen were tenants of the patroon. Yet all evidence indicates that tenancy neither degraded Albanians nor made them servile to their landlord. William Smith, Jr., remarked in the 1750s that rents in Rensselaerswyck had "as yet been neither exacted nor paid." According to my own study, rent arrears persisting ten to twenty years were not uncommon. Underscoring Smith's observations, Anne M. Grant, a long-time resident of Albany county, discusses the temper and attitudes of the Patroon's tenants:

> You may suppose the tenants did not greatly fear a landlord, who could neither remove them, nor heighten their rents. Thus, without the pride of property, they had all the independence of proprietors. They were like German Princes, who, after furnishing their contingent to the Emperor, might make war on him when they choose.

More Albanians became dependent on the patroon for their livelihood over the course of the eighteenth century. Yet, as my discussion has demonstrated, this economic situation was not translated into political subordination on the part of Albany tenants. The interaction of the Van Rensselaer patroonship and Albany town on several levels represents a rare but interesting anomaly in modern history where political forces were more important than economic forces.

Sung Bok Kim came to this country in 1960. He received a Master's degree in American history at the University of Wisconsin (Madison) and a Ph.D. at Michigan State University. From 1968 to 1973, he taught at the College of William and Mary and University of Illinois. Currently, he is professor of history at SUNY at Albany and chair of the department. In addition to a prize winning book (1978) on New York Agrarian Society in the 17th and 18th centuries, he has published several articles on the American Revolution in prominent national journals. His present scholarly interest is in the interaction between the military and non-military segments during the Revolutionary Period.

Further Readings

Bielinski, Stefan. *The People of Albany, 1650-1800*, Unpublished Manuscript.

Bonomi, Patricia U. *A Factious People: Society and Politics in Colonial New York.* New York: 1971.

Grant, Anne. *Memoirs of an American Lady.* New York: 1901.

Howell, George Rogero, and Jonathan Tenney. *Bicentennial History of the County of Albany, N.Y. from 1609 to 1886.* New York: 1886.

Kenney, Alice P. *Stubborn for Liberty: Dutch in New York.* Syracuse, New York: 1974.

Kim, Sung Bok. *Landlord and Tenant in Colonial New York: Manorial Society, 1664-1775.* Chapel Hill, North Carolina: 1978.

Merwick, Donna. "Dutch Townsmen and Land Use: A Spatial Perspective on Seventeenth Century New York." *William and Mary Quarterly* 37 January 1981: 53-78.

Nissenson, Samuel G. *The Patroon's Domain.* New York: 1937.

Norton, Thomas E. *The Fur Trade in Colonial New York, 1686-1776.* Madison, Wisconsin: 1974.

Van Laer, Arnold J. F. *Early Records of the City and County of Albany and Colony of Rensselaerswyck.* 4 vol. Albany: 1916.

Wilcoxen, Charlotte. *Albany in the Seventeenth Century: A Dutch Profile.* Albany: 1981.

The first Manor House, built 1660 by Jeremias Van Rensselaer.

The Van Rensselaer Manor in North Albany, built 1765.

The pursuit of religious freedom brought many groups to America, perhaps none so unique and curiously successful as the Shakers. Economic and political turmoil breed new sects that offer new hopes. Although the Shakers were but one of several utopian communities of the eighteenth and nineteenth centuries, their "experiment" was significant in number, duration, and legacy.

Forced out of England under religious persecution, Mother Ann Lee and a small group of followers who believed her to be the Messiah settled near Albany in 1775. Their pacifism and celibacy brought them further persecution here. Shaker principles included the separation but equality of the sexes, confession of sins, separatism from the world, and community ownership. They believed that religion should not be divorced from secular concerns, but rather should permeate all thought and action.

Initial suspicion about the Shakers gave way to curiosity, then respect. The Shakers became known for their honesty, diligence, and inventiveness. Their community was noted for its absence of racial discrimination and a devotion to industry. The Shakers were far from passive: They developed a strong economic system and were receptive to new innovations, many of their own creation. The goods they produced were of the highest quality and esteemed for their simplicity and beauty.

The Shakers had no difficulty attracting converts with the security and protection they offered this unsettled country. But the Shaker communities rapidly declined after the Civil War, for reasons more complex than their celibacy. The development of steam manufacturing, the lure of the West, relaxed social stigmas against women working, and the establishment of orphan asylums by government and other religious groups all diminished the number of converts. Financial losses and rifts within communities led to the demise of the Shaker religion. Yet their legacy is significant and can still be found in their old communities. As Eldress Emma King concluded, "The material homes may fail but the Shaker experiment is no failure. The eternal principles upon which it is founded are just as true and strong as they ever were. The good lives on forever."

THE SHAKER TRADITION

Donald Emerich

Look closely at a Shaker chair: it is eighteenth century in form, with a ladder back and a clearly American look. It was made in the 1840s and represents what cultural historians call recidivism, a reversion to an old form without concern for modernizing or creating more ornate forms.

The Shakers valued innovation, as evidenced by the tilting buttons sometimes found on the back of their chairs. Like most Shaker innovations, however, tilting buttons were not patented. The Shakers were reluctant to claim their own inventions, and regarded them as collective property.

The Shakers improved on the eighteenth century form and raked the chair. Its visible slant and its seat made of spongy wool tape or listing made it more comfortable than its eighteenth century counterpart. This chair illustrates the simplicity, preservation of form, innovation, and comfort of Shaker furniture.

Shaker chairs were made for use within the community. The Shakers did not begin large-scale chair manufacturing until the 1860s. This chair became a prototype,

however, once mass production was incorporated in Shaker industrial ethics.

The Shakers emerged after a small split in a Quaker meeting in Manchester, England, in the 1740s. At that time, a group of radical Protestant refugees arrived in Manchester from France. With the growing textile industry in Manchester, these refugees had no difficulty finding work at the local mills. There they came in contact with a disillusioned group of Quakers who were concerned about the growth of middle and upper classes in their midst, and who feared that an interest in commerce would supercede that in worship. This small group of Manchester Quakers subsequently broke away from the larger, and, under the influence of the "French Prophets" (Protestant radicals who believed in speaking in different tongues and worshiping through dancing and whirling), they became known as the Shaking Quakers. This was later shortened to Shakers, a designation which, while pejorative, was readily adopted by the Shakers themselves. Once they became an American church, the Shakers called themselves the

United Society of Believers in Christ's Second Appearing. Indeed, they believed that just as there were two Christs and two Gods (God the Father and Holy Mother Wisdom, or Sophia), so the Christ Spirit had come twice to the world--first in the person of Jesus, then as a millhand named Ann Lee. Although there is no evidence that Ann Lee claimed to be Christ, there is no question that her followers made such a claim.

After Ann Lee joined the Manchester Quakers in 1758, the group endured mounting persecution. In time, she was recognized as the group's spiritual leader. Reputed as a psychic, she saw a revelation that the church would grow in the New World as a great tree of life. Soon afterward, in 1774, nine English Shakers landed in New York City. The following year, one of the more prosperous of the group brought back more Shakers from Manchester, raising their American number to a dozen by 1776. At that point, the Shaker church in Manchester vanished from history, its leadership lost to the group in America.

The Shakers initially settled in New York City. Evidence suggests they migrated to New Jersey, perhaps in search of advice from their friendly enemies, the Quakers. In 1776, three of the brethren made their way to the Manor of Rensselaerswyck where, according to Quakers back in New York City, inexpensive land was available. The dozen resettled in Albany County in 1776 and leased land from the patroon in what was then known as Niskayuna, "the place where the corn grows." When townships were first laid out in Albany County, this territory was designated the town of Watervliet. Thus, for most of their 163 year history in the Capital District, the Shakers lived in an area considered part of the Town of Watervliet. In 1895, however, when town lines were redrawn, the Shaker settlement became part of the Town of Colonie. Perhaps the most accurate geographic label for our local Shakers, then, is the Watervliet Shakers of Colonie.

During their first four years in Albany County, the Shakers were faced with hardships they had not anticipated. Without realizing it, they had leased a wilderness of dense forest and swamps with a history of malaria. Gradually they began to drain the land and cultivate it into attractive and prosperous property. The fruit of their labor can be seen today in the Ann Lee Pond and the Shaker Creek running between the pond and the Mohawk River.

Before long, the Shakers began to attract attention. In 1779, only three years after their move to Albany County, the Shakers received their first American-born convert. Although Eleanor Vedder never lived in the Shaker village itself, she espoused Shaker principles. Four of her granddaughters are buried in the Shaker Cemetery, which was established at the Ann Lee Home in 1835 to provide burial space for Shakers from all over the country.

In 1780, responding to a revelation received by Mother Ann, the Shakers decided to reach out to the world. The Shakers called this "the opening of the testimony." Over a four year period, Mother Ann, together with her English followers and some new American converts, traveled extensively throughout New England, establishing Shaker societies in Harvard and Hancock, Massachusetts; East Canterbury, New Hampshire; Enfield, Connecticut; and Sabbathday Lake, Maine.

During this period, the Shakers suffered severe persecution--mobbings, stonings, and every kind of violence imaginable. When Mother Ann and her brother were disinterred in 1835 and reburied in what is now the Shaker Cemetery near the Ann Lee Pond, there was evidence of fractured arms, legs, ribs and skulls. Both Mother Ann and her brother, William, died in August 1784. Church leadership remained in the hands of the English born Shakers until 1785, at which time the Shakers became an American church.

By this time, Shaker doctrine had begun to evolve into a fairly stable system, with celibacy as a well established tenet. Existing marriages were dissolved when people converted to the church. The Shakers were also pacifists, in the Quaker tradition. Indeed, when their liability to the draft came up during the Civil War, they sent a delegation to Washington to meet with President

Lincoln and the Secretary of War, claiming all former veterans who had renounced their pension plan to become Shakers were entitled to several hundred thousand dollars. Shortly thereafter, the Shakers were granted permanent draft exempt status.

The Shakers also believed in the oral confession of sins. Upon admission to the society, Shakers were to confess to an elder or eldress and, for most of the history of Shakerism, they were required to renew their vows and confess their sins at the end of each year.

The Shakers practiced a form of dance worship which had precedence in the Old Testament, with David dancing before the Lord. The public image of the Shakers more or less coincides with that portrayed by Currier and Ives and other nineteenth century engravers. Choreographed marches and spontaneous whirling were regularly incorporated in Shaker worship services, and drew large crowds of Sabbath observers at the central meeting house which was open to the public. Music, including both solo and choral singing, also played an important part in the service. Prior to the singing and dancing, a sermon was generally delivered for the benefit of "the world's people"--those visiting from outside the Shaker community. This reference to outsiders as the world's people reflects yet another Shaker principle--withdrawal from the world into their own communities. The latter was encouraged particularly after the American sector took over the leadership of the church.

Another tenet basic to Shakerism was the community of goods. Because all property and profit were to be held in common for the good of all, each member of the Shaker community gave all he owned to the church and, at the same time, received ownership of all church possessions. By implementing this practice, the Shakers unwittingly reinvented a form of monasticism prevalent in Europe and the Middle East prior to and during the Middle Ages. In dual-house monasticism, an order of sisters lived together with an order of brothers under the leadership of an abbot or abbess, prior or prioress, or both. In England, for example, an order known as the Gilbertines was founded by Saint Gilbert before the Reformation. Thirty or forty houses of dual monastics lived separately, though generally under a single rule. All Gilbertine houses were dissolved by Thomas Cromwell, under Henry VIII, leaving precious little memory of the Gilbertines in the eighteenth century. The order of the Brigatenes, founded by the daughter of one of the kings of Sweden, had established a house in England under Henry V, which also was dissolved in the 1530s when English monasticism ceased to exist.

Similarly, the Shakers were creating a religious society withdrawn from the world, with two orders, in this case an order of brothers and an order of sisters living together in celibacy under the rule of two elders and eldresses, respectively.

The entire Shaker community was subject to a central house equivalent to the mother house of a monastic order. The first such house was located in New Lebanon, New York. When the Shakers were assigned a post office of their own, the name was changed to Mount Lebanon. Meanwhile the Watervliet Shakers of Colonie were gathered into union and established their own order, the second in the country, in 1787. From that time on, the spread of Shakerism was rapid. By the year 1800, there were three Shaker communities in Maine, two in New Hampshire, four in Massachusetts and one in Connecticut.

As the Shakers grew in number, they had no choice but to launch a building program. The first Shaker meeting house in Watervliet was actually a log cabin. It was here that the Viennese physician Marquis de Lafayette made his visit to the Shakers to learn about healing by "the laying on of hands." The original meeting house was torn down in 1791 when a brother from New Hampshire, who was to build a dozen Shaker meeting houses to roughly the same plan, initiated construction in Watervliet of a meeting house that was later torn down by Albany County in 1927. The meeting house built to replace it is currently being restored by the Shaker Heritage Society, a preservation group concerned specifically with the Watervliet Shakers.

The rapid expansion of Shakerism is also reflected in official census records. Records for the year 1800 show that the original twelve Shakers had grown to 87 over a period of twenty years. By 1840, there were 304 Shakers in Watervliet, and 326 by 1850. It is estimated that there may have been as many as 375 at the period of greatest expansion.

The Shaker village at Watervliet was not unlike other Shaker communities in that it followed a basic plan or format developed at New Lebanon. Those who were most deeply committed to the church and had decided to become members belonged to the First Order. Also known as the Church Family, these members lived at the meeting house itself. This family was not a group of blood relatives. Rather it was a group of fifty to one hundred brothers and sisters living under the spiritual supervision of two elders and eldresses and the industrial-agricultural leadership of two deacons and deaconesses. In some cases, separate deacons and deaconesses were appointed to industry and agriculture. The hierarchy changed over the years along with changes in population and community conditions.

The Watervliet community consisted of the Church Family, i.e. those most deeply committed to the church, and three other families named by their compass directions from the church--the North Family, the West Family and the South Family. The South Family functioned as the Novitiate or Gathering Order. Those who desired to learn more about Shakerism or live in the village were not forced to commit themselves immediately. Instead, before turning over their property and becoming consecrated Shakers, they could enter the Gathering Order and remain there one to three years while testing their ability to bear the cross-- that is, celibacy. This opportunity gave prospective Shakers a feeling for the Shaker lifestyle, which was so far removed from that of the world. In time, the Gathering Order at Watervliet became so large that the West Family also took on responsibility for novitiates. All the while, the parent ministry of the church at New Lebanon was relying heavily on the leadership of the Watervliet Shaker church.

In 1805, Eldress Lucy Wright, an American convert from Pittsfield, received a revelation about a great revival in Kentucky. She sent three Shaker missionaries on foot from New York State to Kentucky. Two of the three were Watervliet brothers. Issachar Bates was a veteran of the Revolutionary War, a former officer who renounced that life for pacifism when he became a Shaker. Benjamin S. Youngs is known to some as a clockmaker. He is also the author of the first and, doubtless, one of the most important Shaker scriptural and historical books. Published in Albany in 1810, *The Testimony of Christ's Second Appearing* went through a number of editions and revisions over the years, remaining one of two or three significant works on Shaker doctrine.

The Marquis de Lafayette was not alone in his interest in the Shakers. Although Thomas Jefferson never visited the Watervliet community, he had several copies of *The Testimony of Christ's Second Appearing* in his possession. With respect to communal property, he wrote: " . . . small societies may exist in habits of virtue, order, industry, and peace and, consequently, as much happiness as heaven has pleased to deal out to imperfect humanity."

As a member of the United States Senate, Martin Van Buren of Columbia County advocated a draft exempt status for the Shakers, pointing out the credit due them for their charities, sobriety and industry. He also made a claim for their common right to petition Congress for a redress of grievance.

Yet another New Yorker, James Fennimore Cooper, spoke in high praise of the Shakers, referring to them in "The Traveling Bachelor" letters of 1824 as "an orderly, industrious sect, and models of decency, cleanliness and morality."

As early as 1839, a Boston paper wrote of the Shakers: "It is impossible to describe the air of tranquility and comfort that diffuses itself over a Shaker settlement . . . the two sexes together bear the burden, if burden it may be, of celibacy . . . . The union

24

of these people, their uniform kindness to each other, and the singularly benevolent and tender expression of their countenances speak a stronger language than their professions."

When Robert Owen came to this country and found his own utopian community at New Harmany, Indiana, in 1824, he discovered workshops for carpenters, jointers, whipmakers, coopers, shoemakers and tailors. According to his observations, the Shaker brothers not only had a choice of trade, but the principle of rotation was practiced so that no one would remain in any one shop or barn longer than was pleasant or practical. By that time, Watervliet was involved in the production of medicinal herbs and garden seed. Indeed, it was the Watervliet Shakers who invented the practice of packaging garden seeds.

Censuses from the first half of the nineteenth century reflect a certain number of blacks and aliens among the Shakers in New York State, Kentucky and Ohio. The Shakers consciously strove for an absence of racial discrimination in their villages. When a slave owner became a Shaker, he then freed his slaves and gave them the option to join the society or go out on their own. Among those who opted to become Shakers was an eldress who was eventually accorded the respectful title "Mother." (Mother and Father were rare titles reserved for leaders.) Mother Rebeccah Jackson led a community of black Shaker sisters for a time in Philadelphia, Pennsylvania, and later returned to minister in Watervliet.

In the 1840s a wave of revivalism swept through the Shaker church. This was a period characterized by revelations and communications from the spirit world. Spirit or inspirational drawings, referred to by some as "gift drawings," were seen in visions and later recorded. When each Shaker village was given a spiritual name by revelation, Watervliet became known as Wisdom's Valley. This name was retained among the Shakers for many years to come.

The population of the Shaker church continued to grow toward the middle of the century, reaching its peak just before the outbreak of the Civil War. After the war, however, it became apparent that although the world was still fascinated by the Shaker movement, few desired to convert and enter the Shaker community. While industry and real estate were flourishing, the Shakers were forced to resort to hired labor. They invented a hermetic sealing process for canned goods which were sold all along the eastern seaboard. By 1905, the Watervliet population had dwindled to 67. It was apparent that the end was at hand. Other Shaker villages had begun to close as early as the 1870s. The local Shakers experienced a surge of new vitality in the 1880s when a Shaker village near Rochester, New York, was sold to the state to become the first public epileptic hospital in the country. The Department of Corrections converted the hospital in 1985 into a security prison and closed off the Shaker buildings to the public. As a rule, the Shakers were concerned that their facilities be used for educational or charitable purposes. In some cases, of course, their plans were reversed by the future owners.

The 2,000 acres of Shaker land in Watervliet gradually began to disperse at the turn of the century. The West Family was sold in 1915. Four years later, the North Family was dissolved. The Church Family was eventually sold to Albany County for $160,000. After the death of Eldress Anna Case in 1938, three sisters rang the bell in the belfry of the South Family dwelling house for the last time.

Little remains today of Wisdom's Valley. The property of the North Family was destroyed by fire in 1926. What remains of the Church Family is still owned by Albany County. Now privately owned, the dwelling house of the West Family has been converted into private apartments. And although the buildings of the South Family still stand, they too are privately owned.

Donald Emerich, architectural historian, has degrees from Michigan State University and has been a resident of Albany since 1967. Emerich was the director of the first National Shakers Studies Conference in 1968 with Hancock Shaker Village and Darrow School. In 1973-74 he was the guest director and catalog editor for a Shaker exhibition at the Smithsonian Institute. Emerich has also been the principal consultant for the Historic American Building Survey. Most recently he was the consultant and catalog writer for the New York State Museum exhibit <u>Community Industries of the Shakers: A New Look</u>, exhibited in 1983-84.

Further Readings

Andrews, Edward D. *The People Called Shakers.* New York: Oxford University Press, 1953.

Community Industries of the Shakers: A New Look. Albany: Shaker Heritage Society, 1983.

Filley, Dorothy M. *Recapturing Wisdom's Valley: The Watervliet Shaker Heritage, 1775-1975.* Albany: Albany Institute of History and Art, 1975.

Lassiter, William L. *Shaker Architecture.* New York: Bonanza Books, 1966.

Melcher, Marguerite F. *The Shaker Adventure.* Cleveland: Case Western Reserve University, 1968.

Richmond, Mary L., comp. *Shaker Literature: A Bibliography.* 2 vol. Hancock, MA: Shaker Community, Inc., 1977.

Rose, Milton D., and Emily M. Role. *Shaker Tradition and Design.* New York: Bonanza Books, 1982.

The Town of Colonie: A Pictorial History. Colonie: The Town of Colonie, New York, 1980.

Classic Shaker chairs combine beauty of form and function.

Overall, Albany has a rich ethnic heritage. Particularly prominent are the Irish. As the first and largest national group to come to America during the period of mass immigration between 1820 and 1920, the Irish followed the same path as most ethnic groups that settled in Albany.

The attraction between America and Ireland begins with the legend of St. Brendan the Navigator who supposedly reached America in the sixth century. The Irish settled in the Albany area in colonial times. Religion was vital to them, and they introduced Catholicism to what was a Protestant America. While contributing to their segregation, religion provided cohesiveness to the Irish community. This strengthened them and led to their eventual success.

Most immigrant groups settle in areas resembling their native land. But the rural Irish settled predominantly in American cities. There they suffered economic hardship and religious persecution. With the advantage of language and a keen political consciousness developed from centuries of conflict with England, the Irish persevered and eventually shaped the future of American cities. This was certainly true in Albany. An Irishman, Governor Thomas Dongan, signed the 1686 charter establishing Albany as a city.

Albany's Irish population grew early in the nineteenth century, as Irish laborers arrived to build canals, turnpikes, and railroads. Thousands more fled the potato famine in Ireland in the 1840s. By 1875, one in six Albanians was Irish-born. They started work in the lumber district and numerous foundries in Albany. By the turn of the century, though, many better educated and more skilled Irish people had attained positions in civil service and the professions.

The Irish made significant contributions to politics, religion, literature, theater, sports, and law enforcement. Prominent personalities in the Albany area included Dongan; Sir William Johnson, who brought Irish settlers to the area before the Revolution; and, in this century, Governor Alfred E. Smith. Michael Nolan was the first Irish American to be elected mayor of a large city in 1878.

By the twentieth century, the Irish were as dominant in Albany as Dutch and English had once been. But the old Irish neighborhoods eventually dissolved. And new ethnic groups arrived, continuing the trend of immigration and assimilation. These dynamic forces have created and sustained the character and color of Albany for three hundred years.

THE MELTING POT

John McEneny

Genealogy is the poor man's treasure hunt. It's a wonderful task because you're never done with it. There's always another generation or another lost maiden name and sometimes, for many Americans, another nationality that was buried in archives, church histories, or maybe a trunk in the attic.

The topic of ethnicity in Albany is so complicated that I know that someone will inevitably be left out. Therefore, I'll give an outline of ethnicity in Albany and bring out some of the things that make our community unique.

To start, we have to remember that Albany was not an uninhabited wilderness at the time Henry Hudson discovered it. In fact, it was occupied by two ethnic groups, both Native American. One was the Mahigan Indians, the River Indians. They called the Hudson "the river that flowed both ways" because of its tide. Indeed, it did appear to flow first upstream and then down. The Mohawks, who were in the process of conquering the Mahigans, guarded the eastern part of the Iroquois Confederacy. This internatioal flavor has always been a part of Albany.

Recently in the Albany *Times Union*, Judy Sheppard wrote about the Irish roots in Albany. Very often, I find myself thinking on St. Patrick's Day, that we Irish set ourselves up. I received a call from one branch of the media on St. Patrick's Day: "We want to do something on the Irish for St. Patrick's Day. Could you direct us to a bar?" Irish drinking is a great legend, and yet few people realize that, like most stereotypes, it is somewhat unfair. The Irish have far less alcoholism than most of Western Europe, and 40 percent of the adult population doesn't drink at all. They are members of a group called the Pioneers. The nondrinking Irish were a very important part of nineteenth century Albany, ironically. St. Joseph's Parish of Arbor Hill has the largest temperance society of any parish in the United States, but they also have the other extreme whose per capita consumption makes up for the other 40 percent.

What impressed me with Sheppard's article, in addition to its fine quality, was that the author went to Charles Gehring, Joe Meany, Steve Balinshy, and some of the people familiar with the original source documents. So much of our history has changed since I was a boy, because people have been sensitive enough to care. We have gotten away from the simplistic histories taught in the early part of this century, where everybody came here to be melted down in the melting pot. In the older histories of Albany, take any ethnic group--Irish, Polish, Italian, or any religion you can think of--turn to the index, and you'll find usually only one reference, because it was popular then to discount "hyphenated Americans." Americans in the nineteenth and the early twentieth centuries were scared that the number of immigrants would completely change the nation's makeup. They feared that the United States as they knew it would be lost, taken over by one ethnic group or another. Benjamin Franklin led one of the major forces in the late 1700s to push for public schools everywhere. One of the major reasons was that Franklin, based in Pennsylvania, was afraid that the country would turn into a German-speaking country rather than an English-speaking country. He felt that making English the official language, and having a public school system to make sure that that was carried out, would keep America America. This meant, in the minds of many, to Anglicize the country. People have been Anglicizing names ever since.

Back in the early or mid-1960s, ethnicity was still not much of a popular subject. The Hibernians might have had 65 members, the Polish club seemed to be living off weddings, and the various groups seemed to be just hanging on. It seemed a vestige of ethnicity in the twilight of an era that would soon pass. Yet today as we drive out in the Pine Bush, we see temples of ethnicity, such as the Italian Club and the Polish Club. We see the great charities of groups that were once considered ethnic, and probably still are--the Daughters of Sarah Home, the Teresian House. And we find that people in the 1980s are proud of

their heritage, as they should be. We now accept "hyphenated Americans." In this same movement, women often keep their maiden names because they like to be loyal to their family. They should be allowed to express that, and not be questioned about their patriotism.

There's been a tremendous rebirth of family, local, and ethnic history. I think a lot of questioning went on during the Vietnam era: Why are we here? Where have we been? There was a resentment in the late 1960s and early 1970s against the tendency to homogenize us. This tendency toward regional planning, toward a transient society where people transfer from one job to another, is breaking up families and neighborhoods A lot of these trends have upset people. They began to look back at their families, neighborhoods, and the identities that made them what they are.

In the New Netherlands project, original Dutch manuscripts are being translated. During this period of Dutch Albany (1614-1674), buried within the records we have found people who are not Dutch. According to one estimate, 50 percent of the people who lived in Dutch Albany were in fact Northern Germans, Danes, Hugenots, French Protestants, British, Irish, English, or Welsh. The first Irish came in the 1650s, as well as the first Italians and Polish. These were token numbers, but by the time you add up that experience, literally hundreds of people from other lands accepted and assimilated the Dutch way of life.

When the British came, that process continued and ironically, the colony that we had here was built to be a money maker. It was not chosen for religious freedom (though individuals certainly came here later for that reason), but was an economic colony. It was, in fact, one of the most prosperous items the British hoped to obtain. It hadn't been as prosperous for the Dutch because they had the expense of founding to take care of, but the British did not want to upset the applecart, so they kept all the Dutch officials in the city of Albany, and the magistrates were all re-appointed. They kept as an established church, for a number of years, the Dutch

Reform Church. It made sense. And they introduced more and more people from the British Isles.

Our 1600s and early 1700s history of Albany concerns groups who speak Dutch, identify with the Dutch way of life, but represent nationalities from all over the globe. It concerns both free blacks and slaves, from Africa and often from Brazil. These people were international. Albany was one outpost, stuck in the middle of somewhere. People would go to the next colony and then to the next. Other people would come in as well. Portuguese names show up repeatedly, going back to the days when Indonesia and other places were up for grabs for the various countries of the world.

What happened to the early ethnic groups? What happened to people who weren't Dutch or British by the time of the American Revolution? Unless they formed a church, a rallying point, they became assimilated. Michael O'Brian, longtime Secretary of the American-Irish Historical Society, has a number of writings on early Irish in Albany and what happens to their names. The Hogans get a double "oo", the McGinneys are mentioned as McGinnus, a Gerrett turns out to be a Fitzgerald. We can spot the Irish, once we're sensitized to look for them, but how much easier is it for people of German heritage to get lost with all the Dutch. So we start with an international community. If a group didn't form a church, its chances of maintaining an identity were small.

When the British came, they brought soldiers from all over the British Empire, including Scotland and Ireland. The Scots set up the Presbyterian Church. There was no Catholic Church in the colony of New York until St. Peter's on Barkley Street in New York in 1784. The second Catholic Church was St. Mary's in Albany in 1796. In the back of St. Mary's, you'll find the original cornerstone which has a skull and crossbones, the names of three trustees, and the date 1796-97. The same foundation is there today, but the original church faced the other way. That's why they call it Chapel Street. Then two other churches were built on the same foundation,

extending it back all the way up to Lodge Street, so called because the Scottish soldiers wanted a masonic lodge, and they built it on Lodge Street.

The major group of this time probably is the Irish, an early group which arrived in small numbers after the Revolution. They were relatively elite, and had at least enough money to pay their own passage. Sixty years later, landlords would pay passage costs just to get people off their land before they starved. The early people came from all over. In the 1700s the Irish were assimilated and today we have what is commonly know as the Scotch-Irish myth, because when somebody in the fifth generation is Protestant, there's the assumption they came from Ulster. This has never been the case. If you know Irish names, you can tell what part of Ireland a person has come from. Sullivans don't come from the north, but rather the south.

I was in Ireland for the first time two years ago. I found interesting things that I didn't expect. For example, the people looked very different from west to east, and north to south. Generally, the chance of Norman or English blood in Irish from the south is high. My wife is half Irish and, all through southern Ireland, people resembled her rather than me.

The Irish are proud of their last names and tend to put them outside on their shops. Irish storefronts are fascinating, unless they become Americanized and turn to plastic, and that happens, as it does all over the world. In general though, most people hang painted wooden signs with just their last names, and you can tell the names of the people in the village as you go through. You see popular names like Murphy, Kelly, Sullivan, and Walsh. Drive through Cork or by Lakes of Killarney and you're inundated by these names, but go north and you never see the name again. At the A.O.H. very few people have heard the name McEneny.

People came from all over Ireland during this period and followed distinct patterns of settlement. Without a Catholic church, they either became Anglicized or, once the Presbyterian Church was set up (by their fellow Celts, the Scots), quite a number of Irish went into the Presbyterian church, giving credence to the misconception that everyone was Scotch-Irish. Still others would go and join the Dutch Reform Church because that was almost the only church out in the rural areas, and when you married a Dutch Reformed woman there was a tendency to become Dutch Reformed. So there was a lot of mixture, and a loss of identity.

What I've said for the Irish goes for the Palantinate Germans. Once there was no more Palantinate German church, and they were not congregated in the Cherry Valley area or Schoharie, they intermarried and their names get lost with Dutch names.

The first major influx of immigrants into Albany after the American Revolution was the New England Yankees, people who would bring descendents like Erastus Corning I. Most of them were poor, and did not belong to any particular church. Bible reverence was strong among them and they came here and built churches. They created a greater diversity in American Methodism, the Baptist church, and various other Protestant churches. They were very charitable: The Albany Medical Center and the Parsons Child and Family Center were set up by the New England Yankees. They were, as the stereotype sometimes unfairly will point out, Puritanical. Lotteries were a very popular way of funding government back in the early 1800s, but the New Englanders disapproved and pressured the legislature to wipe it out. They also formed our banking system.

The Irish and the Dutch had much in common. They were both family oriented. The Yankees were different: We think of Erastus Corning and of Featherstonhaugh who bankrolled the railroad. They were individuals, and we think of what each did. On the other hand, when we deal with the Dutch and the late Alice Kenny, it reminds us of the Gansevoorts of Albany. Which Gansevoort was she writing about? She talks about the Ten Eycks as a family. The Dutch functioned almost as a corporation: The families worked as a group. They had contacts up and down the Hudson Valley. It was not so necessary in the family value system for an individual to become a

millionaire. What was important was that the family went on and that the group prospered. I think the Irish could identify with that and, even in more modern times, when we think of the Conners in north Albany and the O'Connells and the Ryans, we think of families. Now and then, great individuals come up and you think of them, but they bring families to mind.

The Yankees wouldn't do that. They would make alliance with other New England families and you soon learned who was married into the Olcotts and that sort of thing. It would be hard for anybody to name the many brothers and sisters of Erastus Corning. They didn't function the same way. The Dutch considered them too cold, too businesslike. The Yankees considered the Dutch to be unbusinesslike people who did not value education enough. Education was important to the Yankees and they were the driving force, along with many upper-class Dutch families, to get a good public school here. Actually the school wasn't quite public, and it wound up being the Boys' Academy, which was begun with funds from the city of Albany. Eventually they expanded into a Lancaster school system which is where we get the name Lancaster Street. Eventually, it became part of Albany Medical College and then was torn down. This was a real public school: A classroom was similar to ours today, whereas in the true academy system (as in Albany Academy) we have smaller classes and several teachers. But it was the Yankees who brought us these institutions that not only served the need of their day but survived.

The Irish are often wrongly stereotyped. First, they were looked upon as newcomers. People said they ran out of potatoes and then they all came at once; that they didn't have any education, put tremendous strain on the system, and built huge slums; and by sheer numbers of their votes wound up taking over the government. It's a convenient scenario but untrue. Yankee versus Irish rivalries which show up in such works as *The Last Hurrah*, demonstrate a chasm between the two classes of people. The book is patterned after Boston. To show you how good the good will was in the mid and late nineteenth century, all the bridges were toll bridges out of Boston. This was intended to keep all the poor people inside Boston, and this is what made Boston so Irish. They couldn't afford to leave, so they took over the government.

Albany was never that bad. During the know-nothing movement, there was an Albany Protestant employment agency in the late nineteenth century, but it was very brief. There was individual resentment here and there, but you get that with any group. There wasn't convent burning or narrow bigotry in Albany because the established elite were there. People who came in were fully accepted by the Yankee-Dutch stock. These were people who came here during the Revolution, people who later fought, like James Mahar, in the War of 1812 as a leader of a group, the Irish Greens. There were enough Irish to form a military group that would take part in the wars against the British, conveniently out in the western part of the state in the Niagara Frontier.

The Irish in Albany in the 1820s, 30s, and early 40s were people like E. B. O'Callahan, whose documentary *History of New York* is a marvelous contribution which preserves Sir William Johnson's and Governor Clinton's papers. This was fortunate, because the State Library burned in 1912 and a lot of that original material was lost or damaged. Also of this period was Tracy, who lived in the Schuyler mansion. These were established, lettered, educated people who valued education. Both Tracy and O'Callahan were state librarians, and are the founders of the state library system we enjoy today. They present a totally different image from that of people coming with little education.

These people built the Erie Canal from 1817-1825 and started on the Champlain Canal in 1823. Next came the first railroad in the United States in 1831 which started here in Albany. The steamboat also started here, in 1807. A lot of Irish came over here at those times because of those transportation linkages. Many came poor, to a nation that was labor-starved and desperately needed workers. It was a nation that was

being built. Rresentment against them then was minimal. When there's work to be done and no one to do it, labor is always welcome: People who come during a depression, on the other hand, are resented. A lot of the Catholic-Protestant rivalries which occurred toward the latter half of the nineteenth century were not there in the earlier part. The second St. Mary's Church, which was built from 1829-30, was designed by Philip Hooker, a local architect, and the cornerstone was laid with complete masonic rites, attended by a number of prominent Irish-Catholic. This era of good feeling would change in the next 30 years.

In the 1830s, when the city was ten percent Irish, two out of five aldermen were Irish. Clearly, the Irish made important political alliances. Next, with the Cornings, they started their own newspaper. The way to political success was to own your own newspaper. Mayor Corning used to say, "Never argue with anyone who buys ink by the barrel," and in the nineteenth century they bought ink by the barrel, and newspapers made no pretense at being impartial.

Around the same time, the Germans came to Albany, among them German Jews. They became involved in political activities. They came with higher levels of education and of sophistication in dealing with government than the Irish. They came in the 1830s and after, and their great waves of immigration were centered on the revolution of 1848 and Bismarck's creation of a united Germany in 1866. But they, too, were well established in Albany before that. There were different waves of German immigration. One goes all the way back to the Palantinate Germans that Queen Anne brought over in the 1720s, who settled near Germantown, in Columbia and Dutchess Counties. They also went through the Schoharie Valley out to Fort Plain, Cherry Valley, and Palantine Bridge. There was a German-speaking Lutheran congregation here from the 1670s, barely tolerated by the Dutch Reform Church and the British.

The Germans are the forgotten group. In the four-county area--Albany, Rensselaer, Schenectady, and Saratoga--the largest ethnic group is Irish. Albany is 26 percent

Irish. The second largest group is German, at 19 percent. Not only are the Germans the second largest group in the city of Albany today, they're number two in Albany county and in every other nearby county except Saratoga. The Germans are often overlooked, because blacks, Italians, and other groups are more visible. The English are third largest in the four counties, except for Saratoga.

There are many groups of Germans. The early group that came over with the Dutch are the ones Charles Gehring is finding out about today. Another group is the very early Germans that came over in the 1830s, before mass immigration. And then other Germans came after 1866 in greater numbers. The great diversity of the German people is amazing, and they produced as many as seven weekly newspapers around 1900, sometimes published daily, in Albany and Troy.

The south end produced an alderman around 1890, Alderman McCann, who had to face the fact that his constituency was half German and half Irish. One would think he'd be damned if he did and damned if he didn't. It didn't work that way as McCann used to have all public announcements, including the *Albany City Record*, produced in two languages, and literally thousands of official documents would come out of the city of Albany in the German language. That's how respected the Germans were. Members of the Hohenzollern would come over here and take a tour of Albany and stop in at the German lodges.

About half of the Germans were Catholic and half were Lutheran, but some further split into other Christian groups. Also, there was a very strong German-Jewish community that founded the Adelphi Club, and was a highly intellectual, well respected group. Most owned stores in downtown Albany with names like Stuhlmakers and Steefles. Generally, German-Jewish merchants did well in the city. There was a whole German community on Central Avenue. The original St. Anthony's school, the one that's a free school now on Elm Street, was a German Protestant Church. There was a diversity of religion within the German community, and there were several churches in the nineteenth century. The Germans from the truck farms on Sand Creek Road used to come to Central Avenue to go to church. The open wagons would stop diplomatically in the middle of Central Avenue and half the people in the wagon would go to Our Lady of Angels and the other half would go over to St. Johns. The Germans lived with this phenomenon for a long time; half would go one way, half the other, and then they would go home on the same wagon as neighbors. One problem was that Germans who came over to the Lutheran churches in this country expected everything to be in the German language. But Albany Germans were people who had been here two hundred years, and they hadn't spoken German since the 1700s.

The two World Wars hurt the Germans. The government promoted anti-German feeling, wiped out the German language from the schools, and got rid of German books in the libraries. Caught up in wartime hysteria, many Germans changed their names, not just for convenience but because of discrimination. Just when things were coming back, World War II began. The census asked ethnicity in 1980 for the first time. Prior to 1980, if you were second generation, you were already homogenized as an American. This was the first time anybody was asked to fill out his or her heritage, and it was a surprise that Germans were the second largest group in virtually every community around here, at 19 percent.

Other groups came later in the nineteenth century to these same neighborhoods. The south end was part German and part Irish and at the far south end was the German community. Some of the Yankees lived on the wealthier streets, and any new immigrant group would be in the back streets. These neighborhoods were not solidly one nationality. You could see the diversity from all the church spires. There was actually a Dutch Reform, German-speaking church on Jay Street for recent arrivals, that became a black Jewish Synagogue. Reverend Delaney was a black southerner who came up here, became Jewish, and started a society of Albany Jews that's been here continuously since the 1890s.

Next came the Italians, the Polish, and the second wave of Jewish immigration all at about the same time. Early Italians tended to be artists and teachers. Albany does not have the Italian or the Polish presence that Schenectady has. Ethnically, by the way, Schenectady County is a standoff. Irish, Italian, German, and English are all about 20 percent. This is because when GE was being founded in the 1880s, Schenectady was little more than a village that moved up to city status. What happened in the 1880s is that, just as the Irish had been lured to come here and work on the Erie Canal, Polish, Italian, and French Canadian workers were recruited to come to this area to the industries, but at this time Albany didn't have the expanding industries. Poles and Italians went to the American Locomotive Works and GE in Schenectady. The French Canadians were given jobs in French-speaking mills in Massachusetts, and in Cohoes. Each of these groups could only afford one church. Originally, there were neighborhoods for the Italians in at least two major areas. (The Franciscans, by the way, used to do a lot of the writing back to Italy because many of the Franciscans spoke Italian, and some of those old letters are in Our Lady of Angels.) But basically they were downtown like most immigrant groups, around Sheridan Avenue, and down in the St. Anthony's area. Well into 1907, an Italian church was created, but only one because the bulk of Italians were in Schenectady, not Albany. Other Italian neighborhoods were being founded at the time, but when a family moved, and immigrant families moved constantly, the Italian housewife and mother would want to move near the church. Then that church would build a school, and that was one more reinforcement.

The same happened with the Poles. They started worshipping in their own language at Christian Brothers Academy downtown. They were scattered, some in the south end and some in the north end. Many lived in Sheridan Hollow. They built a church in the 1890s, just above Northern Boulevard. And so a Polish neighborhood built up around Northern Boulevard, Sheridan Avenue, down into Sheridan Hollow. The Bowery area around Central Avenue was home for the Germans and three or four blocks above the armory was Cork, an Irish neighborhood.

Greeks and Armenians came after World War I and moved to the south end. They all had a difficult time.

Rarely in Albany can you find a Jewish uptown family that comes from Arbor Hill. Only a few exist. Likewise, it's unusual to find an Italian family in Albany that comes from Arbor Hill, and usually you can name the one or two because they're such notable exceptions. There is something magic about Western Avenue: nobody ever crossed it in the years they built the uptown neighborhoods. Arbor Hill people went up into West Hill and then to Pine Hills. If you were in the south end, as you went for newer housing stock you went up Second Avenue, to Whitehall Road, and then over to New Scotland Avenue. The neighborhoods that were created were mixed.

Dan O'Connell's father, Johnny O'Connell, ran a bar on the corner of State and Pearl of the South End, or what was called "the attitudes corner." Diagonally across was Lanahan and MacWorth's grocery store to feed the hungry. O'Connell didn't run the neighborhood Irish bar and he didn't want to. He made sure that he published his menu every day in German. He was certainly Irish, but he wanted to speak German. And when politics changed in Albany (which it does every seventy years or so), he was ready. He knew a lot of people because he knew the two major groups. Today if we had an ethnic block and people were voting just Irish and German, he'd still get a third of the vote. It would be one-third because many of the part-Irish people are also part-German. There are so many Irish-German marriages in the city of Albany because the neighborhoods ran alternate streets. Children have a way of doing things to aggravate their parents, hence there was always a lot of social activity.

The public school brought people together, but not strongly in Catholic

Albany, because Our Lady of Angels had a German-speaking Catholic school four blocks away from St. Ann's predominantly Irish Catholic school. We now realize the melting pot didn't work. We refer to America of that time more as a stew, because although some people got melted down, there were still large pieces. Ethnic groups were mixing, but not with every ethnic group indiscriminantly.

By the same token, some "odd" combinations are common in Albany. For example, many Italian-Americans marry a Jewish spouse. Look at the neighborhoods, at School 15 in Albany. Westerlo Street used to have the large Italian families and it was a predominantly Italian section in the south end. A few Irish clung to St. John's, but basically there was a strong Italian presence. And then Herkimer Street, where Arnold Proskin comes from, was predominantly Jewish. These streets were packed into tight neighborhoods. Italian-Jewish business mergers were common in Albany, John Trifoletti and Ruby Gershowitz, for example.

Today's newer immigrants bring new challenges. They come with separate and unique histories, as has every immigrant group. We have our newer wave of blacks, and people forget that by percentage there were more blacks at the time of the American Revolution in Albany than today. This is so because of the large number of blacks who did the work to build the colony. But their population never grew. Throughout the nineteenth century, as the population of Albany quadrupled from ten thousand, the black population stayed at about one thousand. When the city population was only 36 hundred, that was a very high black proportion, as they numbered about eight hundred. But there weren't massive numbers of blacks coming up from the South or over from Africa to match the influx of Irish, Germans, or Yankees. The black population just never grew until a wave came up after slavery and another during World War I. Some older black populations around Albany have Dutch Bibles. There are also rural blacks. A community in Kinderhook can be traced back over two hundred years. The

city of Albany today is 16.1 percent black. In 1940, the city was about 1 percent black. By 1950, that had practically doubled. By 1960, it was 6 percent black and by 1970 the figure was 12.8 percent. If black immigration had continued at the same rate, 1980 would have found the city 25 percent black. This did not happen, but the 6 percent in 1960 was of a city of 126 thousand, while today's 16 percent is of a city of 102 thousand, or only 16 thousand people. That is only about two or three thousand more blacks in ten years. The immigration stopped, in part because the South had improved and many people moved back.

Irish immigration was unique. For most ethnic groups, men came over in the largest proportions. There was a desperate shortage of women. This was common in French Canada, for example, and totally different from the English-American experience. Irish were not like that. Irish immigration was actually 50 percent female, especially after the famine, so there was an opportunity to keep the culture alive, and often women carry on culture. Also unique for the time was that Irish women outlived Irish men.

Culturally, the Irish are very verbal, hate to get up in the morning, and like to start work no earlier than nine o'clock. They'll gladly work late, though. There's a reason for this. Ireland is very far north and has long twilights. You don't get up that early, but you stay up a long time to talk, hence storytelling and song are probably the greatest arts known to the Irish. Consequently, they become people oriented, and gravitate toward social work and religion.

In nineteenth century Ireland, you couldn't own land, couldn't own a horse worth more than a certain amount, and couldn't own many other things. The penal laws were unbelievable for Irish Catholics (virtually all of them), and consequently, the type of community they sent over here gravitated toward politics. In Ireland they were denied government participation until 1832, and they were denied education throughout the 1700s. This was similar to the situation for blacks. And this country offered an amazing amount of freedom for the Irish. That they could run for office, vote for the people they wanted, send their children to school, and purchase land (and they purchased land at an inordinately high rate as it was such a novelty) was a thrill to them. The women often went into teaching and men often found employment in blue collar jobs. They established colleges at an amazing rate. The number of college presidents today who are Irish is inordinate, and again, it's that value system; social work and education were things that mattered. This breaks down as the Irish get older and intermarry, losing a lot of their ethnic identity, but the Irish still haven't turned out a lot of nuclear scientists.

What happens with downtrodden people? (Surely, the Irish were downtrodden.) A lot of signs warned, "Irish need not apply," but we must look beyond the initial difficulties. I tend to think they did fine when there were jobs around, and they had a hard time when jobs were scarce, and people reacted accordingly. But the world they left behind had absolutely no opportunity at all. It was a worthless existence from an economic point of view. People did have land in parts of Northern Ireland and it was planted, but the British gave up in disgust and they sent over lowland Scots, who literally displaced people from their land and carved up a whole new area. That's why we have difficulty in Northern Ireland today. Those people are different and they validly feel that they're British, and they've been British for seven to ten generations. They've never thought of themselves as Irish, they've thought of themselves as an extension of Scotland or England, always part of the British Empire. In the rest of Ireland, the Irish were allowed to own land or rent land and pass the lease on to their children. A very common custom there is for people to live on land for generations and never own it. The way the law read, and this was enforced, if the oldest child was a Protestant, then the British law would take effect, which said if you had eight acres, one child got eight acres. If the oldest child was Catholic and the second child was Protestant, the second could opt for it. If the family stayed together, as it normally would, the old Gaelic law would take effect and the eight acres would become eight farms. Consequently, emigration looked attractive, and the long-term social solution to the problem, according to the British government, was emigration: They'll leave, and then the farms will be larger. And they left for America.

John J. McEneny is a fifth generation Albanian who has maintained a lifelong fascination with his hometown. He majored in history at Siena College and earned graduate certificates in community development and public administration from New Mexico State University and the Kennedy School of Government at Harvard University. He has been a Peace Corps volunteer in Columbia, South America. McEneny was Albany's commissioner of Human Resources and is the author of a book on the history of Albany entitled Albany, Capital City on the Hudson, 1981. He is an avid preservationist and lectures widely on government and local history.

Further Readings

Dinnerstein, Leonard and David M. Reimers. *Ethnic Americans: A History of Immigration and Assimilation.* New York: New York University Press, 1977.

Eiseman, Alberta. *From Many Lands.* New York: Atheneum, 1970.

Griffin, William D. *A Portrait of the Irish in America.* New York: Charles Scribner's Sons, 1981.

Kennedy, William. *O Albany!* New York: The Viking Press, 1983.

McEneny, John J. *Albany: Capital City on the Hudson.* Woodland Hills, CA: Windsor Press, 1981.

Shannon, William V. *The American Irish.* Rev. ed. New York: The Macmillan Co., 1966.

Thernstrom, Stephen, *et al.,* eds. *The Harvard Encyclopedia of American Ethnic Groups.* Cambridge: Harvard University Press, 1980.

Albany's Central Avenue has always been a meeting and working place for immigrant groups.

Ethnic pride in Albany--a melting pot since the beginning.

Each of Albany's ethnic communities contributes in its own way to Albany's diverse profile.

INDUSTRY AND
TRANSPORTATION

It was not enough for a colonial society to be self-sufficient. In return for protection and needed goods, the settlement had to return a profit to the mother country. So America was established as much in pursuit of an improved economy as religious and political freedom. Communities were generally set up in places which offered some means for making a living and opportunities for trade with other settlements.

Urban cultures are complex. Each community member provides services upon which other members depend. And the more complex and organized a community becomes, the greater the economic opportunities and the interdependence of its members.

Transportation of goods and availability of raw materials largely determine the success of a settlement. Thus, Albany's location in a principal waterway was crucial to its early success as a fur trading center. The community grew and prospered in proportion to the abundance of resources and the establishment of turnpikes, canals, railroads, and steamboat lines. Albany's position as a major crossroads and its proximity to such natural resources as Adirondack iron ore and white pine ensured the establishment and growth of iron, lumber, livestock and brewing industries in the nineteenth century. The strength of these industries, coupled with Albany's role as state capital, provided an abundant variety of job opportunities which, in turn, brought other industries and businesses. Albany grew at an enormous rate and became a financial and publishing center.

Instrumental to Albany's growing importance in the nineteenth century as a manufacturing, commercial, and political center was the career of Erastus Corning (1794-1872). A prominent manufacturer, merchant, banker and politician, Corning had a tremendous impact on the city. The political and economic influence of the Corning family continued throughout the twentieth century.

Advances in manufacturing and transportation elsewhere and the depletion of natural resources contributed to the decline of industry in the Albany area. The economic emphasis in this century gave way to the service and maintenance of government bureaucracy, the area's largest employer today.

MAKING A LIVING: MERCHANTS, MANUFACTURERS, AND BUREAUCRATS

Kendall Birr

Making a living is a serious business. Though we "live not by bread alone," surely, without bread we die. Hence, from the beginning of history, humans have been required to wrest a livelihood from an often reluctant environment. How can we enlarge our income? How can we equitably divide the fruits of our toil? How can we bring our wants and desires into line with our income? In short, making a living is surely one of the most elemental and universal of activities.

How did making a living in Albany differ from the same task in Springfield, Massachusetts; Des Moines, Iowa; or San Jose, California? To answer that question, two themes recur: Albany's location and its status as a state capital since 1797. These factors were important from the beginning, for as John McEneny observes in his history of Albany (1981),[1] the city "was an intersection of commercial and political traffic" even before the arrival of Europeans. Why was location so critical? Albany stood at the head of navigation on the Hudson River and at the eastern end of the most

practical gap in the great barrier to east-west movement posed by the Appalachian mountain chain and its extensions. The city stood astride the most economical trade route between the Atlantic Ocean and the great American interior. Its location afforded immense opportunity for commercial activity.

Indeed, the location promoted initial settlement when the Dutch West India Company established a trading post at Fort Orange in 1624. In the seventeenth and eighteenth centuries, Albany evolved as a commercial, political, and military center. Its economic welfare depended on three factors. First, was the fur trade. Albany became a way-station between North American trapping sites and European fur centers such as Amsterdam. By the late eighteenth century, the importance of the fur trade began to wane as trappers moved farther west in search of fur-bearing animals and as Albany merchants faced increasingly stiff competition from Montreal merchants. Second, Albany merchants cultivated the upper Hudson River area, collecting livestock, growing wheat, flour, and lumber, and exchanging these goods for imported manufactured goods. Such trade probably constituted the most stable part of Albany's economy during these years.

Finally, while trade was the heart of Albany's economy, that economy was occasionally affected by political and military events. Farmers and merchants in the eighteenth century had mixed feelings about war. On the one hand, war could be destructive, introducing an undesirable element of uncertainty into business affairs. On the other hand, if one could avoid the destruction and disorder associated with battle itself, there were economic opportunities to be had for provisioning troops. In the mid-eighteenth century, during the French and Indian Wars, Albany was the headquarters of the northern department of the British Army and, as such, served as a troop assembly point, provided winter quarters for troops, acted as a quartermaster supply center, and provided rear echelon hospital facilities.

Such activities made Albany one of the leading cities in the new American republic which won its independence by 1783. The city's population in 1790 was only about 3,500, about a tenth the size of New York City, in a new nation numbering fewer than four million. Ranking sixth in population in the country, Albany could look back on a record of economic success.

Then, after 1800, the city moved forward spectacularly. Its 5,000 residents in 1800 grew fivefold by 1830, reached 62,000 by the eve of the Civil War, and topped 90,000 in 1880. The city's growth reached a plateau at that point. It took another 30 years to reach 100,000, then slowly inched up to its peak in 1950 before beginning its recent decline. What caused that growth between 1800 and 1880? New people poured into the city in response to rapidly expanding economic opportunity. And Albany's economy took off.

How do we explain this period of extraordinary economic growth? It was a complex process, but basically Albany citizens took advantage of a unique set of circumstances related to the city's location,

and people flocked to the city to take advantage of job and business opportunities. Perhaps the process is best illustrated through the business career of one of Albany's most successful citizens, whose lifetime coincided almost exactly with Albany's economic growth spurt. His name is a familiar one in Albany, for he was the great-grandfather of the late mayor,[2] the first Erastus Corning.

Corning was born in 1794 in Norwich, Connecticut, and was to die 78 years later in 1872 as Albany's wealthiest citizen. His biography is almost, but not quite, a rags to riches story. He came from English stock who had lived in New England for several generations. Erastus was the fourth child and the third son of the family. Although we know relatively little about the family, there is evidence that his father was, to use the terminology of the day, somewhat "shiftless." Still, the family was well enough off to give Erastus a common school education which was better than that received by most young men of his generation. Perhaps he was given these educational advantages to compensate for his physical disabilities; he fell from his crib in his second year and sustained injuries which forced him to move about on crutches for most of his life. In any event, he continued his education until age 13, even after his family moved from Connecticut to Chatham in Columbia County.[3]

At age 13, Corning took a job as a clerk in a Troy hardware firm in which his uncle was a partner. The job was surely a menial one, but he took advantage of the opportunity to engage in some small commercial operations on his own, notably buying oranges and lemons in New York City and selling them from the stoop of the hardware store where he worked. Seven years later, in 1814, he moved to Albany, taking a position as a clerk in John Spencer & Co., a hardware and iron firm. Two years later, he used $500 he had apparently saved to become a partner in the firm, the remainder of his investment to come from his share of the profits. Both Corning and the firm did well; when John Spencer died in 1824, Corning bought Spencer's share from his heirs and became the sole proprietor of the hardware and iron company.

Corning's mercantile activities were very profitable and were to remain the base of his widespread business operations through the rest of his life. Like most merchants, Corning dealt at both the retail and wholesale level. The latter were far and away the more important part of the firm's operations. Located in Albany as it was, Corning's firm had easy access to imported goods through New York City and the cheap transportation of the Hudson River. In the next decades, both the Erie Canal and, later, railroads provided his firm with rapidly expanding markets throughout upstate New York and into the Great Lakes region. As we shall see, the construction of railroads provided his firm with marvelous markets for its iron goods. Like most merchants of the day, Corning bought goods on credit and in turn advanced credit to his customers. It was no wonder, then, that Corning should soon become involved in the development of Albany banking. And it was all very profitable. Just how profitable, we do not know with certainty, but we do know that by the late 1820s, he was looking about for new investment opportunities.

One of the first investments Corning made was in the iron business, purchasing in 1826 the Albany Nail Factory which, despite its name, was actually located on the banks of the Wynantskill[4] in South Troy. When he bought the company, it was principally a manufacturer of nails and spikes, but by 1837, when he brought in an effective managing partner, John F. Winslow, and changed its name to the Albany Iron Company, it began making axles for wagons and railroad cars. In the 1850s, Corning and Winslow bought another Troy firm which gave them the ability to smelt iron and roll iron rails.

It was a highly successful and lucrative business. Among its more notable achievements were rolling the iron plate that equipped the *Monitor*, the Civil War ironclad that fought the first naval battle between iron ships, and the construction in 1865 of the first successful American plant using the Bessemer process for making steel.

Indeed, the firm flourished until the depression of the 1890s. Corning's success tells us something about the economic advantages of the capital district in the first half of the nineteenth century and about the way in which a successful entrepreneur like Corning integrated his various enterprises. Where did the iron come from? Much of it was imported (again we note the advantages of cheap transportation on the Hudson and the profits that accrued to Corning's hardware and iron firm). But some of the iron was smelted in the area, using Adirondack[5] iron ore brought to Troy by the low-cost transportation of the Champlain Canal. Who sold the iron products? Again, the Corning hardware firm. To whom? In large part, to the expanding railroads.

Thus it was logical that Corning should invest in railroads at an early date. As a merchant, he was always interested in inexpensive transportation to move his goods, and as an iron-maker he was similarly concerned with markets for the products of the Albany Iron Company. He was an initial investor in the Mohawk and Hudson Railroad, operating between Albany and Schenectady,[6] which in 1831 provided the first steam railroad in New York state. He was one of the founders in 1833 and long-time president of the Utica and Schenectady. But, of course, his great triumph was arranging the merger in 1853 of a series of railroads between Albany and Buffalo to form the New York Central. He served as its president for the first 12 years of its existence. At the same time, he invested heavily in railroads in the west. It was said that in the late 1860s it was possible to go from coast to coast on railroads in which Erastus Corning had a substantial investment. Americans seemed little concerned about "conflicts of interest" in those days; hence, Corning regularly used his position as a railroad leader to enhance the sales of the Albany Iron Company and the hardware and iron firm he headed.

In the early nineteenth century businessmen of all kinds and merchants in particular operated by giving and receiving credit. Hence, many merchants including Corning were influential in the development of banks, which sprang up everywhere in the rapidly growing economy of nineteenth century America. Corning helped found the Albany City Bank in 1834 and served as its president until his death. As president, he personally examined all loan applications, a process which gave him immense information about and not a little power over business affairs in the city. Additionally, he helped organize and served as president of the Albany City Savings Bank and briefly headed the National Savings Bank. He had extensive interests in banks in other parts of upstate New York and in Detroit. In all cases, he made certain that the railroads he influenced did their banking with institutions in which he had invested.

Corning, like all successful entrepreneurs in the early nineteenth century, invested heavily in that greatest of all American natural resources--land. Throughout most of his career he was a major land speculator, investing in upstate town sites (Corning and Auburn), agricultural land in nine or ten different western states, and mineral and timber land in Michigan. One speculation is of particular interest. Corning was one of a group of eastern capitalists who in four years and for a million dollars built a canal around the rapids of the St. Mary's River between Lake Superior and Lake Huron (what we know today as the Soo Canal). In return, the state gave them 750,000 acres of Michigan land, including some very valuable mineral and timber acreage.

All of this was immensely profitable. By the time he ran (successfully) for mayor of Albany in 1833, he was widely regarded as one of Albany's wealthier citizens. He became a prominent Democrat, a leading member of the Albany Regency,[7] was four times mayor of the city, and served once as a state senator and twice as Congressman. On the eve of the Civil War, he was estimated to be worth $3 million, and on his death in 1872, his estate was valued at about $8 million.

If Corning was an example of some of the opportunities available to businessmen in the expanding city, his career did not exhaust the story of Albany's economic growth between 1790 and 1880. It all began with location. Citizens supported the various transportation revolutions of these years: the turnpikes in the 1790s, the advent of the steamboat on the Hudson with Fulton's *Clermont* in 1807, the construction of the Erie Canal between 1815 and 1825 and the completion of the Champlain Canal in 1822, and, of course, the building of the railroads in which Corning was so involved.

The construction work itself stimulated Albany's economy; the city's Irish population has its beginning in the workers brought in to dig the Erie Canal. More important, the new transportation built Albany's reputation as a commercial center. Early in the century the city was busy provisioning westward--moving Yankees from New England, populating upstate New York. Numerous jobs became available transferring goods from canal boats and railroad cars to river boats for the trip down the Hudson. Most important, Albany merchants took advantage of opportunities to collect agricultural goods from booming upstate farms and delivering the manufactured goods which enabled New York farmers to improve their standard of living. The merchants in turn with their credit needs turned Albany into an important banking and financial center.

In numerous specific ways, Albany entrepreneurs took advantage of their locational advantages. In the middle of the century, the city developed substantial stockyards to feed and water livestock in transit between western farms and eastern urban markets. Albany's importance as a rail center led to the establishment of the West Albany railroad repair and maintenance facilities. Heavy traffic on the Hudson created jobs for longshoremen and others in the activities of the dock areas. Others began to exploit the pine lands of the Adirondacks and turned Albany into a major lumber center. Availability of New York grain enabled others to establish a substantial brewing industry; as early as 1829, Albany produced some 42,000 barrels of beer, "exporting" about 30,000 barrels to other communities. Corning's career illustrates well the mid-nineteenth century prominence of Albany and the entire capital district in the iron business. These business successes generated jobs and population growth which, in turn, put heavy demands on construction to build the homes, shops, and factories required by a nineteenth century commercial and industrial city. Finally, the growing population generated the retail stores, recreational facilities, and other amenities that made nineteenth century urban life comfortable. It was an impressive growth spiral which in the space of eight decades converted a rather small commercial center on the Hudson to a bustling, modern commercial and manufacturing center.

Yet the evidence suggests it was beginning to come to an end in the 1880s. The rate of population growth slowed noticeably until population began to decline in the 1950s. What brought an end to these marvelous decades of economic growth and civic expansion? The basic answer is fairly simple: the locational advantages which had fueled Albany's growth in the early nineteenth century began to disappear. The process was slow but certain; it took nearly a century for its effects to be fully felt, nevertheless, they were felt. In the early twentieth century, the elements of decline were hidden from contemporaries; the overall economic environment of the city was sufficiently attractive that when one kind of economic activity died, another entered the city to take its place. A successful urban economy generates its own momentum.

Still, with the advantage of hindsight we can see the forces of decay at work. The most attractive stands of Adirondack pine were exhausted by the twentieth century, and lumbering largely disappeared as a major Albany activity by World War I. The iron and steel industry moved westward, closer to the incredibly rich and inexpensive Lake Superior iron ore; Albany's sources in the Adirondacks could not compete. The major wheat growing areas moved out of the Genesee country[8] to the upper mid-West and the Great Plains, and Albany merchants lost a significant trade. Refrigerator cars on railroads beginning in the 1880s doomed Albany as a stockyards center; cattle flowed into places like Chicago, were slaughtered, dressed and partially cut, and were then shipped to urban centers like New York City

with no need for an Albany layover. By the 1880s, the Hudson River and the Erie Canal, which had given Albany some initial advantages, were losing the battle with the railroads for traffic. Activities (and jobs) in the port area of Albany declined.

Some of the losses have been very recent, of course. The shift from steam engines to Diesel-electric locomotives made the West Albany shops of the New York Central obsolete in the post-World War II years. The nationwide revolution in brewing in the last two decades doomed almost all local breweries including those in Albany. Deregulation of banking and the internationalization of banking and finance in the very recent past have produced mergers which have lowered Albany's importance as a financial center.

In the face of all these negative developments, why was not Albany's economic decline quicker and more radical? In large part because the state and federal governments came to the rescue, and Albany's status as a state capital began to play a more important role in the city's economic life. The fact that Albany was the capital of the Empire State had always had some economic impact on the city. It guaranteed a larger than average legal profession, and it stimulated various support services: hotels, restaurants, etc. Albany's status as a state capital *may* have been a factor in making the city a major center for the printing industry. It is also interesting to speculate on the economic impact of the generation-long construction of the state capitol; some local workmen apparently had virtually lifetime jobs on the project.

Still, major impacts came only in the 1930s with the rapid enlargement of both state and federal governmental functions. Albany benefited doubly; not only did it have the center of state government in the city, but many federal programs were operated through the states, and state capitals like Albany became major centers for federal offices. The results are evident enough. In recent years, federal and state governments had become the leading employers in the area; state buildings--the so-called State Campus, SUNY at Albany, and the Nelson A. Rockefeller Empire State Plaza--dominate the city's skyline; local business is stimulated to provide various support services for state agencies and workers; and Albany banks have continued to flourish in part because of the heavy flow of state funds through their accounts.

Still, the outlook in 1985 seems at best uncertain. A half century of cheap gasoline led to the universal use of the private automobile; that in turn led almost inevitably to the flight to the suburbs and the concurrent decay of the central city. While Albany is doubtless grateful for the economic stimulus provided by the state, it also complains with justification of the erosion of the city's tax base with the spread of government buildings across the face of the city.

What can we learn from all of this? We need to learn that a community's prosperity can be a sometime thing, based on unique but temporary advantages. When those advantages disappear, the city may die unless its citizens can respond in some creative fashion. Albany cannot return to the flush economic times of its nineteenth century past. It *must* look to its future.

What might that future look like? Forecasting is hazardous, but I believe that one can see some large, impersonal social and economic forces at work, shaping the city's economy in the twenty-first century, forces that are unlikely to change radically in the near future. First, I believe we will continue to hear more about the "capital district," or some such entity, and less about Albany. The city is part of a major long-term process of regionalization that is not likely to be reversed. The *fact* of regionalization has been recognized by newspapers and public utilities, for example, but the equally intractable fact of local political jurisdictions often interferes with creative action. If the processes of regionalization continue, the prospects for the revival and rehabilitation of downtown commercial areas appear gloomy. But if downtown Albany is successfully revived, it will be something different from the bustling center of entertainment and retail trade it was as late as the 1950s. I must enter one caveat to this particular generalization. Regionalization has grown from cheap gasoline and the pervasiveness of

the personal automobile. The world supply of petroleum is limited, and fuel prices will inevitably rise as we move toward the twenty-first century. *If* gasoline prices should rise to a level of, say, $3.00/gallon, will people in the capital district begin to abandon the suburbs, turn to high-density housing in the city, abandon the personal automobile, and create conditions for efficient, convenient mass transit? Perhaps, and if all this should happen, Albanians may yet see in the year 2020 a downtown Albany providing services similar to those provided in its heyday a half century ago.

Second, people in Albany will come to the uncomfortable realization that less and less of their city's economic future is in their own hands. Important decisions affecting the economic welfare of Albanians will be made by corporate executives in remote places who are more concerned about the profitability of a proposed plant in Albany than about its economic impact on the community. The city will be more and more at the mercy of executives of multi-nationals, federal and state officials, and bankers headquartered in New York City with agendas other than the city's economic well-being.

Third, while I have argued that Albany's economic woes stem from the loss of its nineteenth century locational advantages, the loss has not and will never be complete. Albany remains an important transportation center with excellent railroads and the New York State Thruway close at hand. It should continue to show strength as a regional distribution center, and while the Port of Albany's future may be limited, nevertheless it has a future.

Fourth, government activities will continue to provide an economic base for the community. The next decades are not likely to see vigorous growth in public employment, but I don't believe there will be sharp cutbacks either. And this means that economic activities servicing government agencies will remain strong: the legal profession, the financial community, and so on.

But the best resource for the economic future of Albany is the quality and talents of its people: businesspeople, technologists, educators, workers of all kinds. Those resources are considerable, both in terms of the people who are actually here and the ability of the educational system to improve quality and sharpen talents.

In the final analysis, one of the most certain predictions about Albany's economy in the twenty-first century is that it will be very different from that of earlier generations. Albany, along with the rest of America, is moving into a "post-industrial" era, an "information" society. Skills, education, and the ability to serve effectively in an infor-mation-oriented society will mark the difference between economic success and failure. It is peculiarly appropriate, then, that this series of lectures should be sponsored by the SUNY Albany University Libraries and that this particular talk should be held in the State Museum. Libraries are the ultimate data bases, the repositories of the information on which the economy of the future will be based. The economic future of the city is inextricably linked to these important institutions.

Kendall Birr is a professor of history at SUNY Albany. His field of interest is American economic history, particularly the history of technology. He has published two books and numerous articles on American technology, and professionally uses Albany as an interesting case study of a community's relationship to different stages of economic and technological change. He received his B.S. from Cornell College and his M.A. and Ph.D. from the University of Wisconsin.

Endnotes

1 McEneny, John J. *Albany: Capital City on the Hudson.* Woodland Hills, CA: Windsor Press, 1981.

2 Elected Mayor of Albany in 1941, Erastus Corning II (1909-1983) remained in office until his death in 1983.

3 Columbia County is southeast of the Capital District on the east side of the Hudson river.

4 The Wynantskill Creek.

5 The Adirondacks are a mountain range of the Appalachians in northeastern New York, north of Albany.

6 Schenectady, home of the General Electric Company, is located on the Mohawk River west of the Hudson and north of Albany.

7 Albany Regency. Headed by Martin Van Buren, this political machine dominated New York State for a quarter century. In Albany itself, the Regency established the pattern for machine-type rule.

8 The Genesee River in western New York State flows northward into Lake Ontario.

Further Readings

Cochran, Thomas C. *Frontiers of Change: Early Industrialism in America.* New York: Oxford University Press, 1981.

Cochran, Thomas C., and William Miller. *The Age of Enterprise: A Social History of Industrial America.* New York: Macmillan Co., 1942.

Groner, Alex. *The American Heritage History of American Business and Industry.* New York: American Heritage Publishing Co., 1972.

Kennedy, William. *O Albany!* New York: The Viking Press, 1983.

McEneny, John J. *Albany, Capital City on the Hudson.* Woodland Hills, CA: Windsor Press, 1981.

Neu, Irene D. *Erastus Corning: Merchant and Financier, 1794-1872.* Ithaca: Cornell University Press, 1960.

Taylor, George R. *The Transportation Revolution, 1815-1860.* New York: Rinehart, 1951.

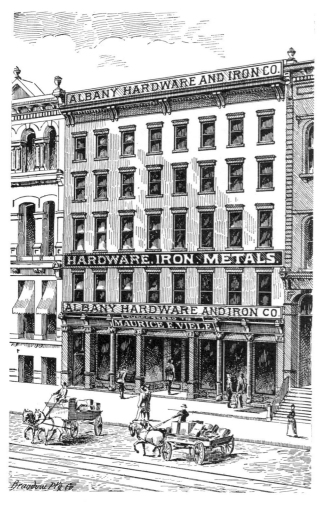

Erastus Corning and Albany Hardware and Iron Company, the man and his work.

ERASTUS CORNING.

[Third and present president of the Albany Cemetery Association.]

Transportation is how we get ourselves, our goods, and our property from one place to another. The city of Albany is the crossroads of the northeast and, therefore, transportation figures largely into the area's history.

A fascinating form of transportation is "electric traction." Here vehicles are powered by electric motors supplied with electricity from distant generating stations, of which trolleys are a good example. Trolleys were the result of experiments made on electric-powered vehicles supplied with energy from wires. They offered the advantages of electric propulsion: quiet operation, no fumes, and faster acceleration. Trolleys also could accommodate curb loading, but were less flexible than buses and required overhead wires for a return circuit. The costs of the trolley bus and motor bus depended upon local particulars, including traffic volume and cost of electric power.

Though Albany's trolley era ended in 1946, interest in trolleys is still keen. Trolleys were gradually replaced by buses of the United Traction Company until 1972 when CDTA took over. This history of the United Traction Company was compiled from various primary sources including the author's collection of photographs, clippings, memorabilia, and personal recollections.

GETTING AROUND: EARLY TROLLEY TRANSPORTATION

Fred B. Abele

A key factor in the development of any community is transportation--its ability to move about. From the beginning, Albany and its neighboring communities enjoyed a good path of commerce on the Hudson River. Passengers and freight were carried at first in sailing vessels, and later, for a century and a half, by steamboats. Initially, roads were crude, following paths blazed by Native Americans of the area.

The era of the turnpike, circa 1800, offered greater opportunity for travel between cities. The Cherry Valley Turnpike, originally Company of the Great Western Turnpike, opened in 1800. This route is now Western Avenue in Albany.

Additional improvement came with the railroad. The Mohawk and Hudson Railroad opened from Schenectady to Albany in 1831. Others soon followed to the east, north, and south.

The communities themselves were too small for anything but horse drawn wagons and carriages. By the Civil War era, however, the growth of cities and factories began to generate employment, and the need for reliable public transportation became apparent.

The notion of a steel wheel on a steel rail, with reduced friction, had already been implemented on the railroads. This increased efficiency and made it possible to haul larger and heavier loads. Thus, the horse drawn streetcar came into existence in Albany and nearby communities.

The corporate beginnings of the United Traction Company lie in highway-oriented street transportation. Its origins can be traced to the Watervliet Turnpike Company, chartered by the New York State Legislature in 1828 to build a turnpike from the city of Albany to the village of Green Island. After the road was built, a stage line used it for a brief time.

On 15 April 1862, the legislature approved a change in the company such that it included a street railway. The name was changed to the Watervliet Turnpike & Railroad Company.

The line was built as a double track line, beginning at the South Ferry (south of the Dunn Memorial Bridge), and running north over Broadway to the North Ferry (North Ferry Street). It was opened on 4 July 1863 after a test run. By 1864, the line reached the Albany Rural Cemetery, and a year later it had reached 25th Street in Watervliet. A branch was built over Albany's North Ferry Street to the ferry and north through North Albany's lumber district along what was the original Erie Canal.

On 14 September 1863, the Albany Railway was established. Beginning with the difficult hill, the company immediately tackled State Street. A contract was made on 16 October 1863 for a 3.5 mile line west from State and Broadway. The first segment of this line, running from Broadway to Congress Hall in the capitol vicinity, was opened on 22 February 1864.

Albany Railway extended the State Street line to West Albany, and built a line over North and South Pearl Streets to Kenwood, then the site of the Huyck Mill and later Kenwood Mills, until it burned in the 1890s. Additional lines were built on Clinton Avenue, Hamilton Street, Madison Avenue, and Lark Street. Stables and a car barn were built on Central Avenue near Lexington and on South Pearl Street at Gansevoort Street. During the 1870s, stone for the new capitol was shipped from Maine, and hauled up State Street on four-wheeled flat cars over horsecar tracks.

In 1889, the New York State Railroad Commission approved a change from horsepower to electric power, and on the evening of 27 April 1890, car number 75 made a test run for officials from State and Broadway, up State Street, Washington and Central Avenue, to the Quail Street barn. Regular service began the next day and electrification pushed forward.

The horsecar barn on South Pearl Street was converted to a power house where coal-fired generators produced the 600v DC power required to operate electric cars. This continued until 1918, when the transition to purchased power was made.

Early cars were 26 feet long with a single, four-wheeled truck and open vestibules. They were operated by a motorman and a conductor who collected fares and re-versed the pole at the end of the line. They were heated with stoves. Summer cars with open benches were also in operation.

The Belt Line, established over a combined route on 29 July 1894, was the most popular of the open cars. For a 5-cent fare, one could take a refreshing ride on a hot summer evening, leaving the car at the same point one boarded.

The first electric cars were color-coded, as had been the horsecars: red for West Albany, green for Hamilton Street, yellow for Clinton Avenue, and so on. Due to inflexibility in assigning cars to routes, this was soon discontinued. Signs were color-coded, however, during the period trolleys were in existence.

Many horsecars were converted to snow plows and sand cars. Express service between Albany and Troy was set up in 1894 to carry package freight. It is suspected that some of the express motors had been converted from closed horsecars.

The first double truck cars in the area (180 series) were acquired in 1898 from J. M. Jones Son's of Watervliet. They survived until 1934, after five rebuilds.

In 1892, Albany Railway leased the Watervliet Turnpike & Railroad, giving it entry into Watervliet and Troy. Neighboring Troy had its own trolley system, known by that time as the Troy City Railway. Unlike the routes of Albany, Troy lines radiated from the city to nearby communities and were a consolidation of the Troy and Albia Horse Railroad, Troy & Lansingburg Railroad, and Troy & Cohoes Horse Railroad.

On 31 December 1899, the Albany Railway, Troy City Railway, and leased Watervliet Turnpike & Railroad consolidated to form the United Traction Company, effective 1 January 1900. Cars were then integrated into one roster of equipment, augmented by 25 new open and 25 new closed cars purchased in 1900.

In 1901, the new company was hit by a strike over low wages and poor working conditions. At the same time, it received an order from the New York State Railroad Commission (prior to the PSC takeover in 1907) to provide closed vestibules on all closed cars, thereby insuring the protection of the crews. This work was performed in the North Albany shops.

By agreement with United Traction in 1901, cars of the Schenectady Railway's new line to Albany reached downtown Albany and terminated on lower State Street, east of Broadway. That same year, cars of the Albany & Hudson Railway & Power Company (later Albany Southern Railroad) entered Albany on United Traction rails in Rensselaer and Albany, and over the old Greenbush bridge. Albany Railway had extended its electrical trackage to Rensselaer in 1897.

Until 1904, all cars had been purchased from local builders--J. M. Jones Son's of Watervliet and Gilbert Car Company of Green Island. This pattern was broken in 1904 with the purchase of 10 cars from J.G. Brill Company of Philadelphia.

Stove heating gave way to underseat electric heaters made in North Albany by the Consolidated Car Heating Company. Car trucks were manufactured by the Taylor Electric Truck Company of Menands, and wheels by the Albany Car Wheel Company of Menands.

In 1905, United Traction acquired the Hudson Valley Railway, an interurban line consolidated from several smaller companies in 1901, and branching out from Troy to Glens Falls, Lake George, and Warrensburg.

In 1906, the Delaware and Hudson Railroad bought United Traction and maintained control of the company through 1928. At the same time, United Traction took responsibility for the Troy and New England Railroad, which had been in operation since 1895. This company was in operation from Albia to Averill Park and was acquired by the D & H in 1905. In May 1904, the Cohoes Railway Company was leased by United Traction, which already controlled its stock.

The parent company, Delaware & Hudson Railroad, formed a proprietary company called Northern New York Development Company. All new cars were purchased for United Traction by the company and leased to United Traction Company.

In 1913 the Delaware & Hudson Building and Plaza were constructed, which Schenectady, Hudson, Troy, and Cohoes subsequently used as a turn around and layover point.

After World War I, the effect of the automobile on receipts was felt sharply. As employees were demanding more money, the Delaware & Hudson was losing money. They proposed that one-man crews replace the two-man crews then in use. In 1921, a bitter strike broke out with violence lasting several months. Many strikers were left without employment, and bitterness persisted for years. In 1921, the company acquired, by lease, eleven one-man Birney Safety cars from Watson Manufacturing Company of Springfield, and received permission from the Public Service Commission to convert all city cars to a one-man operation. The last of these was the Albany-Troy car in 1924.

In 1922, all routes were numbered and color-coded, and by 1923, a bright color scheme of red, cream, and tan replaced the drab olive, light green and gray in use at the time.

The completion of the Barge Canal in 1918 and the abandonment of the old Erie Canal spelled doom for the Lumber District, the last of the horsecar lines, which was abandoned in 1921. Use of open cars was discontinued in about 1920.

Revenues continued to fall. In the early 1920s, the cities of Rensselaer and Cohoes passed ordinances to repave the streets over which trolley cars were run. Railroad law required that the Traction Company bear the cost of paving in the area between the rails and two feet outside the rails. In addition, there would have to be a large outlay for new rail and ties. As a result, the Traction Company explored other types of vehicles which did not require track.

The first of the Albany division lines to go was the number 11 Broadway-Aiken Avenue route. This occurred when Broadway was repaved north to Partition Street, and Aiken Avenue from Columbia to Riverside Avenue. Two custom built buses, numbers 51 and 52, were then used in that area.

Because the law prohibited traction companies from operating buses, a separate company had to be formed. On 14 April

1924, Capital District Transportation, Incorporated, was set up as a subsidiary to operate the buses.

Cohoes devised a different solution when it was decided in November of the same year that Columbia Street was to be repaved. The number 2 "C" Belt route was abandoned and trackless trolley buses were substituted. Four of these were purchased from Watson Manufacturing Company of Springfield.

Apparently these vehicles were not considered efficient. Plans to use them for the new Western Avenue route in 1925 were scrapped in favor of gas/electric buses, run on a gasoline engine generator which supplied power to an electric traction motor. The substitution took effect on 24 August 1925, when the Western Avenue route opened and the number 4 Country Club route was cut back to Manning Boulevard. The roadside track on the south side of Western Avenue was to be relocated to the center of the street for continued trolley operation.

New track was installed on Clinton Avenue from Pearl to Quail in 1928, and the street was repaved. In the same year, Hamilton Street was repaved and new track was installed from Grand Street to Lark Street. An ambitious program was launched to rebuild and refurbish cars which had survived the massive scrappings of 1925-1928.

On 28 November 1928, after several years of financial difficulties, the Hudson Valley Railway subsidiary closed down its operations. On 31 December 1928, Delaware & Hudson Railroad divested itself of all trolley holdings, including the United Traction Company.

In 1929, United Traction took delivery on its last trolley, a modern foot-controlled lightweight which was on exhibit at the American Electric Railroads Association convention in Atlantic City before it was shipped back to Albany. Built by Cincinnati Car Company, its aluminum body was both quiet and smooth. Although it was rumored to be the first of an order of 30, circumstances dictated otherwise. It was fondly dubbed the "Queen Mary" by the operators.

In December 1929, service ceased when the last car of the Albany Southern left Albany for Hudson. The company had become Eastern New York Utilities Corporation, acquired by New York Power and Light Corporation, which was interested in the power houses and transmission line in use today.

From 1931 to 1933, all lines in Troy, Cohoes, and Watervliet were motorized. In July 1933, the last car bound for Schenectady (number 562) left Albany in the gray dawn of a Sunday morning, the victim of a state plan to rebuild Route 5 and replace the old New York Central underpass. In February 1934, the West City Line route was abandoned for the same reason. The bus line then became number 1 Central Avenue.

On 4 February 1934, cars were operated for the last time on the number 9 Albany-Cohoes Route. Likewise, victims of proposed road and bridge widening and the UTC rail network were reduced to the City of Albany.

In 1936, the UTC assumed operation of the independent Slingerlands, Delmar and Elsmere Bus Line (SDE) and extended it to Berne, Voorheesville, and the communities along Delaware Avenue.

Only five trolley routes remained after 1934. In 1936, scrapping of the 600 series cars reduced the number of cars to 38, and the company was committed to converting to an all bus operation, as quickly as possible. Although abandoning these five routes was planned for 1941, it was postponed because of World War II and the freeze on bus allocation imposed by the Office of Defense Transportation (ODT).

Shortly after its release from Delaware & Hudson ownership, the company went into receivership. This was also encouraged by the Depression. In 1942, once the requirement for a separate bus company had disappeared from the statutes, a merged, reorganized United Traction Company, Incorporated, came into being. This company comprised all former subsidiaries.

In 1942, Crane Car 3 was rebuilt, decorated, and launched as "USS Navy Recruiter." As part of a ceremony commencing on lower State Street, it toured the city streets on a patriotic assignment and blew its air whistle, the last such whistle to be heard in Albany.

Early in 1946, permission was requested of the Public Service Commission and the City of Albany to substitute buses on the five remaining lines. On 21 July 1946, the last trolley excursion ran over all the remaining operable trackage. On the night of 10 August 1946, trolley operation ceased on four of the lines. The last car departed Quail Street at 11:10 P.M., returning at 11:40 P.M. The orderly crowd of more than 100 people who made the trip paused to sing "Auld Lang Syne" and then quietly left the car.

Finding itself in serious financial straits during the early 1920s, the United Traction Company had turned down a request for a trolley line up New Scotland Avenue. Residents organized and formed the Woodlawn Improvement Association Transit (WIAT) which operated a fleet of nine open, custom-built buses with side curtains. In 1925, this was superceded by the Albany Transit Company, which began operation with a fleet of AB Mack buses.

The company enlarged its scope by adding the Washington Avenue and West Albany routes. These routes coincide, for the most part, with today's CDTA routes 2, 12 and 13. Buses were originally two-toned green with a yellow stripe, later white, and finally gray, at which time the operation was nicknamed the "Gray Line." United Traction absorbed the operations of this company in 1948.

In 1971, United Traction operations were sold to Albany County, and on 15 August 1972, to CDTA, ending nearly three quarters of a century for the woven emblem so familiar to Albany riders.

Fred B. Abele, now deceased, was an engineer with New York State Department of Transportation and well-known local historian. As the author of a book on the planning, construction, and operation of the Mohawk and Hudson Railroad, and as a collector of photographs to accompany his collection of data, Fred Abele was well qualified on this topic. He was also president of the Guilderland Historical Association, and volunteered for the McKownville Fire Department. Abele published the Guilderland Historical Calendar each year, drawing upon his vast collection of photographs for this project.

Further Readings

Hilton, G. W. and J. F. Due. *The Electric Interurban Railways in America,* 1960.

Klapper, Charles. *The Golden Age of Tramways.* 1961.

Linecar, H. W. *British Electric Trains.* 1949.

Miller, J. A. *Fares, Please!* 1941.

Owen, W. *The Metropolitan Transportation Problem.* 1956.

Owen, W. *Strategy for Mobility.* 1964.

Stone, T. R. *Beyond the Automobile: Re-shaping the Transportation Environment.* 1971.

Taafe, E. and H. L. Gautheir, *Geography of Transportation.* 1973.

Williams, E. W. *Future of American Transportation.* 1971.

This bustling center for the region has always reflected the latest transportation technology

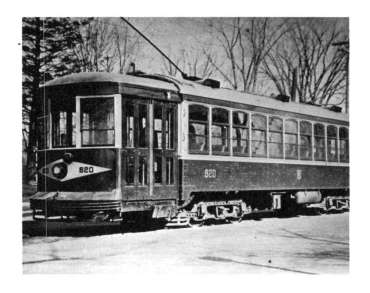

In 1982 the Port of Albany celebrated its golden fiftieth anniversary. These fifty years represent a mere fragment of time in Albany's history as a major inland port. We might tell this history starting with the arrival of Henry Hudson in 1609, though the river had been important to the Indians long before the arrival of the Europeans. Early "port" activities centered around the lucrative fur trade; later, as settlements grew and prospered, a true port was established to facilitate the importation of goods and supplies.

In addition to mercantile trade, Albany was an important passenger port from its earliest settlement. A ferry system across the river was established in the mid-seventeenth century. Before the development of railroads and thruways, sloops and steamboats provided passenger service between Albany and New York City. The Hudson River Day Line transported and entertained generations of travelers until 1948.

For many years Albany's bustling port was situated directly at the center of the city's waterfront, and by the end of the nineteenth century, it presented a sorry face to those entering the city by boat. Docks, warehouses, and piers cluttered the riverside, and the thousands of boats entering the Erie Canal through the Albany Basin each year only intensified the mayhem. The convergence of major rail and navigational lines in the early nineteenth century spurred Albany's growth as a metropolitan center, but also contributed to the aesthetic deterioration of the waterfront. Many motions were initiated to beautify the riverfront, which lay along the base of State Street in plain view of many, including those in the Capitol building. The construction of the Delaware and Hudson Railroad building at the foot of State Street in 1914 was a major step toward dismantling the dilapidated port area and regenerating the downtown district of the city.

The next improvements of Albany's waterfront were the establishment of a deep ocean channel in 1927 and the subsequent creation of the Port of Albany in 1932. Shipping Concerns and dock facilities were relocated to the south of the city, enabling Albany to enter its fourth century as a major inland port.

THE PORT OF ALBANY IN THE DAYS OF SAIL AND STEAM

Richard W. Wilkie

In the fall of 1609, when Henry Hudson navigated his ship to a point opposite the present city of Albany, there was no port, no city. In 1614, though, at a small island fort, the Dutch initiated a lively fur trade with the Indians. During the age of sail, the early fur trade grew to include such items as flour, fish, tar, horses, and above all, lumber. Sloops and schooners brought rum and sugar from the West Indies, and hardware, wine, and yard goods from Europe. Having reached the city of Hudson, these goods were frequently off-loaded to smaller craft and sent on to Albany.

In 1642, the first ferry between Albany and the east shore began service, and Albany quickly developed as a major port for passengers: In the seventeenth and eighteenth centuries, the only convenient means of travel between Albany and New York was by Hudson River sloop.

In 1807, commercial steam passenger service began at Albany when Robert Fulton's original vessel, the *Clermont*, was enlarged and renamed the *North River*. After 1863, the Day Line from Albany became a regional institution. Until the mid-nineteenth century, however, packet sloops carrying passengers or freight competed quite well with the steamboat.

During that early period, Albany's waterfront was actually the port. Warehouses, freight, and passenger docks were shadowed by hundreds of masts and spars all the way north to the famous lumber district along the final one and one-quarter miles of the Erie Canal. The Albany Basin was created by 1820 with the erection of a pier attached to a bridge at the foot of State Street, and by a second pier running north to the Erie Canal's southern terminal. By 1890, there were ferries to Bath and Greenbush, and two railroad bridges as well, because Albany had become a major railroad terminal. A smaller bridge from the foot of South Ferry Street across the river to Third Avenue in Greenbush (now Rensselaer) is shown in the Beers map of 1894, an important commercial shoreline map.

The fact that Albany rests at sea level meant that the geographic position was strategic when the waterways west to the

Great Lakes and north to Lake Champlain were completed. The Erie Canal, begun in 1817, was opened to barge travel by Governor DeWitt Clinton in 1825; and the present barge canal system, completed in 1918, added the Champlain, Oswego, Cayuga, and Seneca Canals. These developments place Albany and its port at the junction of several thousand miles of important waterways.

All the conditions necessary, then, for a truly great port at Albany were present: convergence of canal and rail traffic, a growing network of roads, and nearly a third of the nation's population within a radius of 250 miles. All conditions were present, save one: The shifting shoals and sandbars extending 30 miles south of Albany allowed no conventional ship to pass.

The Hudson River below Troy is not a river at all, but a tidal estuary; therefore, ocean vessels could sail to the bay just north of the present city of Hudson. If these vessels when loaded could float in relatively shallow water, they could then sail all the way to Albany. So it was "shoal draft" schooners and the famous Hudson River sloops that gave rise to an Albany "seaport" 124 nautical miles from the sea.

The lithographs, paintings, and photographs of the Albany waterfront in the nineteenth and early twentieth centuries show these "shoal draft" watercraft: the depth of their keels below the waterline was shallow enough to enable them to navigate over the sandbars below Albany. Steamboats and their barges seldom "drew" more than eight or nine feet. In fact, according to Captain Collyer, an author of *Sloops of the Hudson*, the largest sloop ever to sail the Hudson, the 220-ton Albany-built *Utica*, probably drew only about nine feet.

Even so, the sandbars in those years caused no end of stress for even the best pilots of shoalcraft. Benson Lossing, in his descriptive 1866 account of the Hudson, mentions the sight of from 20 up to sometimes 50 craft fast aground on one of the worst bars, the Overslaugh, just south of Albany. This was not rare evidently, and he says, "The amount of profanity uttered by the vexed sailors was sufficient to demoralize the whole district." If Albany were to fulfill

her promise as a major world seaport, something would have to be done about the sandbars.

The first effort to overcome these navigational problems may have been the erection of a large dike around 1790 near Papskanee Island; previous attempts may have been made, however, since the earliest known maritime chart of the Hudson, that of Joshua Lorning in 1756, indicates a preferred channel of at least four feet depth from Albany to Claverack (Hudson). During the period 1853 to 1863, a number of dikes were built between Albany and New Baltimore. They were supposed to achieve a minimum channel of eight feet which would still allow only about 12 to 14 feet of draft at high water.

Around the mid-nineteenth century, an interesting controversy was set in motion between the proponents of dikes and canal supporters: William J. McAlpine in 1852 had drawn plans for a ship canal to run from a lock at New Baltimore to a projected ship basin about where the present port of Albany lies. In the short run, proponents of the dikes won out. But by 1913, it was finally clear that the channel between Albany and the city of Hudson would have to be dredged to allow passage of the new deep draft motor vessels.

The invention of diesel power and the construction of deeper draft ocean carriers meant the end of the shoal draft era of commercial sail and steam at Albany's port. Gone were the days, for example, of the freight sloop Canaan, built in Albany in 1826, which had made a memorable passage to Providence, Rhode Island, carrying lumber.

In 1915 Congressman Peter Ten Eyck successfully sponsored a bill in Congress to survey the Hudson for the purpose of dredging a deep water channel. By 1923 it became incumbent upon the Deeper Hudson Committee of Albany and Troy to prove the feasibility of deepening the Hudson River. The committee raised the $20,000 necessary for the survey. In 1924 their plan for a deep channel was approved by the Army Corps of Engineers and in 1925 was signed into law by President Calvin Coolidge. That was a keen moment of joy for the men who had worked so hard, since the Rivers and Harbors provided over $11 million to dig a 30-mile ocean channel 27 feet deep at mean low water and about 400 feet wide from Hudson to Albany. In April of 1927 the great dredges began to work, and the channel was finished in June of 1931.

Governor Alfred E. Smith had signed a bill in March of 1925 creating the Albany Port District Commission which then directed the building of a good portion of what we know today as the Port of Albany. The 200 acres of land set aside on Albany's shore transformed Westerlo's Island into 4,000 feet of dockside, and the 100 acres on the Rensselaer side into a 605-foot dockside designed to handle huge shipments of lumber. The entire landsite of the port was raised some 18 feet to allow major ocean freighters to load and discharge cargoes from around the world. The Port of Albany with its new grain elevator and first two sheds was dedicated in a gala celebration on 6 and 7 June 1932.

Richard W. Wilkie, *associate professor of rhetoric and communications at SUNYA, received his Ph.D. at the University of Michigan. Wilkie's fields are rhetorical theory, theory of argument, political rhetoric of left radical movements, and discourse analysis. He and his wife Lee are well-known folk singers in Albany and collectors of Hudson River songs.*

Further Readings

Hislop, Codman. *Albany: Dutch, English, and American.* Albany: The Argus Press, 1936.

Kimball, Francis P. *The Capital Region of New York State: Crossroads of Empire.* 3 vols. New York: Lewis Historical Publishing Co., 1942.

McEneny, John J. *Albany: Capital City on the Hudson.* Woodland Hills, California: Windsor Publications, 1981.

Port of Albany 1932-1982: Golden Anniversary Celebration. Albany: Golden Anniversary Committee, 1982.

Sears, Mary Hun. *Hudson Crossroads.* New York: Exposition Press, 1954.

ALBANY POLITICS

The city of Albany has a long history of machine activity. While urban political machines vary in form and operation, they are nevertheless quite similar. The political machine is actually a political party that becomes rooted in favoritism and the use of material inducements. Typically the political machine has a tight, hierarchical organization with party agents at the grass roots level and systematic distribution of patronage among its members.

In order to understand the nature of machine activity in America, a distinction must be made between two types of political organizations prevalent in American cities. Party organizations which combined all the essential features of a machine with a neighborhood focus are known as "factional" machines. The factional pattern developed when several ward-level machines would compete with each other and "regular" political groups for city power. By contrast, when city politics is effectively and durably controlled by a single machine, the "dominant" pattern is at work.

Because of the variation of machine organization in American cities, the evolution of machine politics in America is difficult to trace. Most scholars agree, however, that political machines first took hold in post-Civil War cities, flourishing by the turn of the century and declining in the mid-twentieth century. Research indicates that it was the factional pattern which emerged first, as early as the mid-nineteenth century, and became the more common form of organization politics.

Machine activity peaked at the turn of the century. It is estimated that over the entire period of organized machine activity, at least one half, and perhaps far more than one half, of all sizeable American cities experimented with bossism.

MACHINE POLITICS

M. Craig Brown

When it comes to politics, Albany resembles, even now, what historians think American cities were like a century ago. The elements of "machine politics"--powerful political leaders, strong party organizations, numerous and dutiful ward politicians, and a political style based less on issues than the exchange of jobs and favors for votes--continue to be as prominent in discussions of Albany as is the picture sketched of cities in the decades before the turn of the century. As a result, attempts to understand the origins, development, and amazing persistence of Albany's machine politics seem to offer an unusual opportunity to enlighten us about Albany while at the same time illuminating the American urban past.

The answers to many questions about Albany's politics, buried in public and private records and preserved in the recollections of participants, will be provided, if at all, with standard historical methods. Nonetheless, as a complement to traditional approaches, it might be useful to consider how Albany compares with other American

cities. This broader point of view can show how Albany is similar to or different from other places, and point to possible explanations of Albany's political pattern. Before we can implement this comparative strategy, however, it is important to be clear about what we mean by machine politics--a term that is used with little precision.

What is Machine Politics?

To properly understand machine politics we must look behind the political rhetoric that has made it possible to attach the label, "boss," to a bewildering array of city politicians. Nor were bosses and their machines necessarily bad or corrupt. Among social scientists, the politician machine has instead come to be regarded as something much more neutral--a political party wherein a very personalized style of generating support sustains an elaborate grassroots organization.

As political parties, machines run candidates for office and strive hard on behalf of the ticket--without electoral success the benefits of holding office cannot be placed at the disposal of the organization. Machines pursue success in a style that is distinguished by a heavy emphasis on "specific material inducements"--a lofty way of describing concrete rewards like jobs and political favors--to generate support. The political use of jobs and favors is certainly not confined to machine politicians, but they exploit patronage and payoffs on a scale that is quite distinctive. Moreover, this variety of political favoritism animates an organizational hierarchy that reaches from the boss down to ward and neighborhood politicians acting as representatives to the voters the machine seeks to serve.

It would be a mistake, however, to think all political machines were equal. Some machines combined all the necessary ingredients at the neighborhood level, either foregoing or enjoying limited success at city-wide influence. Good examples of these factional machines are those that "specialized" in the needs of a particular ethnic group. Other party organizations combined the elements of machine politics on a city-wide scale, effectively and durably controlling a city's politics. These dominant machines varied considerably among themselves, but all of them actually "bossed" an entire city.

How to Recognize a Political Boss

Keeping these distinctions about machine politics in mind, we sifted the histories of the 50 largest U.S. cities at 1900, looking for descriptions of party organizations composed of bosses and ward politicians and fueled by patronage and favoritism. Thirty cities, Albany among them, were well enough described to allow us to judge the nature of their politics from 1870-1945--a period usually thought to have witnessed the rise and fall of machine politics. Before trying to use these data to draw the larger picture of machine politics and how Albany fits into it, however, we should be more concrete about the three basic outcomes of our search for boss politics in a given city at a given time.

First, we sometimes concluded that, for some period, a city was without political machines. This generally occurred when someone stated plainly that there were no machines, described an alternative political style (e.g., "reform" or domination by an economic elite), or misused the machine label. As we noted above, the term boss has been loosely applied, and in cities like Minneapolis, Minnesota, and Portland, Oregon, there was never enough organization and political style to sustain the liberal use of the label in city politics.

Second, we often found that for a given time a city was characterized by factional machine politics. In the last quarter of Cleveland's nineteenth century, for example, a number of politicians, some were ethnic specialists, built neighborhood organizations on reputations for befriending their constituents. The emergence of these ward bosses was not, however, accompanied by a serious attempt to consolidate control of Cleveland's government until very near the turn of the century. Therefore, in this period Cleveland is classed with other cities and times having a factional style of machine politics.

Third, we sometimes decided that a political machine was in control of city government. These were not always easy decisions, since machines varied greatly in how much power they wielded in city politics and how long they wielded it. As a result, we developed the specific rule that to qualify as a dominant or city-wide machine, a party organization had to hold control of the mayor's office and a majority on the city council for an unbroken string of three elections. There can be little doubt that a machine controlling the mayor and council for three elections did actually "boss" the city.

We need go no farther than Albany for some of the best examples of dominant machine politics. In the years from 1870 to 1945, three machines emerged in Albany. The first, bossed by D. Cady Herrick, consolidated power in the 1880s. The Herrick machine is poorly described and its beginnings are uncomfortably vague. We use 1884--the first of a string of Democratic electoral victories--as the provisional date of ascendance, pending badly needed research on this period in Albany's political history. Despite electoral success, however, this was not the disciplined Democratic machine that

68

was to come later. Indeed, after only a decade in power, Democratic control in both the council and the mayor's office was broken by a "reform" administration. The Democrats bounced back in 1895 and 1897, but, badly divided and ripe for a final upset, they were through as an organization.

In 1899, the Republicans, led by William ("Billy") Barnes, finished what was started five years earlier and opened a period of Republican hegemony that was to last more than 20 years. Barnes, the grandson of Thurlow Weed, used his position as a newspaper publisher to harass the Democrats and revitalize the Republican party. Barnes had started his rise as the Republican state committeeman and the leading Albany Republican. Called the "boy leader," after gaining control of the city he went on to play a prominent role in state and national Republican politics. Becoming, in effect, a boss *in absentia*, Barnes and his local organization faltered as the 1920s approached. Finally, in 1921, the reorganized Democratic party terminated the dominance of the Barnes machine and opened a new era of Democratic control.

The Democratic victory in 1921 had its immediate roots in Dan O'Connell's upset election in 1919 as an assessor. He was the lone Democratic winner. Seizing the momentum of that victory, Dan, in association with his brother Ed and the patrician Edwin Corning, took control of the Democratic party and then the city. Dan O'Connell gradually became the undisputed boss and the Democratic machine tightened its hold on Albany. In the 17 elections between 1921 and 1981, the organization enjoyed success without exception. The machine survived the death of Dan O'Connell in 1978, passing the reins to Erastus Corning, Albany's perennial mayor. The death of Corning in 1983 has left the future of the organization somewhat clouded but by no means bleak.

Machine Politics in Thirty American Cities

In all, we examined 76 years of politics in each of 30 cities. Most of these city-years were characterized by machine politics. Nearly two-thirds were accounted for by machines of either the factional or dominant type, and only seven cities failed to make contribution to this total by remaining untouched by either variety of machine politics. In 1870, around half the cities had either a factional or dominant machine, but this proportion increased sharply until the early 1890s when, for nearly a decade, about eight in ten cities had machines of some kind. Thereafter, machine politics declined to its low point in 1945.

So far the overall pattern of machine politics fits the standard historical renditions quite well. The rise of machines to prevalence in the three decades before the turn of the century is widely predicted and is usually attributed to the social and political disarray accompanying urbanization, industrialization, and immigration. The decline after 1900, also commonly expected, is thought to have resulted from a political environment made less hospitable to machines by reform efforts and the gradual assimilation of the foreign born. However, carefully separating factional and dominant patterns sheds new light on the history of machine politics.

Factional machines greatly outnumbered dominant ones. Of the city-years accounted for by machine politics, about seven in ten were due to factional machines. This means that the overall trend in machine politics is largely a trend in factional machine politics. As a result, historians who describe machine politics in the fashion we noted above may actually be providing a description and an explanation of the factional variety of the phenomenon.

We found only 25 dominant machines. Included are the famous city bosses: Tweed in New York, Chris Buckley in San Francisco, Jim Pendergast in Kansas City, as well as less well known George Aldridge in Rochester and Tom Dennison in Omaha. These machines consolidated control in 17 (57%) of the 30 cities, enjoying periods of domination ranging from the necessary minimum of three to as many as 17 elections. The so-called Tweed Ring in New York was the first instance of machine domination and from this point (1865-66) on. Machines became, by fits and starts, more and more prevalent until the early 1930s when, with about one third of the cities ruled by a boss, dominant machine politics peaked. Thereafter, dominant machines declined until 1945 when around two in ten cities were under machine control.

Dominant machines were thus present in numbers and times, perhaps for reasons unanticipated by most historians. As a result, new explanations are needed for these important developments. Perhaps Albany's experience can provide some promising clues.

How Albany Compares

How does Albany contribute to the pattern of machine politics in American cities? Table 1 presents comparisons across cities of various aspects of machine politics. To increase the validity of these comparisons, groups of big and small cities are created. Albany is, in turn, separated from its small-city peers.

First, consider differences between big and small cities. In several respects, big cities are, as most historians would probably predict, much more prone to machine politics. First, all 14 big cities had one kind of machine or the other at some point between 1870 and 1945, while only a little more than half the smaller cities did. Second, in big cities 90 percent of the years between 1870 and 1945 were characterized by machine politics--almost twice the average of smaller cities. Third, bigger cities were also much more likely to see factional machine politics develop into domination by a political boss.

When it comes to the durability of machine control, however, size differences are not so clear. Despite being more likely to have had a dominant machine, bigger cities spent about the same amount of time as smaller cities being controlled by a political boss. As the last row of Table 1 shows, this is because dominant machines in small cities typically lasted somewhat longer than their big-city counterparts (23 versus 15 years).

It thus appears that while big cities were more likely to experience machine politics and machine domination, small cities were easier to control once "dominated."

Small cities may not have been particularly inviting to machines, but if a machine managed to gain the upper hand, it typically controlled a city for nearly a quarter of a century. This is a very surprising result in light of most discussions about machine politics and one that has particular relevance for Albany.

It takes only a glance at the comparisons in Table 1 to appreciate Albany's exceptional political history. Albany was in the bare majority of smaller cities that experienced machine politics of one type or the other, was characterized by machine politics throughout the *entire* period 1870-1945, was among the minority of small cities that developed a dominant city boss, and was under the influence of a dominant machine about four times as long as the average of other cities, big or small. Only two other cities, both large, had three episodes of machine domination. And the O'Connell/Corning organization, though it continued beyond the period of interest in this study, represents America's most durable urban machine. Albany is, in many ways, the archetypical machine city.

What accounts for Albany's exceptional political style? For a variety of social and economic characteristics that are often thought to be associated with machine politics, Table 2 compares Albany to other cities, retaining the distinction between smaller and bigger cities. Interestingly, Albany started out in 1870 as a larger than average "small" city, lagged behind by 1890, and ended up as a small city among small cities. The population growth figures graphically demonstrate the dynamics of Albany's slide in the size hierarchy of American cities: Albany always grew at a substantially slower rate than its thriving small-city cohort. In the density of its population, Albany was not consistently different enough to explain why it differed politically from other cities.

Nor was Albany much different in the "foreignness" of its citizenry. In the "Irishness" of its foreign born, however, Albany was, for at least four decades, both relatively and absolutely high. The Irish concentration among foreign born might be a profitable object of further investigation.

The same is not true of homeownership and the emphasis on manufacturing in the local economy, since in these characteristics Albany is indistinguishable from other cities.

In short, while there is certainly nothing dramatic enough in Table 2 to completely explain Albany's politics, there are more small pieces to the Albany puzzle and the larger one about machine politics in America. We conclude by turning to these puzzles.

Conclusions

From what we can tell, Albany is an "unexceptional" city, save for its exceptional record of machine politics. As a result, Albany is not an easy city to explain. It is not so hard, however, to dispense with some explanations. It is clear, for example, most of the traditional ideas offered by social scientists are not of much promise here. It is also clear that the almost irresistible urge to explain local politics by the personal qualities of the politicians involved--Herrick, Barnes, O'Connell, Corning--should be resisted. Albany has been controlled by four bosses, and the differences among them in style, personality, and background belie a single explanation. Even the incredible O'Connell/Corning organization prospered before Corning, after O'Connell, and may yet continue beyond Corning.

If Albany's political history is distinguished by powerful organizations, perhaps qualities of these organizations hold the key to understanding Albany. Though beyond the scope of this report, our preliminary explorations suggest that the "organizational" explanation is at least suspect. The O'Connell/Corning machine, for example, was no more disciplined, organized, or service-minded than many other organizations that were much less successful. The O'Connell/Corning organization was distinctive mainly because it worked so well.

To finally understand Albany, we need to find out why the pattern of dominance prevailed virtually without interruption from machine to machine. What is it about this city that lends itself to the inertia of dominance? Is it the emergence of an ethnic political configuration more than a century ago that somehow replicates itself? Or is it the manifestation of what William Kennedy has called a "patroon psychology"?

Even if we do not fully understand all the details of Albany, as a small city it may still have a general message about understanding the history of urban machine politics in America. That message revolves around the ability to govern small cities. Traditional explanations of machine politics stress the link between the chaos and complexity of social change and the growth of bosses. This report shows that these social forces may push a city towards a mixture of factionalism and short-term dominance. In smaller and simpler cities like Albany, control, once achieved, can be sustained. Of course, nowhere else has this control been quite as sustained as in Albany.

M. Craig Brown is a sociologist specializing in the quantitative study of organizations and cities. He received his B.S. in mathematics and statistics from Colorado State University. After receiving his M.A. in sociology from Colorado State University, he attended Cornell University where he received his Ph.D. in 1976. He was assistant professor of Sociology at SUNYA, and he currently works for New York State. In addition to publishing articles on the sociology of organizations, Brown has directed a three-year project, funded by the National Science Foundation, studying urban progressive reform and the evolution of urban political machines in U.S. cities from 1870-1945. Brown is writing a quantitative historical account of the distribution of political machines across cities and over time. Albany is one of the focal cities in this study.

Further Readings

Callow, Alexander B., Jr. *The City Boss in America.* New York: Oxford University Press, 1976.

Clark, Terry N. "The Irish Ethic and The Spirit of Patronage." *Ethnicity*, 2 (1975), 305-359.

Greer, Scott. *Ethics, Machines, and the American Urban Future.* Cambridge: Schenkman, 1982.

O'Connor, Robert Emmett. "William Barnes, Jr.: A Conservative Encounters the Progressive Era." Ann Arbor, Michigan: University Microfilms, 1972.

Robinson, Frank S. *Albany's O'Connell Machine, An American Political Relic.* Albany: The Washington Park Spirit, 1973.

Teaford, Jon C. "Finis for Tweed and Steffans: Rewriting the History of Urban Rule." In *The Promise of American History: Progress and Prospects.* Baltimore: John Hopkins Press, 1982, 133-49.

Table 1

Machine Politics in Big Cities, Smaller Cities, and Albany

Machine Politics 1870-1945	Group of 14 Bigger Cities	Group of 16 Smaller Cities	
		All 16	Albany
Percent With Either Type of Machine	100%	56%	Yes
Average Percent of Years With A Machine of Either Type	90%	48%	100%
Percent With a Dominant Machine	71%	44%	Yes
Average Percent of Years With a Dominant Machine	20%	17%	74%
Among Cities With a Dominant Machine, How Many Years Did The Boss Last?	15	23	10 22 60 + ?

Table 2
Characteristics of Big Cities, Smaller Cities,
and Albany at Each Decade From 1870 to 1940

Characteristic/Group	1870	1880	1890	1900	1910	1920	1930	1940
Population (Thousands)								
Bigger Cities	296	398	679	771	992	1,217	1,464	1,511
Smaller Cities	36	55	101	131	197	252	332	358
Albany	69	91	95	94	100	113	127	131
Population Growth (Percent)								
Bigger Cities	68	42	53	31	26	26	18	2
Smaller Cities	179	115	187	41	58	25	24	4
Albany	11	31	5	-1	6	13	12	2
Population Density (Hundred Per Acre)								
Bigger Cities	-	-	15	16	19	20	21	21
Smaller Cities	-	-	12	11	13	12	13	13
Albany	-	-	15	14	15	10	11	11
Percent Foreign Born								
Bigger Cities	37	32	32	27	27	23	19	15
Smaller Cities	27	23	23	18	19	16	13	10
Albany	32	26	24	18	19	16	14	12
Percent Foreign Born--Irish								
Bigger Cities	35	29	21	17	11	8	8	7
Smaller Cities	42	33	21	17	11	8	7	6
Albany	60	53	43	39	25	17	13	10
Percent Homeowners								
Bigger Cities	-	-	27	26	28	30	37	30
Smaller Cities	-	-	29	28	34	36	43	36
Albany	-	-	27	26	27	29	37	31
Percent Employed in Manufacturing								
Bigger Cities	-	-	18	15	13	14	11	9
Smaller Cities	-	-	13	12	10	12	10	7
Albany	-	-	14	13	10	10	6	4

William F. Barnes, "boy leader" of the Albany Republicans.

Daniel P. O'Connell

Erastus Corning II

The modern history of Albany cannot be told without reflecting on the career of Erastus Corning II. His 41 year tenure as mayor had its roots in the early nineteenth century with the political and business activities of his great-grandfather, Erastus Corning I. The family fortunes waxed and waned through the years, but ultimately the same shrewdness that made them successful politicians also contributed to the Cornings' survival as keen businessmen.

The connection between the Irish Catholic working-class O'Connell family and the Protestant aristocratic mayors of Albany was established at the end of William Barnes' Republican machine in the 1920s. This and a long-term friendship between the O'Connells and Cornings largely contributed to the solidarity of the Albany Democratic Party at the time.

As the youngest elected mayor of Albany, at 32 Erastus Corning was no stranger to politics. With politics as a well-established way of life for the Corning family, it was natural for Erastus to assume political office, first as a convention delegate, then as a state assemblyman, later as a state senator, and finally as mayor.

While often controversial, Erastus Corning's tenure was never successfully challenged in the polls or anywhere else. His service as an army private in World War II did much to restore the popularity of the Democratic party after Governor Dewey's lengthy investigations into corruption in the Albany machine.

While often characterized as the public voice of the O'Connell faction, Erastus Corning nonetheless maintained a firm hold on Albany politics long after the death of Dan O'Connell. His influence on Albany was profound and, to this day, many citizens remain loyal to his memory. His death marked the end of the longest tenure of any American mayor.

THE CORNING LEGACY

Ivan Steen

In late May, 1983, a major era in the history of Albany came to an end with the death of Mayor Erastus Corning II in a Boston hospital. For more than forty-two years, Corning had served as the chief executive of his native city. A large portion of the city population knew no other mayor. Visitors may have been bewildered by a campaign slogan that read: "Keep the Mayor Mayor," but Albanians certainly knew what it meant. Erastus Corning occupied his office longer than any of his predecessors, and longer than any mayor of any city of substantial size in the United States during the twentieth century.

What might account for this unusual political longevity? At this point, we have no conclusive answers; to find them we must make a careful study of Albany politics and the role played by Corning. Although this study is under way, a great deal of research remains to be done. We can, however, provide background and suggestions to account for this political phenomenon.

During the first few decades of the twentieth century, Albany was dominated by

the Republican organization of William F. Barnes, Jr. The local Democratic Party, weak and divided, was unable to achieve any success until 1919, when Daniel P. O'Connell was elected to the Board of Assessors. Working closely with Edwin Corning and his brother Parker, the O'Connell brothers, Dan and Edward, managed to oust the faction loyal to Patrick McCabe and take control of the Albany Democratic Party the following year. Their candidate, William S. Hackett, was elected mayor in 1921. Hackett enjoyed great popularity and served from 1922-1926, when he was killed in an automobile accident during a visit to Cuba. His successor, John Boyd Thacher II, who was also very popular, held office from 1926-1940. When Thacher was elected Childrens' Court Judge in 1940, Herman Hoogkamp took over for the remainder of Thacher's mayoral term. In 1941, Erastus Corning II was elected mayor, holding office from 1942-1983.

During all these years, the Democratic organization faced few serious challenges and remained in firm control. It successfully weathered charges of corruption and election fraud, including several state investigations. One of the keys to the success of the party was the steady stream of able and popular men who held the office of mayor. It is interesting to note that in a city which might be characterized as working class, immigrant, and Catholic, its mayors had been, until 1983, aristocratic, native Protestants.

Mayor Corning's family background was crucial both to his development and his popularity. The Corning family connection with Albany dates to about 1805, when Erastus Corning, Sr., and his parents moved to Chatham from Connecticut. By 1814, the then 19 year-old Corning moved to Albany, and made a fortune through his activities as a hardware merchant, iron manufacturer, railroad developer, land speculator, and banker. He became a major political figure in Albany, serving as mayor in the mid-1830s, state senator from 1842-45, and congressman from 1857-59 and 1861-63.

Although less is known about his son, Erastus Corning, Jr., clearly he was not as active in politics as his father, nor was he as shrewd a businessman. By the time Erastus Corning, Jr., died, the family fortune had dwindled considerably. It was left to his two sons, Parker (1874-1943) and Edwin (1883-1934), to re-establish the family's financial position. This they did with considerable success.

In 1895, on graduating from Yale, Parker Corning and James W. Cox founded the Albany International Felt Company, where Parker served as chairman of the board until his death. Not long after Edwin graduated from Yale in 1906, he and Parker became active in Ludlum Steel, a remnant of the old Corning iron interests. Located in Watervliet, the company prospered with Edwin Corning as president and Parker as vice-president. In 1927, Ludlum Steel and Krupp Steel of Essen, Germany, entered into a patent pooling agreement whereby Ludlum became the exclusive U.S. manufacturer of a new hardened steel known as nitralloy.

Edwin Corning was also treasurer of the Albany Felt Company, a director of the State Bank of Albany, a trustee of the Albany Savings Bank and a partner in the brokerage house of Gurnett and Company. Parker Corning, in addition to his positions with Albany Felt and Ludlum Steel, was a director of the State Bank of Albany, a trustee of the Mechanics and Farmers Bank of Albany, a director of the City Safe Deposit Company, and a partner of Gurnett and Company. In January 1932, Gurnett and Company suspended business and notified the New York Stock Exchange of its inability to fulfill obligations as a result of customer failure to meet calls for margin. The company was suspended by the New York Stock Exchange and the New York Curb Exchange, resulting in heavy liquidation of stocks in which it had considerable interest. One of these was Ludlum Steel. Thus, the Great Depression dealt a serious blow to Corning family financial interests.

Both Parker and Edwin Corning were very active in politics. As noted, the Cornings, in alliance with the O'Connells, were responsible for ousting the Barnes machine. Edwin Corning headed the Albany County Democratic organization at the time. Two years later he became a member of the state Democratic committee. In 1922, Parker Corning was elected to Congress, and served seven terms. He aided his district in many ways, with legislation creating the Port of Albany, approving the Parker Dunn Memorial and Troy-Menands bridges, and erecting a new federal building in Albany. Parker Corning was uncomfortable with New Deal philosophies, however, and opposed some of its important legislation, including its banking and tariff policies, the N.R.A., and the A.A.A. He considered himself a "constitutional Democrat" and observed the Democratic Party taken over by people he considered "collectivists"; indeed, almost Communists. Consequently, Parker Corning decided not to seek re-election in 1936.

Meanwhile, Edwin Corning's success with the Albany Democratic organization and his friendship with Al Smith were earning him statewide attention. In 1926, with support from Smith, he was elected chairman of the New York State Democratic Committee. Later that year he became the Democratic candidate for lieutenant governor and was successful in his election bid. While serving as lieutenant governor, Edwin remained party chairman. When Al Smith decided to run for President in 1928, Edwin Corning was mentioned as a possible successor. Since he had recently suffered a stroke, however, he declined. In August of 1928, he resigned as chairman of the State Democratic Committee. After completing his term as lieutenant governor, Edwin Corning stepped down from politics, and in 1934, died at the age of 51.

Erastus Corning II was the product of a family deeply rooted in the Albany business and political scene. At home, Corning recalled, where the principal topic of conversation was politics, he acquired a love for politics from his father. His formal education began at the Albany Academy, which he attended from 1917-22, where his favorite subject was arithmetic. He remembered his first political battle, as the only Democrat in his class: "I got so mad at one guy for making derogatory remarks," he related, "that I took off after him, and like a dumb kid will, [ran] head on. I missed him, and hit the tree with my head. That's politics." After a few years at the Albany Academy, at the age of 12 he was sent off to Groton, his father's old school. There he had an excellent academic career, ranking at the top of his class regularly. His closest competitor for academic honors was his good friend, Joseph Alsop. Corning's favorite subject was mathematics, for which he won an award. Active on the school publication, *The Grotonian*, he served as business editor. He had a part in the senior play, for which he was described by a student critic in *The Grotonian* as a "natural actor." Corning also participated in athletics, earning a letter in baseball. He played right field, but rarely made the starting lineup, though in the last game of his senior year, he was put in as a pinch runner so he would have enough playing time to earn his letter. Not altogether successful, he was caught trying to steal second base--a good lesson for a future politician.

When choosing a college, Corning was told he was free to enroll at any college he wanted, provided it was Yale. Although Corning originally expected to room with Joseph Alsop, the latter decided to attend Harvard, leaving Erastus without a roommate for his freshman year. Corning was a good student at Yale, though he seemed less interested in academics than at Groton. Hunting, fishing, and golf afforded greater appeal than his studies. Nonetheless, his grades were good enough to qualify him for Phi Beta Kappa in his senior year. As a freshman, he tried his hand at boxing, enjoying little success. According to the *Yale Daily News*, although he fought well, he "was forced to the ropes in the first round," and his opponent proceeded to gain the decision. The 1932 Yale yearbook noted that Corning's career plans were to enter manufacturing. One might presume he considered working at his father's company. By that time, however, the Depression had hit Edwin Corning and Ludlum Steel quite hard. After returning to Albany, then, he founded the insurance company with which he was associated throughout his life.

While his father's death in 1934 was a great loss, it was not long before Erastus Corning II became actively involved in politics. In 1934, he was a delegate to the Democratic state convention, and in the following year he successfully ran for election to the New York State Assembly. Obviously, as a freshman assemblyman he was not well known to the editors of the 1936 *Red Book*, in which his official biography is entered under the name "Edwin Corning II." He spent an uneventful year in the Assembly, serving on the committees of Affairs of Villages, Canals, and, perhaps of greater interest to him, Conservation. It was during his Assembly term that his uncle Parker announced his decision not to seek re-election to Congress. By the end of July, the Albany County Democratic Committee named William T. Byrne their candidate for Congress. Byrne had been serving in the State Senate since 1923 and was both party whip and chairman of the powerful Judiciary Committee at the time. Erastus Corning II was selected as the Democratic candidate to succeed Byrne, and George Foy was nominated to replace Corning in the Assembly. Corning won an easy victory over his Republican opponent, J. Palmer Harcourt, in November, 1936, and in 1937, he moved to the State Senate.

The freshman senator's committee assignments were: Commerce and Navigation; Finance; Internal Affairs; Conservation; Cities; Civil Service; Pensions; Public Printing, Revision and Engrossed Bills; and Reapportionment. Conservation, again, seemed to be his principal interest. Of particular interest to him was a bill passed by the legislature and approved by the governor creating a temporary state commission to make a survey of the scenic, historic, and commercial assets of the Hudson River Valley. Corning served on the commission, chairing it briefly. Although the Hudson River Valley Survey Commission's recommendations were not implemented immediately, many were ultimately approved and carried out. Corning was justly proud of his work in this area. It might be presumed that Corning played a role in the legislature's defeat of a bill in 1939 calling for a legislative investigation of Albany City and County. Serving in the State Senate in those days was hardly a full-time job, and Corning was regarded as one of the less vigorous members of that body. Nonetheless, the position gave him political experience and public exposure.

In 1940, the same year Erastus Corning II was re-elected to his last term in the State Senate, Mayor Thacher was elected judge of the Albany County Children's Court. Ordinarily, Frank Harris, as president of the Albany Common Council, would have succeeded Thacher as mayor; but Harris would have been required to resign his state position to do so. Instead, Harris resigned as council president and was replaced by Herman Hoogkamp, who was then designated mayor. In August, 1941, Albany Democrats chose Erastus Corning II as their mayoral candidate. Corning's family background, six years in elective office, and his relationship with Daniel O'Connell were among the factors affecting this choice. With Corning's resignation from the

legislature, the party chose Julian B. Erway as its candidate to replace him. The Republicans selected Benjamin R. Hoff, a self-proclaimed political novice, to oppose Corning for the mayor's office, and the American Labor Party entered Morris Zuckman as a candidate. Corning won a landslide victory over his opponents in what was generally conceded to be a dull campaign. Indeed, the Democrats won every major office in the county. On 1 January 1942, Erastus Corning assumed the office of Mayor of the City of Albany. At 32, he was the youngest mayor in the city's history. Sworn in by State Supreme Court Justice Francis Bergan, Mayor Corning's first official act was to administer the oaths of office to city officials, among them Alderman Richard Conners.

Corning's early popularity was enhanced during the Second World War, when he entered the army as a private in the infantry. In Corning's absence, from April 1944 to September 1945, Frank Harris served as acting mayor. After a brief stay at Fort Dix, New Jersey, Corning was sent to Camp Blanding, Florida, for basic training, an experience he seems to have enjoyed. After completing basic training, he passed up the opportunity to apply for Officer's Candidate School. Believing that the war would soon be over, he was reluctant to spend the remainder of his military service in training, preferring to do something more constructive. The young mayor kept in touch with events in Albany and, when home on furlough, spent much of his time at city hall as an advisor on municipal matters. By October 1944, he was in England and from there went to France and Germany, where he was involved in combat with the Second Infantry Division. Mayor Corning returned home a local hero in September 1945.

As mayor of the upstate Democratic stronghold, Corning played an important role in New York State politics. His name became especially prominent in 1946, as his party was putting together a ticket to challenge Thomas Dewey for the governorship. At a time when a sizeable percentage of the state's voters was recently returned servicemen, a politician who belonged to that category would be an asset to the ticket. The Democratic party choice for governor was Senator James Mead; the nomination for lieutenant governor went to Corning. Corning reluctantly accepted the nomination, but ran a spirited campaign and was considered a stronger candidate than the lackluster Mead. Nonetheless, Dewey defeated the Democrats. From that point, Mayor Corning devoted his attention to Albany without seeking any elective office other than mayor.

As mayor of the state's capital city, Corning had to deal with the governor and other state officials on a regular basis. The Albany Democratic organization was of considerable interest to these officials, particularly when the governor's office was occupied by Republicans. None of those governors was more concerned with the city's Democratic organization than Thomas E. Dewey, the celebrated crime buster, who had promised action against the O'Connell faction in his 1942 election campaign. Dewey launched what was to be the most extensive investigation into Albany politics, in 1943. The effort continued through 1946, but no major evidence of corruption was uncovered and only a few minor convictions were recorded. Corning was in the military for a good part of the investigation. However, there is no doubt that of all the men who occupied the governor's office during Corning's long tenure as mayor, Dewey was the one he liked least.

Mayor Corning's dealings with Nelson Rockefeller were quite significant, as Rockefeller's building aspirations were in large part focused on the city of Albany. Rockefeller managed to acquire more than ninety acres of land adjacent to downtown Albany for his government complex, displacing several thousand loyal Democratic voters in the process. Raising money for construction, however, was quite a different matter. The usual procedure would have been to seek the state voters' approval of a bond issue. It was doubtful that such a large sum of money would have been authorized for Albany by the citizens of New York. Corning came up with the financial scheme permitting the construction of the Empire State Plaza by raising the money through Albany County rather than New York State bonds. Under this agreement, the land and buildings would belong to the county and be leased to the state for an amount equal to county interest and principal payments. The property was to be returned to the state once the bonds were redeemed. The state would make other payments to the city and county, including payments in lieu of taxes. In this way, Nelson Rockefeller was able to build his state office complex, but Erastus Corning could exert considerable influence; specifically, pressure could be brought to bear on the Rockefeller administration by holding up a bond issue.

Throughout the years Corning was mayor, the Democratic organization faced few serious challenges. The greatest threat came in the late 1960s, when the Republicans succeeded in electing a congressman, a state senator, two assemblymen, and the county district attorney. Despite predictions that the downfall of the Democratic organization was at hand, the triumph proved to be short-lived. The most serious challenge to Mayor Corning came in 1973, when Carl Touhey lost the election to him by little more than 3,000 votes. Other predictions of the demise of the Democratic organization came with the death of Dan O'Connell in 1977. But Corning rapidly managed to take control of the organization, retaining that control until his death.

Questions concerning Democratic political longevity in Albany and the role played by Erastus Corning II are not fully answered, though some background and suggestions have been provided. The story of these years must be reiterated and analyzed with scholarly detachment. What evidence might a scholar use to reconstruct and interpret events? There are newspapers, but the press reflects considerable bias. This is most evident to any reader of Albany's newspapers. Official documents also fail to reveal a complete story, at best telling us what happened without specifying why it happened. Personal correspondence is often a useful source of information for historians. In the case of twentieth century politics, however, correspondence generally provides little insight. Diaries and memoirs do not appear to exist for this period of Albany's history. The key to the questions of how and why lies with the people who made the decision or who were close to those who did. Unfortunately, many of the major decision makers are no longer living. Obviously, only Daniel O'Connell or Erastus Corning II would have been able to answer certain questions. There are other individuals, however, who might provide insight for Corning and his involvement in Albany politics. The Erastus Corning Years Oral History Project has been established to develop and preserve the tape-recorded memoirs of these people.

Oral history is one of the oldest methods of historical investigation, employed since Herodotus' investigation of the Persian Wars. Historians have a tendency to rely primarily on documentary sources, however, since most members of the profession deal with time periods beyond the human life span. For earlier eras, the written record generally yields sufficient evidence to enable the historian to piece together stories and draw reasonably reliable conclusions. Eighteenth and nineteenth century men and women often wrote very candid letters and kept intimate diaries. In more recent years, such documents are rare. Ironically, our age generates more paper than any other, but in many ways that paper is less valuable to the historian. Modern human beings put very little of themselves on paper. Writing takes time, and time is in short supply. The telephone has become the preferred means of communication for most people, and few people keep diaries. Politicians, in particular, are reluctant to commit themselves to paper, for fear that such paper will eventually haunt them. The problems of historical research caused by a shortage of useful written material can be overcome, to an extent, by employing the tape recorder. The gathering of oral history memoirs has come to be widely accepted as a research methodology.

The first and most important phase of the oral history process takes place before the interview begins, consisting of extensive and meticulous background research. Based on this research, the interviewer, prior to each interview session, prepares an outline of topics to be covered and sends a copy to the interviewee. This serves as the basis for the interview, though the interviewer must be prepared to ask appropriate follow-up questions or to probe the interviewee on other topics. Following the interview, a verbatim transcript is prepared from the tape, and a copy is sent to the interviewee. The interviewee carefully reviews the transcript for accuracy, correcting misspelled names, answering any questions posed by the interviewer, and adding marginal notes for clarification. A final copy of the interview is prepared, incorporating these corrections and comments. The tape, the verbatim transcript, and the final transcript are all made available to researchers. Until the project is completed and the necessary papers regarding disposition of the material have been signed, interviews must be considered confidential. Ultimately, however, all material is accessible to the public.

This is the procedure employed by the Erastus Corning Years Oral History Project. Oral history memoirs, when combined with existing primary documents, newspapers, and other traditional sources, will enable historians to reconstruct this vital period of Albany's history. Only then will we be able to move beyond myth and partisanship and come to understand the phenomenon of Erastus Corning II's four decades as mayor of Albany.

Ivan D. Steen received his Ph.D. in history from New York University in 1962, and is a specialist in the history of the American city. He has published eight articles, delivered numerous scholarly papers, and taught a variety of courses in that field. In addition to serving as an Assistant Professor of History, he is also the director of the Oral History Program at the State University of New York at Albany. One of the goals of that program is to document the recent history of the Albany region, particularly the Erastus Corning years.

Further Readings

Kennedy, William. *O Albany!* New York: The Viking Press, 1983.

McEneny, John J. *Albany: Capital City on the Hudson.* Woodland Hills, California: The Windsor Press, 1981.

Robinson, Frank S. *Albany's O'Connell Machine.* Albany: Washington Park Spirit, 1973.

Solomon, N. *When Leaders Were Bosses: An Inside Look at Political Machines and Politics.* Hicksville, New York: Exposition Press, 1975.

A meeting of the 1963 Albany Democratic Committee
(from left: John Pennock, Eugene Devine, Daniel P. O'Connell, and Mayor Erastus
Corning)

Albany has always offered an interesting perspective on political culture. Curiously, the reaction to Albany's insular society has not always been one of shock and dismay, rather sometimes of interest and amusement. To an observant, conservative young student encountering the ancient, accepted regimen of the city in the late 1950s, Albany provided endless instruction and fascination with its "infinite capacity to persist in its own ways."

The student's attitude did not differ greatly from those held generally, nor did the city's self-concept differ much from that of the nation as a whole. America in the 1950s had a sense of unity. Society was self-regarding and self-regulating. Politics operated in stable, comprehensible patterns. Political machines thrived on voter satisfaction.

Yet if one looked, one could see flaws in the democratic structure, even in the 1950s. During the Kennedy administration, changes were made in this structure. America began to work on the problems of injustice and discrimination. Even this student, now an employed, dutiful, tax-paying resident of Albany, could see that change was necessary. Indeed, a great deal was wrong with the city. Albanians had long recognized these wrongs; the issues long ago had been decided. But Albany, as always, resisted change. Clearly, if change were to occur, it would have to come from higher forms of government. Thus, the courts and federal government applied pressure.

Albany serves as a microcosm in which we can more closely observe life in America. The city provides abundant opportunity for observation, instruction, and introspection.

POLITICAL TRADITION:
LIFE AMONG THE DINOSAURS

Richard H. Kendall

This commentary on the course and conduct of public affairs is singularly dependent upon my own observations during the years I lived in Albany. I would like to recall what I observed in Albany, how I responded, and how I interpreted the public life I encountered.

Living in Albany in the late 1950s and throughout the 1960s was a formative experience in understanding political behavior. It forced me to come to terms with my own preconceived notions about society and government and was a crucial part of my education. I remain self-conscious about its impression, particularly during the late 1960s, when a decision seemingly had to be made regarding the "new politics" of that tumultuous time. This chapter then, is not formal, but a personal statement about an aspect of my own history of which "experiencing Albany" is irrevocable. While such personal reckoning is subjective on one level, the past itself is objective and has its own compelling integrity. Whatever the context of inquiry, therefore, we are bound to tell the truth about the past.

My experience in Albany began in 1954, when I arrived as a freshman at the Teacher's College--the "Albany State" from which the present State University at Albany developed. The college then occupied buildings which today comprise the downtown campus on Western Avenue. I lived in a rather old house on Thurlow Terrace, which had been converted to a small dormitory in the fifties. Thurlow House, as we called it, quartered some thirty students and was superintended by a resident couple who were "house mother" and "house father." Breakfast was served at 7 a.m., dining room doors closed at 7:30, and the table was cleared at 8:00. Dinner was at 5:30, sharp, and quiet was enforced after 11 p.m. No alcohol on the premises. I mention these details only to indicate, apart from considerations of Albany itself, the larger culture of the 1950s and early 1960s, as represented in the etiquette of college-as-parent. This profoundly differed from the changes which occurred during the cultural revolution of the late 1960s, on through the 1970s and 1980s. If, as I might suggest, Albany and its politics are a remarkable anachronism--"the place where time stands still"-- remember the vividness of this image of Albany is heightened immensely when we think of the scope and quickness of changes encountered in contemporary America, from the Great Society to the Great Communicator.

The issue here, though, is not a trick of relative speed and appearances, but comparisons and judgments. Even in those placid years of our "previous culture," the substance of Albany as revealed in its public life marked the city as different from what I had known and come to expect growing up in a small city in the mid-Hudson Valley. My introduction to Albany's culture and politics came shortly after my arrival, getting acquainted with my fellow students over beer. There was to be no drinking in the dorm, but the old Washington Tavern was only a few blocks away, and the smaller, extraordinarily murky Ockie's was even closer. On tap exclusively in Albany was an arresting example of the brewer's art, Hedrick's Beer, Albany's "machine beer" which, by command order of the powers-that-be, every bar in town had to serve in order to do business. At my first taste, I was assured by solemn upperclassmen that this beer was the source of the story of the beer sent for analysis to the Cornell Veterinary School which brought the reply, "Your horse has sugar." The fact that Albany politics produced this infamous brew was generally seen as an apt comment on the politics. Still, it seemed an atavism of a society from the saloon era, or an aspect of Prohibition. This was the first "official" commodity I had encountered in the land of free enterprise, consumer sovereignty, and the Bill of Rights.

In linking Hedrick's beer to the Bill of Rights, I do not necessarily mean that its peculiar properties violated the guarantee against cruel and unusual punishment, though this is arguable; rather, this public nuisance was a constant reminder of the apparatus of enforcement lurking behind its inevitable presence. The beer would lead to a discussion of law and law enforcement in Albany, which is to say, a discussion and a warning about the police. In short, the Albany police had an earned reputation for hitting people; it was an integral part of their style. An upperclassman returning to Vanderzee Hall (at the corner of State Street and Sprague Place), had once been overtaken by a police patrol car and hit by an officer who bolted out of the car, no questions asked. Later, when a phone call was made by the College's Dean of Men, the student was released from custody; the police had been responding to a complaint about a disturbance in the area, but admitted they had the wrong man. As a souvenir, the student had a chipped front tooth.

In the 1950s, the use of force was not a common form of police misconduct in America, as I was aware at the time. (Restraint of the police by federal courts, part of the sweeping changes of the Warren Court, was several years in the future.) I also knew the police were different where I came from and that informed opinion nationally condemned such practices which were indefensible, not to mention dangerous. Of all the things I learned to associate with the culture and politics of Albany, it was the license of the police which came nearest to my nerve of fear and loathing, not merely because of potential violence, but for the feeling of helplessness before it. As victim or observer, the fact of vulnerability and helplessness in the face of force is debilitating, dispiriting and in opposition to the ideas of republican government, virtue, and liberty. Such an estimation emerged only over several years of observation and thought, rather than direct experience. As a college student, I had no connection with the Albany police and no substantive connection or involvement with the city's public life. In the late 1950s, the voting age was still 21, and the excitement of student activism, one of the many lively surprises of the following decade, was not yet revealed. As far as I knew and could testify, the police were noted not for action, but inaction, having removed themselves from that staple of municipal police work, enforcement of traffic laws. Triple-parking downtown, drag racing uptown--where were the cops? They were in their Buick sedans, undoubtedly the least suitable police cruiser one could contrive. It was a truly ludicrous hunk of Detroit iron: the two-speed Dyna-flow transmission squandered the output of once mighty V-8s now hopelessly untuned; the soft suspension responded carelessly to stone-block pavement and potholes; the whole machine, in agitation and distress, whining and revving, bounding and swaying, strained to break 45 mph. What were the thoughts--and who were the thinkers--which produced this unembarrassed display of in-eptitude, foolishness, and low comedy? Of-ficial beer, police battery, boulevard Buicks on street patrol--what kind of a city was Albany, content to present such emblems to the world?

The answer came with the realization that whatever Albany was in public was con-sonant with the private ways of its citizens. Government in Albany, or as one learned quickly to say, the "Albany machine," was not distinct from those it governed, and did not impose an unwelcome rule on a subdued and alienated people. In a broad and func-tional way, the men and women who com-prised the "machine," who held elective of-fices and posts in the Democratic party, were enthusiastically and inseparably part of the community. All the stories about the five dollar vote, "registering the graveyard," peeking in the voting booth to insure party loyalty, and intimidating the odd independ-ent-minded stray do not account for the consistent and crushing majorities in all the elections for local offices.

That governance in Albany was firmly anchored in democracy and reflected the will of the people was first suggested to me by my freshman year history professor at the Teacher's College. Discussion of political history rested on the premise that people get the kind of government they deserve, and Albany was a convenient and conclusive ex-ample. At first I failed to understand how anyone deserved poorly paved or unplowed streets, manipulated property assessments, colluded purchasing practices, or that dread-ful beer. Who would vote for that? The point, as I came to see, was not an issue, an electoral event, partisan triumph, per se; it was the larger matter of the historically conditioned disposition of a community ex-pressing its life through politics. The lesson,

new to me in its explicitness, was that poli-tics is culture, and people recreate their pri-vate ways in public life. Obviously, the content of the culture is crucial. I had grown up in a community with effectively delivered public services and regularly con-tested elections. I saw politics as a public activity which examined, criticized, and re-flected upon government in order to make it do its job, much in the same way (so I thought) the telephone and power companies did their jobs. Reflecting on the history of Albany, I realized that while my own cultur-al baggage disposed me to a view of gov-ernment which may be characterized as "public-regarding," Albany's culture pointed in quite the opposite direction. Politics and government in Albany were an extension of the social consciousnesses and revelations of members of its community. Essentially, Albanians made no distinction between pri-vate and public ways. Did they deserve what they got? Yes, for what they got was none other than themselves.

As an undergraduate interested in the study of American history, I knew that Albany was not, historically speaking, remarkable. Similar communities and political cultures were actually the norm in the nineteenth century, and common until the Second World War. Indeed, as noted below, this type and level of consciousness was retained in all of the south. But the history of American politics demonstrated that from the turn of the century onward, the trend was to alter this consciousness and redefine government according to a "public-regarding" conception: an honest, efficient provider of public services and programs, with an internal, constitutional structure designed to prevent its use for private benefit and enrichment. The history of modern American politics, especially at the local level, was of *reform*. What hap-pened to reform in Albany?

Albany of the 1950s was fashioned by the O'Connells and their allies, who wrested con-trol from the perversely stubborn and high-handed Republican boss, William Barnes, in the early 1920s. The Barnes organization was by all accounts a near perfect embodi-ment of all the illegal, immoral, and fattening practices for which American machine politics were notorious. As such, it was a prime target of reformers in the Progressive Era before the First World War. Indeed, the demise of Barnes shortly after the war should have marked a characteristic, though overdue, victory for Progressivism. This would have placed Albany within the flow of change which was reshaping America. Instead of reform, the electoral successes of the Democrats in Albany brought a new and extraordinarily effective version of that which was being displaced in the larger society. Thus with the next several elections, Albany did not become worse--rather, it stepped aside and let the world pass. I can still remember the sense of revelation when I saw that the circumstances behind Progressivism were identical to circumstances of contemporary Albany politics and government. The political culture of Albany in the 1950s was akin to that of the eras of Robert La Follette, Hiram Johnson, Theodore Roosevelt, and Woodrow Wilson. Albany was an historical survivor, having managed the trick for so long as to confound one's sense of the probable.

The notion that Albany's public life was that of another America--perfectly real and animated, yet by popular consent frozen in the dance of time--was demonstrated conclusively for me in the early 1960s during the reform campaign of the Reverend Hudnut and the Citizens United Reform Effort. Here re-enacted in Albany was the archetypical American story of a campaign for political reform: an aroused middle-class citizenry tries to throw out the old, corrupt machine and install a new, civic-minded government. These earnest challengers recited habitual instances of cronyism, graft, peculation, judicial favoritism, manipulation of tax pools, spoliation, police mis-, mal-, and nonfeasance, and general incompetence and inefficiency in city affairs. "Be rid of all this and have an honest government, efficient in the delivery of public services," was the appeal on which municipal reform swept America during the Progressive movement. The classic confrontation of two sensibilities of government (one public-, the other private-regarding) had been played out many

times. No doubt the words spoken in Albany differed little from those spoken by reformers fifty years before, when the face of American politics changed.

Mayor Corning was returned to office in the election, as was the usual slate of Democrat candidates. The margin of electoral triumph for the Corning-O'Connell organization was not unusual: the customary three to one superiority over approximately 15,000 votes cast for the challengers. Except for the campaign oratory (which seemed to have involved the reform minded talking to themselves), nothing much appeared to have changed. The past remained undisturbed. Why? The answer (and I remember thinking that answering this question was very important) was that the reformer's list of chronic civic wrongs was common knowledge to the community and, for many years, had been subject to whatever scrutiny and judgment people chose to give it. Fundamentally, the consensus of public opinion in Albany did not regard the aforementioned abuses as sufficiently wrong to turn out the government. The behavior and practices under criticism were venal transgressions; they were not shocking and did not outrage the majority. They, in fact, fell within the range of behavior considered realistic. This was not mere abstraction; in a relatively homogeneous city with a familiar, often benign spoils system affecting numerous families, this world was real and immediate to virtually everyone. Ultimately, the reformers condemned the transactions by which the community lived, and knew itself. They demanded that the community condemn itself for its settled ways, and become something other than what it was. More than an appeal for good government, the issue transcended politics. Ultimately, the community was required to transform its essence. But Albany was incapable of self-transformation, which was a self-contradiction in Albany's culture, particularly its political culture.

This understanding was illuminated by a story told by another of my teachers about his introduction to Albany politics in the mid-1950s. This teacher had come to Albany from the midwest, where he had been active in the United Auto Workers' no-nonsense brand of Democratic politics. In a desire to continue his party participation, he sought out the local Democratic committee and attended one of its meetings. He offered his help at the grassroots level, as he had in UAW country. When the committee recovered from the shock of the intrusion, they informed him that his help was neither needed nor wanted. Politics in Albany was unabashedly tribal, the powerful expression of the collectively initiated: No Innocents Need Apply. The necessary condition upon which this political culture rested was the insularity of the people--ingrained, reflexive, possibly religious in sanction. (In this respect, Albany is the subject not of politics or history, but of anthropology.) Change was not a part of Albany as the people with alternative ideas were not sufficiently present where it mattered--within the tribe. Explaining this insularity would require giving a demographic and social history of the city beyond this chapter's scope, although anyone who has experienced the city can imagine the reasons involved. For all those who found expression within the Corning-O'Connell dispensation, life's possibilities were bounded by concentric rings, first of the city, then the county (with its judicial and prosecutorial offices), and most remotely, the state judicial district stretching south. Beyond that horizon lay the unknown, as represented in the following quintessential story of Albany's parochialism and isolation: Years ago, prominent Capital District Democrats gathered for a display of partisan achievement, at which Mayor Corning was asked to introduce each of the notables. In his typically practiced and graceful public style, the Mayor, without notes, identified and duly complimented each in turn, stopping only at the very end when he turned to a person whose name, rank, and very presence stumped him. After a moment's hesitation, he apologized for not knowing this fellow Democrat and asked the man to introduce himself. The unknown politician was none other than Sam Stratton, the newly elected mayor of Schenectady. Schenectady was far to the west and, Democrat or not, simply a different tribe, another world.

This was the Albany to which I returned from graduate school in the early 1960s in order to teach at my alma mater. The Teacher's College was then beginning its rapid growth to university status, anticipating its move to the new campus under construction on the site of the former Albany Country Club. As a registered voter living and working in the city, I had to ask myself what I thought of its politics. While I confidently knew right from wrong and naturally disapproved of those who did not know or care, I was not sufficiently involved in the life of Albany to be offended on a personal level or to be moved to action. I felt I had no stake in the community, unlike those who, over the years, had given their votes continually to the organization's candidates. In this sense, I was still an observer in Albany. Moreover, if I had any political ideas or prejudice, I think I was wedded to the notions of localism and pluralism with an instinctive preference for social stability, based on my regard for majority opinion. Temperamentally, I was a conservative who saw society as an organic product of slow, cumulative growth. I was skeptical of social engineering, change for abstract reasons, and any elitist ordering of society "from the top down." If I had had to state a rule, it would have been, "If it ain't broke, don't fix it." And Albany, for all its intractable, self-regarding venality, did seem to work well enough. For Albany, was that not precisely the point?

Even as I said this, I was increasingly aware that although it had served well enough in my own growing up, my conceptualization was already more tenuous. Those were the climactic years of the black civil rights movement which, since the *Brown* cases ten years before, had successively battered down the many forms of racial segregation in the South, and stood poised at the triumph of the Civil Rights and Voting Rights Acts of the mid-1960s. What the civil rights movement had overcome, with the help of federal courts, was the elaborate arrangement of laws and customs which the white south had erected community-by-community. The problem of a prolonged, unconstitutional racial caste system, arose when intractable white majorities deeply resisted any changes in their belief that people should live together while remaining apart. Without discussing society in the American south during the eight or nine decades after Reconstruction, I simply invoke the civil rights struggle of a quarter century ago. Observing and pondering that struggle, bearing in mind the underlying history, allowed for a new appreciation of the ideal of localism and a more accurate picture of Albany. Although Albany was essentially a Southern city in its culture, it was not whimsical or quaint in the least; nor was it the object of condescending indifference.

My purpose here is not to describe Albany's civil rights activities in the 1960s or the city's shortcomings; others have done that with feeling. I want to emphasize that the civil rights movement challenged the premises of localism and majoritarianism throughout America and, by its moral and constitutional claims, forced one to take a closer, more critical look at the prevailing social and political order. The persistent and often inspired resistance of local majorities to the imperative national standard of civil rights subjected the fundamental character of those communities to painful scrutiny. Just as they were ethnically self-conscious, conforming, and insulated, so was Albany. In the context of an America pulsing with self-transformation, breaking a pattern of racial relations ingrained for over a century, the proposition of a community inured against change was futile and vicious. In a society which defined itself through movement, and change, this proposition was truly reactionary.

By the middle of the sixties, then, I understood that Albany's political culture was not a hopeless anachronism or a providentially available specimen of Tammany Hall in its classic form: the "honest graft" of George Washington Plunkett, the courthouse sage remembered for the creed, "I have seen my opportunities and took 'em." Its culture permitted the vast injustice and pathology embodied in the now defeated system of racial segregation. I am not commenting on the racial situation in Albany at the time; I am emphasizing the importance of recogniz-ing the unconscionable and destructive implications of self-regarding localism. Functionally, the crucial, and perhaps tragic, point is that these communities are not self-correcting. There comes a time when the need cannot be denied, and national standards must be imposed on the local setting. Otherwise, the politics and governance of the community might never rise to a consciousness that knows right from wrong. The south, for example, mandated racial classifications in the public life and prescribed second-class citizenship for the racial minority; this in a nation whose constitution was colorblind and without separate classes. This same phenomenon was apparent in Albany in the lost distinction between stealing and not stealing. Granted, racism and reflexive venality are not the same thing. But in America, the fundamental flaw of character and the ensuing disorder in the moral universe are the same. I felt then the full impact of the admonition of the Progressive muckraker and reformer, Lincoln Stephens: "Corruption is not compulsory."

American society saw vast changes during the late 1960s and much of the 1970s sufficiently broad to mark a cultural revolution. The effects of these changes on the nation's political culture, as revealed in the transforming tendencies which have driven the nation's political culture for the past two decades, are readily apparent when one notes the difference between the politics of 1960 and of the mid-1980s. In 1960, according to Theodore H. White's *Making of the President* election studies, "the largest and most important division in American society (was) . . . between Protestants and Catholics." White shows how far, and with what unpredictable complications, we have come from that measure of disposition and alignment in his recent summary of the period 1954-1980, *America in Search of Itself.* The central and dominating political fact of this period was the imposition of "order from the top down" through the directives of the federal bureaucracy, courts, and Congress. The federal system of our traditional constitutionalism and the localism sheltered within it eroded beyond recognition.

If, given my own ideological predilections, I should have been opposed to this crucial and continuing alteration, I was not. Ever before me, was the example of Albany, instructing and reminding me of the essential disability lurking in localism of the problematic capability of local majorities to reform themselves, should they need to do so. For some issues, only national standards provided the appropriate answers. The federal system, together with the localism it nurtured, was a device and a convenience, rather than an end itself. The object of American politics and government is a republican liberty which is not subject to local option. Observing Albany encouraged me to think about the purposes of government, to heed the history I had studied and taught. Thus, I became reconciled to the rationalizing impulse which prevailed during those years. My experience in Albany recast an important part of my own political consciousness; I remain pointedly aware of the personal significance of those years in Albany.

When I moved out of the city in 1972, the Albany Democratic organization was as robust as ever. The stirrings of the sixties had brought no fundamental change; the revolution in the larger culture passed by in the same way as the Progressivism of long ago. The abiding political cultures of Albany remained intact: it continued to escape history.

Marked by the passing of the patriarchs, the story of Albany politics over the last decade or so lies beyond my subject. Yet, on the ground that residence in the county permits continued observation of the city, let me note that change has made a cautious, guarded appearance in Albany's politics and government in just the past year or so. Tantalizing in prospect, carefully hedged with deeply solicitous regard for the ancient pieties and interests, but real nonetheless, this change has come in the only way possible for this particular culture: from the top, and as the fortuitous result of an arranged succession. When Thomas Whalen succeeded Mayor Corning, who died in the office to which he was first elected in 1941, it turned out that Albany "got lucky once." In a culture which is not self-transforming but staunchly hierarchical, internal peaceful change *can* occur if the man at the top is ready, willing, and able to chart a new course. For Albany, as I have tried to demonstrate, there could be no other way.

And what is the point of this new departure? Apart from the political and administrative skills indicated in news accounts, the quality that so strikingly distinguishes Mayor Whalen's conduct of office is that he understands the difference between stealing and not stealing, and acts accordingly. In the Albany long known, this must be accounted as a revolutionary break. Mayor Whalen may well be the best and most interesting thing to happen to Albany since Dan O'Connell threw out that rascal, Billy Barnes. It seems like only yesterday.

Richard H. Kendall, *associate professor at SUNY Albany, first came to Albany as a college student in 1954, staying five years and receiving a B.A. and M.A. from the then New York State College for Teachers--the old "Albany State." After receiving a Ph.D. in history at Yale University, he returned to Albany to teach and has been on the SUNYA faculty since 1963. During the 1970s, Kendall served in the university administration and, since returning to teaching in 1980, has offered courses in American military and constitutional history. He is preparing a study of the "American Military Role in Vietnam, 1965-1969."*

Further Readings

Kennedy, William. *O Albany!* New York: The Viking Press, 1983.

_____. *Ironweed.* New York: The Viking Press, 1983.

_____. *Billy Phelan's Greatest Game.* New York: The Viking Press, 1978.

_____. *Legs.* New York: Coward, McCann & Geoghegan, 1975.

McEneny, John J. *Albany: Capital City on the Hudson.* Windsor Publications, 1981.

Morris, Charles R. *A Time of Passion: America 1960-1980.* New York: Harper & Row, 1984.

O'Neill, William L. *Coming Apart: An Informal History of America in the 1960s.* New York: Times Books, 1972.

Robinson, Frank S. *Albany's O'Connell Machine: An American Political Relic.* Albany: The Washington Park Spirit, Inc., 1973.

White, Theodore. *America in Search of Itself: The Making of the President, 1956-1980.* New York: Harper & Row, 1982.

When it comes to politics in Albany, there's always another opinion.

The 1960s was an age of protest, even in Albany.

ARCHITECTURE

Comfort and privacy have always been principal considerations in the design of American domestic interiors. Pragatism has helped define American style and taste. While European high style remained ideal for the elite American, most Americans looked for more moderate styles. Elements of a new decorative style appeared tentatively. Full acceptance was hindered by provincialism, isolation, and, most important, economics.

Even the most sophisticated American homes were not furnished entirely in high style. A single object, such as a chair, a picture, or a statue might represent high style. Rooms were furnished slowly, since furniture was costly and difficult to acquire. Objects were obtained locally or imported from Europe. Often interiors showed much incongruity and contrast of style, class, and quality. Yet a great deal of individualism could be seen in American homes.

The notion of high style, that is, concepts of design that were identifiable, highly sophisticated, fashionably acceptable, and beyond popular consumption, was radically affected by the mass manufacturing of the 1830s. While high style objects were still created through individuals and craftsmen, a sense of standardization prevailed by the 1880s. American interiors underwent a democratization. Mass-produced furnishings rivaled shop-made objects and contributed to the disappearance of the regional craftsman. A kind of popular high style developed, with quality goods available to the public through mass manufacturing, better transportation, and widespread circulation of catalogs.

Mass production brought revivalism: Borrowing or imitating styles from the past became popular, and the concept of "matched sets" was rejected. The centennial celebration of 1876 stimulated a sense of nostalgia and antiquarianism, though preservation did not catch on until the 1920s when the collection of antiques began.

Albany homes were representative of these trends. Albany tastes kept pace with styles, and transportation aided acquisition. Excellent examples from all periods can be found in Albany's historic houses and public buildings, notably the Schuyler mansion, Ten Broeck mansion, Executive Mansion, and perhaps New York's most complete record of early domestic life, Cherry Hill. After five continuous generations of Van Rensselaer family occupancy, Cherry Hill was established as a museum. This provides a rare glimpse into the evolution of American taste.

DOMESTIC INTERIORS: MAKING A HOME IN ALBANY

Douglas G. Bucher

Interior design during the eighteenth and nineteenth centuries was marked by a wonderful richness. This chapter will try to describe some of that quality, focusing on examples of Albany interiors during that vital and ever changing period. It is difficult to talk only about Albany because few illustrations exist of Albany interiors as they appeared in the late eighteenth and early nineteenth century. We must rely on written descriptions, paintings, old photographs, and most importantly on our own detective work undertaken in the rapidly vanishing examples of early domestic architecture in Albany. The examples in this chapter offer a sense of what was taking place during this age of transition inside both domestic and public buildings.

Albany was a city of many different characteristics in the late eighteenth and early nineteenth centuries. There was the old Dutch city with gabled houses facing the street, and the young Georgian city with its typical English inspired brick houses with classically detailed doorways. These two very different styles soon co-existed with the delicately detailed buildings of the emerging Federal style. This riotous justaposition of styles is nowhere better illustrated than the watercolors by James Eights.

In most houses during the late eighteenth century the floorboards would be exposed and present an austere, scrubbed appearance unless the family could afford to buy some sort of carpeting. Oriental carpets were rare but not unknown. More likely, they had an English-manufactured, Turkey-patterned carpet or some other form of woven domestic or imported carpeting, either wall-to-wall or set in the middle of the room.

Vivid and bold, multi-colored wallpaper was common and, although it had to be imported from England or France, most middle class homes had some wallpapered rooms. Wallpaper was manufactured in Albany as early as 1793. During this period, interiors might feature woodwork painted in bright tints, including Prussian blue pigment, which was popular but expensive. This pigment becomes darker with successive brushing, and this created intentional contrasts between sections of paneling or moldings.

Cherry Hill preserves a wonderful series of eighteenth century interiors that have been modified and shaped by several generations. Constructed in 1787 for Philip Van Rensselaer, both the house and its contents survive today as an outstanding example of eighteenth, nineteenth, and twentieth century lifestyles. Albany is fortunate to possess such a treasure.

Figure 1 (c. 1880) is a remarkable photograph which extends through the length of the house, and includes the north parlor, the center hall, and the south parlor in the distance. The later nineteenth century taste for the juxtaposition of periods and styles is well illustrated. The spatial configuration dates from 1787, but in the 1830s Solomon Van Rensselaer remodeled these rooms in the fashionable Greek Revival style, adding black marble mantels and broad openings fitted with sliding doors. The woodwork was grained in 1872 and the wallpaper and red patterned carpet probably were installed then. The mixture of furnishings includes an English sidechair, c. 1700; a New York Kneehole chest, c. 1760-90; a classical armchair, c. 1815-25; and a center table in the hall, probably purchased by Solomon Van Rensselaer in 1834. Preserved at Cherry Hill is a unique collection of wallpapers used in the house from the time of its construction to the mid-twentieth century.

The Van Rensselaer manor house, one of the grandest but least known American houses of the eighteenth and nineteenth centuries, was unfortunately demolished in the late 1890s. The house was constructed in 1765, in the then novel Georgian style, by the Van Rensselaer family. In 1819 Philip Hooker, Albany's famous architect, remodeled and enlarged the house for Stephen Van Rensselaer III. Hooker added wings on either end of the house. They contained a drawing room, library and dining room. Extending between the wings, a covered piazza was built on the garden facade. This delicate porch is recorded in an 1839 drawing of the house by Thomas Cole. In 1843 Stephen Van Rensselaer IV engaged

Richard Upjohn to extensively remodel the manor house in the rather foreboding Classical style familiar to us from old photographs of the house.

Figure 2 shows the rich and palatial drawing room in the east wing added by Hooker. It opened into an equally impressive library through a wide, heavily draped doorway. The bold plaster cornice and massive door trim are characteristic of the work of Hooker. The drapery, suspended from an elaborate gilt pole, seems to be contemporary with the creation of the room. The medallion Brussels carpet was woven to fit the room. William Paterson Van Rensselaer ordered a similar carpet in 1841 from Glasgow, Scotland, for Beverwyck, his new palace on the east bank of the Hudson.

The dining room, shown in figure 3, encompassed a large portion of the west wing. The woodwork resembles that seen in the drawing room and may be from the designs of Hooker, although the overall Victorian heaviness of the architecture may also indicate that it is the creation of Upjohn and was that architect's attempt to blend the new with the eighteenth century trim in the center portion of the house. The dining table and chairs, c. 1830, may be attributed to Duncan Phyfe. The massive sideboard was created some thirty years later. The wallpaper and ormolu gasolier would date from 1843 to mid-century.

In the eighteenth century and earlier, interior design was individual to each country or region. By the end of the eighteenth century, interior design became more international. As more people traveled and design publications became plentiful, far-flung interiors began to share the same characteristics of color, arrangement, and furniture design; sometimes it was difficult to tell what country one was in simply by examining a room's interior adornments. A middle class drawing room in New York City had much the same character as a similar space in London or Berlin.

Moving to the Federal period, beginning about 1790, domestic interiors began to show some interesting innovations, such as unusually shaped rooms, spiral stairways, and delicately detailed woodwork and plasterwork. Elegant interiors were the fashion even in smaller homes, with patterned wall-to-wall carpeting, horsehair upholstery on the furniture, and wallpaper with elaborate borders outlining the ceiling as well as the woodwork. Bright yellow paint was popular both for interiors and exteriors. Many of Albany's houses, including Cherry Hill, Ten Broeck mansion, and the Schuyler mansion, were painted yellow at this time. As the Federal period ended and the Greek Revival period flowered about 1820, the delicate and stylized classical detail of the Federal period gave way to the more correct classical detail of the newly emerging style and houses began to resemble Greek temples with the added amenity of windows.

Ten Broeck mansion, possibly designed by Philip Hooker in 1798 for Abraham Ten Broeck in the Federal style, was remodeled extensively in 1850 in the Greek mode. Many of the details familiar today, such as the classical front and rear porches, were typical features of the new style. The interiors vividly illustrate Greek Revival style, with massive columns, deep plaster cornices, and marble mantelpieces.

The mansion's parlor, shown in figure 4, underwent a transformation between the late 1870s and the early 1900s, when the photograph was taken. The Ionic columns and architrave are part of the 1850 renovation and still dominated the parlor in the 1880s. Suspended from an angular gasolier, c. 1870s, was a small glass bell which kept the kerosene lamps from soiling the ceiling. The room contained an Oriental corner with faux bamboo furniture so popular in the 1870s. By 1890 the room had been transformed into an elegant high style drawing room, the type popular during the 1880s. Most of the furnishings were new, including the Empire Revival tables and chairs with overtones of the Napoleonic age. Figure 4 shows a room that had come full circle. The 1880s clutter has been removed and the new decor attempts to recreate the room's original appearance, although the heavy Greek woodwork remains. The wallpaper imitates an eighteenth century damask, while the floor is covered in a solid velvet

carpet. The gasolier and an 1840s astral lamp have been electrified. The furniture is both antique and reproduction. This parlor well represents the Colonial Revival style popular at the end of the century.

At the same time as the Greek Revival rage, some Albanians liked to live in castles, and the Gothic style was popular. Albany has several townhouses that were built during this period, such as the Pruyn house and its neighbor on Elk Street and the handsome row facing Madison Place. Their interiors featured very correct or sometimes fanciful interpretations of Gothic woodwork and vaulted plaster ceilings. Joel Rothbone's residence, Kenwood, designed by A. J. Davis in 1841, featured furnishings in the Gothic style. The Pruyn house was furnished in the more popular and comfortable Rococo style.

In the 1850s it was popular to furnish rooms with a plain background--that is, white walls and woodwork--and then introduce a riot of fabrics, color, and furniture.

As the Civil War ended, interiors underwent a striking change. The country prospered and everyone wanted everything. The Renaissance style became popular, and furniture became more architectural in character. Colors became deeper; rich reds, golds, beiges, and blues were popular. Wallpaper-covered walls and ceilings were frescoed and stenciled.

What is now the governor's mansion on Eagle Street was built, c. 1856, as a country house by Thomas Olcott. It was purchased by Robert L. Johnson in the 1860s and extensively remodeled in the Second Empire style. Governor William Tilden moved into this elaborate house in 1875, and after it was purchased by the state, the building was greatly enlarged. The drawing room illustrates a typical 1860s interior with frescoed ceiling and walls by Albany's noted fresco artist Emanuel Mickel, and ornate drapery masking the windows. The profusion of ornament is complemented by the liberal use of color. The massive ebonized drawing room furniture remains in the mansion to this day. Figure 5 shows the dining room, created by the architect Isaac Perry during the 1886-87 expansion of the mansion in the Queen Anne style. The mahogany woodwork complements the rich coloring of the wall coverings and the gleam of the polished brass fender and andirons. The polished hardwood floor is partially covered by a large rug. The original dining table and chairs are still used in the room.

The arts and crafts movement and the aesthetic style began influencing Albany interiors in the 1860s and 1870s. The movements, fostered by men such as Charles Eastlake, William Morris, and Christopher Dresser, were marked by fine craftsmanship, the use of patterns derived from nature and geometry, and the popularity of stained glass. The library at Judge Muhlfelder's residence, designed by Alexander Selkirk, and shown in figure 6, suggests the influence of the arts and crafts movement with its brick fireplace. The novelty of electric lighting can be seen by the use of exposed bulbs. By the end of the nineteenth century, highly polished hardwood floors, frequently covered with Oriental rugs, were favored. Oriental rugs also were placed on tables and made into pillows and wall hangings.

The aesthetic movement flourished in the 1880s, with its emphasis on fine materials, rich colors, stenciled ornamentation, and parquet flooring. Rooms contained built-in nooks for all sorts of ornaments. Collecting was the rage, particularly for Oriental objects. Grand interiors from the 1880s are to be found in the New York State Capitol. Probably the greatest interiors in the building were created by H. H. Richardson.

One of the really grand legislative halls anywhere in the country is the Senate Chamber, with its abundant use of rich material. The wall covering in the chamber is gilded leather, which became popular in the 1880s. The Executive Chamber, known more recently as the red room, was completed by Richardson in 1881. The office featured an Oriental pattern carpet, an enormous polished brass gasolier and walls covered in embossed paper imitating leather. The room has recently been restored so that it now appears much as Richardson intended it. During this period, the elaborate drapery treatments from earlier in the century gave way to simpler forms, although there was extensive use made of elaborate needlework and applique.

Another example of Richardson's work is Albany's City Hall, constructed between 1881 and 1883. A limited budget prevented the completion of the interior in the rich manner typical of this architect, but Richardson's influence could be seen in the original configuration of the mayor's office, with its paneling and decorated ceiling. In 1916 the architectural firm of Ogden and Gander was retained to remodel the interior of Albany City Hall, and the result was more restrained than Richardson's bold polychromatic exterior. The transition is evident in the view of the mayor's office shown in figure 7. The furnishings were designed to complement the architecture.

The 1890s ushered in a number of changes in interior design. This was the great age of the Newport mansions, in which people were trying to evoke the past with grand, European inspired interiors, filled with ornate but often fake antique furniture. Any style was possible and money was the only limitation. Very often these recreations were surprisingly accurate to their European model. Even simple homes aspired to these trends. Stamped metal ceilings in a variety of styles were popular both in houses and public buildings, and often took the place of more expensive plaster or wood ceilings. Often, what appeared to be carved woodwork or stone would turn out to be mass-produced plaster ornament masked under a coat of paint.

Just about anything imaginable could be part of a room's interior in the 1900s. Interiors during this period tended to represent a culmination of nineteenth century taste, using many different styles.

An excellent example of this culmination can be found in the Dutch Revival mansion constructed in 1900 and now occupied by the Rockefeller Institute at 411 State Street (figure 8). The interiors reflect a multiplicity of styles--no two rooms feature the same period. The Georgian inspired drawing room opens into a French salon which in turn leads to a Classical music room and a paneled Tudor dining room. This single house contains a history of style.

So, from these views of Albany interiors, we can trace the history of taste that fashioned the people, the homes, and the grand city of Albany.

Douglas G. Bucher, associate with Mendel, Mesick, Cohen, Waite, Hall, specializes in restoration work. A graduate of Rensselaer Polytechnic Institute, Bucher often lectures on the topic of architectural restoration and historic interiors.

Further Readings

Bennett, Allison P. *The People's Choice: A History of Albany County in Art and Architecture.* Albany: The Albany County Historical Association, 1980.

Blackburn, Roderic H. *Cherry Hill: The History and Collections of a Van Rensselaer Family.* Albany: Historic Cherry Hill, 1976.

Mayhew, Edgar de N., and Minor Meyers, Jr. *A Documentary History of American Interiors from the Colonial Era to 1915.* New York: Charles Scribner's Sons, 1980.

Peterson, Harold L. *American Interiors: From Colonial Times to the Late Victorians.* New York: Charles Scribner's Sons, 1971.

Roseberry, C.R. *Capitol Story.* Albany: New York State Office of General Services, 1982.

Seale, William. *Recreating the Historic House Interior.* Nashville: American Association for State and Local History, 1979.

Seale, William. *The Tasteful Interlude: American Interiors Through the Camera's Eye, 1860-1917.* 2nd ed. Nashville: American Association for State and Local History, 1981.

North parlor, hall and south parlor at Cherry Hill, 1882.   Figure 1.
Photo courtesy of Historic Cherry Hill.

The drawing room at the Van Rensselaer manor.   Figure 2.

104

Dining room at the Van Rensselaer manor.   *Figure 3.*

The Ten Broeck mansion's parlor.   *Figure 4.*

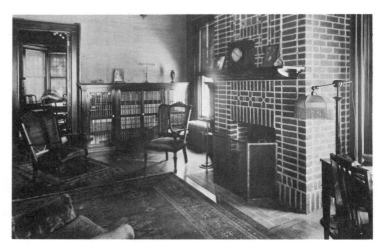

Judge Muhlfelder's library.   *Figure 6.*

Figure 8.

Dutch colonial at 411 State Street.

Figure 5.

The dining room at the governor's mansion.

The mayor's remodeled office.   *Figure 7.*

Architecture represents a skillful blend of need and aspiration, form and function. This pluralistic nature of architecture is evident in American design, which has strived to be practical and efficient while attaining an ideal. Many factors dictate architectural design: topography, climate, resources, technology, and culture shape and direct an architect's perception of the real and the ideal. No other art form has so many restrictions.

These factors have been vital in shaping American architecture. From the beginning, Americans possessed an unparalleled concept of space and an awareness of abundant natural resources. The colonial inhabitants adapted the architectural styles of their homelands to the materials and climates in which they were located. As these colonies changed hands and the country gained independence, adaptations took on a decidely American character. European styles predominated, but were interpreted in materials--wood, stone, and brick-- appropriate to the location. Transportation advances made materials widely available, and the technologies of the Industrial Revolution created new building forms in metal. A growing and increasingly cultivated middle class never lagged too far behind the wealthy trendsetters. These transformations of the social structure can be traced in architecture.

Albany architecture has followed these patterns of assimilation and independence. The rapid growth of the city in the nineteenth century stimulated the construction and demolition of many buildings. The city's growing role as a government and financial center created an architectural heritage that illustrates the American tendency toward grandiloquence in design. Albany's public and private buildings were always grander than necessary: The colossal size of Union Station belied a population of one hundred thousand; the State Education building boasts one of the world's longest colonnades; and Albany's skyline has always suggested a much larger city.

Albany has been home to many fine architects. Philip Hooker, one of the first and most notable, literally built Albany in the early 1800s and shaped its appearance for many years. Few examples of his Federal style buildings remain. Only recently has Albany grown interested in preserving its architectural heritage which, in addition to many fine buildings of all periods, includes fine examples of eclecticism. Albany has its architectural follies and its treasures. But above all, Albany shows a diversity of style.

State capitols represent a unique American building form. As America grew from royal outpost to independent nation, and states emerged from colonies, Americans needed to express liberty and autonomy in their architecture. The multi-functional state house, though often prominently positioned, did not fulfill the lofty visions of legislators.

The term "capitol" derives from the Temple of Jupiter in Rome and was first applied, in 1699, to the Virginia state house. Appropriately, the term expressed the desire to create architectural symbols. The architectural symbols of democracy generally included an imposing portico, balanced legislative chambers, and a tower in the form of a steeple or dome.

Early capitols were often designed by amateur architects such as Albany's Philip Hooker and modeled after earlier styles. Hooker's capitol was classical in design but indecisive in form and function, housing both state and municipal governments. As all capitols are symbolic of their times, so Hooker's inadequate capitol was representative of the declining fortunes of the Federalists.

American capitols were the most costly architectural projects of the nineteenth century. An architect had to be a persuasive lobbyist as well as a talented artist to win the job of designing a capitol. Battles ensued over designs; legislative committees changed architectural plans; and wars interrupted construction. Politics had as much to do with design as architectural dreams.

The New York State Capitol reflects the conflict between these forces. Begun when European forms still dominated American style, the building reflects 30 years of changes. The final cost of over $25 million, double that of the United States Capitol in Washington, was largely due to wavering legislative committees. Vacilliation and political upheaval rendered the final structure antiquated before its completion at the end of the nineteenth century. As style surmounted style, the building became a visible index of its five architects--as much archaeology as architecture.

Despite these obstacles, the New York State capitol was completed, albeit a departure from typical capitol design. Although towerless, the Capitol fulfills its original intention of demonstrating the culture, wealth, and power of the Empire State. It stands as a document to transitions in American building practices, as well as a collection of architectural styles and a magnificent example of the superb craftsmanship of stonecutters, woodcarvers, cabinetmakers, painters, and other artisans.

Current restorations attest to continued involvement with the Capitol. Through rehabilitation and reconstruction, we may uncover and newly appreciate the original form and function of this exquisite building.

GOVERNMENT BUILDINGS: THE PUBLIC FACE OF A CITY

Dennis McFadden

Architect John Mesick says that cities document the values of the cultures which build and inhabit them. Clearly, the architecture of a city is a medium through which cultural values are conveyed. The buildings, streets, and parks built by our predecessors are a key to understanding what was important to them. Similarly, what we build, demolish, and preserve will tell our successors what is meaningful to us. I would like to explore the concept of understanding a culture's values through "urban documentation," looking specifically at Albany and the contribution New York State government has made in defining its character.

A process of interpretation inherent in the claim is that the physical matter of a city can tell us something about itself. Buildings and streets--merely individual artifacts of man, the maker--can be beautiful abstract shapes whose color and texture delight the eye. But without an understanding of their use, the ideas behind their design, and the dreams of their authors, they remain remote from our experience and difficult to understand, though perhaps easy to appreciate.

Recent travel has taken me to two cities I had not visited previously. Recalling these cities, I am struck by the extent to which the combination of my visual memory and a cursory knowledge of each has shaped my impressions of them.

In 1983, I visited Austin, Texas. Three structures particularly impressed me. The first was the capitol building; the second was the tower of the University of Texas; and the third was the university's football stadium. Each structure is large, strikingly designed, and tied to an aspect of Austin culture. The State capitol was built in the 1880s, and like Albany's, is currently undergoing restoration. Architecturally, it is modeled after the U.S. Capitol in Washington, D.C. The University tower is a tall, slender building standing in the midst of an otherwise low campus. The football stadium adds a remarkable enough element to the city skyline when empty. It is even more dramatic when filled with fans.

Each of these elements of Austin's urban landscape would be of visual interest on its own. Each makes a unique and significant contribution to the variety and life of the city's skyline. More significant is the contribution of these structures in relation to the functions and activities associated with them. Suddenly, a reading of the skyline becomes a reading of the life of the city. The roles of government, education, and athletics are obvious. A second level of speculative meaning can be arrived at with knowledge of Austin's capitol relative to the nation's Capitol. As an attempt to secure credibility, or perhaps through boastfulness, the Texas building is seven feet taller than the nation's Capitol.

In contrast to these three distinct structures, there was an inordinate amount of mundane, new construction underway in Austin, with countless cranes creating bland office blocks. While nondescript, these buildings are alarming by virtue of their numbers. The impression was one of tremendous growth in the service sector of the economy, a growth by no means uniformly favored. People in Austin, as elsewhere, feared that the qualities which made their city livable would be lost to growth. It was with great interest, then, that I read a recent article in the *New York Times* reporting that Austin had elected an outspoken environmentalist mayor.

I had no impression of Austin prior to my visit. By contrast, I carried a strong set of preconceptions when I visited Pittsburgh in 1985. Though I had never before visited Pittsburgh, it stood in my mind's eye as the quintessential steel city, undoubtedly because of its image in popular culture. Even recent attempts to portray it as a new city seem to emphasize what it was not, almost as much as what it was, thereby reinforcing the traditional image.

What I discovered in Pittsburgh was a curious mixture of images associated with a variety of other cities. Granted, one finds steel mills and working class neighborhoods, but most of the tall smokestacks are dormant and the air is clear. An unexpected discovery was the city's resemblance to Los Angeles in the multilane, limited access highways cutting through downtown Pittsburgh. Also surprising was the almost Manhattan-like view and layout of downtown Pittsburgh when seen across the confluence of the two rivers. An impressive collection of highly individualized buildings is found in the downtown section, among them H.H. Richardson's Allegheny County Courthouse, and Philip Johnson's and John Burger's PPG Building.

All of the above create the impression of Pittsburgh as a city of vigor. Although it is a city troubled by the problems of the American steel industry, Pittsburgh is nevertheless optimistic about the future. Those who promote the city would have us view it as a livable city of the future; in fact this is the view reproduced on postcards.

Sometimes the things which give a city its identity are carefully orchestrated to create a certain impression, as in the case of Brasilia. Although politics may be the most obvious force to shape a city in this way, it is not the only force. Bethlehem, Pennsylvania, for example, is an eighteenth century city formed and shaped by a religious group, the Moravians. The Moravians were among the first in the country to plan entire urban systems at once. As a result, Bethlehem was one of the first cities in this country to have centralized water distribution. Few cities are so carefully defined on a large scale. More often, the sense of a city results from the cumulative effects of many individual actions, with buildings erected one at a time.

The city of Albany, as seen today, is a collection of pieces of various shapes and sizes from throughout its history. Although we struggle to find anything predating the mid-nineteenth century, we are certain Albany is about to begin its fourth century. Evidence of Albany's early years is limited to the downtown street pattern and the city's relationship with the river. A description of the city, in *Random Recollections of Albany from 1800 to 1808*, written by Gorham A. Worth at the beginning of the nineteenth century, presents the following view of the growing city: "The city of Albany in 1800, though the capital of the state and occupying a commanding position, was nevertheless in point of size, commercial importance, and architectural dignity, but a third- or fourth-rate town. It was not, in some respects, what it might have been; but it was, in all respects, unlike what it is now." The author continues, "Albany was indeed Dutch in all its moods and tenses; early and inveterately Dutch. The buildings were Dutch--Dutch in style, in position, attitude, and aspect. The people were Dutch, the horses were Dutch, and even the dogs were Dutch."

Albany was not to remain a third- or fourth-rate city for long. It was designated the state capital in 1797, three years before Worth took up residence at the age of 18. During the Revolution and the years that followed, the legislature moved about from New York City to Kingston, White Plains, Poughkeepsie, and finally Albany. During this transient phase, New York State government had no capitol building. The capitol was wherever legislators chose to congregate. With the selection of a capital city came a move to create such a building and the impact of state government on the city's physical appearance was inevitable. The idea of a building suitable for government was not foreign to the newly independent states. Capitol buildings had existed before the Revolution. Williamsburg's can be called the first capitol; in 1699, it was referred to as such in official government documents. The eighteenth century saw the design of a number of government buildings. In 1704, Francis Nicholson, then governor of the Colony of New York, erected an office building in Manhattan designed in part on the capitol in Williamsburg. In 1712, the State House in Boston was built. (This is not the same State House that stands in Boston today.) Finally, in 1750, Pennsylvania built a State House in Philadelphia, which later became Independence Hall.

After the Revolution, a number of capitols were built, one of the most famous being Jefferson's in Richmond, Virginia, built c. 1798. Another familiar to many is Bulfinch's Boston State House, part of which still stands today. Capitols in South

Carolina and New Jersey were also built during this period.

In Albany, the legislature met in the Stadt Huys, or town hall. It was a rather simple structure--three stories atop a brick basement with a simple pediment roof, a tower, and cupola above. In 1803, the city Common Council decided that this structure was inadequate. This might seem a strange decision, were it not for the fact that the hall was then used not only by state government, but by the county and city as well. The Council decided to raise $30,000 to build a new capitol with $3,000 contributions from the city and county, and a $12,000 contribution from the state. The balance was to be made up by the sale of the old town hall, and the final cost exceeded $110,000.

The first capitol building in Albany was designed by Albany's Philip Hooker (1766-1836) between 1802 and 1804, and completed in 1809. It was intended to house all branches of state, county, and city government. Government quickly outgrew the building, however, and new structures were built. By 1829, the space problem had become so acute that the city sold its share of the building to the state and built the first city hall, not far from where the present city hall stands today. Sole possession of the capitol, however, did not satisfy the state's hunger for office space. Between 1834 and 1840, a new state hall, known today as the Court of Appeals, was built, replacing an earlier state hall erected at the close of the eighteenth century on the corner of Lodge and State Streets. State hall later became the state museum and, ultimately, in 1870, the geological museum. Even in the nineteenth century, state government buildings were important in downtown Albany. Space continued to be at a premium, and, by the time of the Civil War, legislative committees were forced to meet in private homes and hotels.

All this serves as background to the story of the new capitol, the first state building about which we are well informed. Its history ranks among the tales of political intrigue and architectural competition worthy of a collaboration between John LeCarre and William Kennedy. This building meant much to those who constructed it and, like all buildings, reflects something about the culture that built it.

Design competitions were a common nineteenth century method of choosing architects. In the case of the capitol, two such competitions were held. The first was held on very short notice and attracted only three architects. Because of the meager response, a second competition was held in 1866 and some 30 architects participated in this competition. An analysis of the entries reveals three categories of approaches to the question of how to design a capitol. The first is the traditional approach, which could also be called the Williamsburg approach. Based on the Williamsburg capitol, this approach generally incorporates a central block flanked by wings of offices over two legislative houses, a tall tower, a cupola, and a central portico. This type of capitol is exemplified by Charles Strickland's structure of 1825 in Nashville, Tennessee. The original Hooker building also approximates this idea.

The second approach was based on the nation's Capitol. The reasons are obvious. Initiated in 1803, the nation's Capitol was completed in its first incarnation in 1831 and substantially enlarged in the 1850s. During the Civil War it became a symbol of the Union. Clearly a model for major state government buildings, this approach enjoyed nationwide popularity. California and Texas, for example, followed this model, incorporating the dome, or signature piece, of the nation's Capitol in their capitol buildings.

The jury for the New York competition was not interested in either of these approaches. Perhaps they felt New York should not follow a precedent established by a building built 70 years earlier; rather, the state should look to more contemporary models. These feelings were shared by a number of architects who entered designs in the New York competition based on the Louvre in Paris, which was designed and completed about 1857 as a building of complex visual drama. With its mansard roofs, the Louvre is representative of a whole se-

ries of decorative motifs popular in French architecture of the sixteenth and seventeenth centuries.

Buildings of this third type were favored in the awarding of prizes. The award winning designs were announced in May, 1867, and although no single plan was found totally satisfactory, prizes were distributed to those which came closest. The architect who subsequently began the design of the building, Thomas Fuller, in collaboration with Nicholas and Brown, won a consolation prize of $1,000. Another firm, Schultz and Schoen of New York City, which had come up with a similar design, also received a consolation prize.

The commission which had been created to review the plans, select a winner, and direct the construction of the new capitol, decided to seek a suitable designer from architects outside of the official competitors. Arthur D. Gilman was brought in to put together the best features of the various preferred plans. A long row about how this was to be done and who should be given credit ensued. Curiously, Thomas Fuller emerged in a pivotal position every step of the way. Whenever a new team was suggested, he was invariably part of it. It is worth noting that Fuller was also one of the three who entered the original competition. His desire to work here was obvious. Trained in Great Britain, Fuller designed the Houses of Parliament in Ottawa, Canada.

Fuller's idea for New York's capitol is reminiscent of the Louvre, evidenced by the strong elements at the corners and the tower. Fuller ultimately prevailed and was appointed architect of the capitol in August of 1868. His design is described in the first annual report of the commission on the new capitol. The first paragraph suggests prototypes and sources deemed appropriate for a capitol building in Albany: "In the exterior composition of the design, there is a general adherence to the style of the pavilions of the new Louvre, of the Hotel de Ville of Paris, and of the elegant hall or Maison de Commerce, recently erected in the city of Lyons. Without servile imitation of any particular example, the architects have produced a composition in the bold and effective spirit which marks the most admired specimens of modern civil architecture. The terrace which forms the grand approach to the east, or principal front, will form an item of striking architectural detail nowhere else attempted on such an extensive scale, at least in America." Clearly, those who shaped this building wanted to ensure that the capitol would be a meaningful structure rather than just another office building. New York had emerged from the Civil War an economic and political power. There was a tremendous desire to celebrate that power in a building which, located in the state capital, would encourage pride in the Empire State.

One often hears complaints about how easy it is to get lost in the capitol. I attribute this to the fact that the building is no longer used as originally intended, and continuing efforts to squeeze in more office space have only exacerbated the situation. The story of the selection of a designer for the capitol is one of competing artistic ideals, and the tale of its construction follows suit. Fuller indeed began construction on the building and, although subsequent architects were involved, Fuller defined the plan by building the foundations. Within a few years, however, Fuller was replaced by a triumvirate of extraordinary architectural talents: Henry Hobson Richardson, one of the nation's greatest architects, was joined by Leopold Eidlitz, a fascinating New York architect, and Frederick Law Olmsted, best known for his landscape architecture. The three were brought together in 1875 to review Fuller's plans and evaluate construction to date. Their response was to criticize every aspect of both the design and construction of the building. It was not long before Richardson, Eidlitz, and Olmsted were appointed as Fuller's replacements. By that time, however, Fuller had completed the first two or three stories of the exterior, and the triumvirate set out to impose their concept of a capitol on Fuller's work. Their proposals sparked the "battle of the styles," which ended only when the legislature decreed the building was to be built in the Renaissance style. This did not stymie Richardson or Eidlitz as their creativity al-lowed them to develop a design which preserved their original ideas. By incorporating slightly French motifs, the architects managed to convince the legislature that they had followed instructions. Much of the building we see today carries their mark.

Like Fuller, however, Richardson, Eidlitz, and Olmsted never completed the building. They were replaced by Isaac Perry, a builder from New York State who came to Albany with a solid reputation as a sound, responsible architect-builder. Fortunately, he developed a great affection for Richardson's ideas for the building. Much of Perry's work reflects his interpretation of what Richardson had intended. In light of all this, the last thing we might expect is that the capitol would be a consistent structure, and it does, in fact, vary stylistically. Looking at the building, one detects both a frenetic quality and a very interesting diversity. It has a wonderful visual liveliness. Yet there are consistencies in the building which contrast with the tremendous variety. It is, in total, a fine example of the ideal late nineteenth century public building.

The capitol was to be entered on what is now the second floor. All major ceremonial spaces in the building were located on either the second or third floors; the second floor housed the governor's formal office and the Court of Appeals; and the third floor held the Senate and Assembly Chambers and many conference rooms. The first and fourth floors were intended to be service floors. And the building was to have had a tower or dome. The earliest design allowed for such things as a restaurant and two barber shops (one for the Senate and a second for the Assembly) on the first floor. The fourth floor housed a number of small offices, committee offices, and commission offices.

The capitol was designed with sources of natural light in mind. Because it was built at a time when there was no electric light or heating, natural light and central ventilation were important considerations. Designed around a large courtyard, the building originally had three major sky-lit staircases. If you venture into the staircases today, you will find that they are completely dark and the courtyard is not readily apparent. Clearly, some of the more central elements of the original building design are hidden.

These elements--the idea of an entrance on the second floor, the courtyard as a major organizing element, and the use of a tower or dome--were architectural features built into the original plan, which would mark the capitol as a "symbol building" and, by extension, define the nature of Albany as a capital city.

The capitol, of course, was quickly outgrown. It is important to consider the more recent structures erected in Albany, as they suggest what has subsequently been considered appropriate for a capital city. An interesting sequence began with the construction of the New York State Education Building in 1910. Intended to house the state's education department, including the state library, the education building is stylistically distinct from the capitol. The building makes a compelling argument for New York's commitment to education by virtue of its size and pretense. The Alfred E. Smith State Office Building, built in 1929, is perhaps symbolic of state government's contemporaneity. More recently, the State Campus suggested that state government belongs outside downtown Albany. With the construction of the Empire State Plaza, however, the focus is back on the city. Both of these complexes express an idea about the city as a whole. Both reflect what was considered appropriate for a capital city, from the city's perspective, rather than the building's. What does all this mean? Nelson Rockefeller made a number of interesting comments at the dedication of the Empire State Plaza, all on the theme of Albany as the ideal capital city for the greatest state in the greatest country.

What did Rockefeller mean by this? Let me answer with an anecdote. One day while riding from the railroad station in a cab, I met a woman and her young daughter. As we headed across the arterial beneath that vast stone wall at the approach to the Empire State Plaza, she said, "It's just like Star Wars!" That, of course, is what was intended. Albany was to be the capital of the future.

We might ask where this leads us today: What does this all suggest about Albany in its 300th year? Moving back a hundred years and looking at prints, maps, and photographs of the city, we find an interesting recurring phenomenon. The state builds a rather grand building on a high site in Albany which, for several years, dominates the skyline of the city. This was the effect achieved by the Hooker capitol in the mid-nineteenth century and the capitol in the later nineteenth century. Then, city buildings surpassed state buildings in scale and height. This might cause one to wonder what will happen to the South Mall.

Two recent preservation and restoration developments may signal a change, the first being the D & H Building and the second, the capitol. It would seem that both signal a new direction for New York State government; rather than building new structures, the state is restoring, preserving, and rehabilitating existing structures. In this respect, New York is in step with the times. Interestingly, when the City Strategic Planning Commission recently published their plan, they chose City Hall, rather than a futuristic view of the city, for the cover. Perhaps the tide has turned so that in coming years visitors walking the streets of Albany will sense Albany as a city which has looked both to the past and to the future.

Dennis McFadden, *director of the New York State Commission for the Restoration of the state capitol, is in charge of the educational program and the general program for the commission. McFadden has degrees in the history of architecture and architectural planning from Columbia University. He has worked in the areas of theater, audiovisual planning, and general building restoration in New York City. Coming to Albany in 1980, McFadden has been instrumental in working with the city in the development of current architectural planning.*

Further Readings

Hitchcock, Henry-Russell, and William Seale. *Temples of Democracy: The State Capitols of the USA*. New York: Harcourt Brace Jovanovich, 1976.

The Master Plan for the New York State Capitol. Albany: The Temporary State Commission on the Restoration of the Capitol, 1983.

Proceedings of the New York State Capitol Symposium. Albany: The Temporary State Commission on the Restoration of the Capitol, 1983.

Rosberry, C.R. *Capitol Story*. 2nd ed. Albany: New York State Office of General Services, 1982.

Seale, William. "Glowing Revival for 'Most Beautiful Room in America'." *Smithsonian* (November 1981): 146-53.

Capitol interior.

Fuller and Laver's 1869 design for the Capitol.

The first Capitol (1809), designed by Philip Hooker.

Richardson/Eidlitz/Olmstead design (1876).

The Alfred E. Smith Building (1927), by Sullivan Jones.

The nineteenth century Senate Chamber.

Twentieth century restoration of the Senate Chamber.

Always grand, the Capitol and the Education buildings.

ALBANY ART

The Hudson River School of painters was a group of nineteenth century landscape artists who worked largely in New York and New England. The Hudson River School was born in 1825 when John Trumbull, William Dunlap, and Asher B. Durand "discovered" three of Thomas Cole's landscapes in a shop window in New York City. The name of the school was coined at the turn of the nineteenth century by a critic who sarcastically associated them with the Hudson River to emphasize their parochialism.

Thomas Cole founded the Hudson River School. Like most of his colleagues, Cole had a simple background. Born 1801 in Lancashire, England, he worked as a calico designer and engraver's assistant before coming to America in 1818. He worked in Philadelphia as a wood engraver, then an art teacher, itinerant portraitist, wallpaper designer, writer, and general artist-handyman. His assets in 1825 were his dissatisfaction with his so-far spotty career, his love of the countryside, and his new-found dedication to landscape painting. Cole's individual performance, success, and public recognition became the model for other artists and draftsmen as they followed him into landscape painting.

First-generation painters of the Hudson River School included Thomas Doughty (1793-1856) and Asher B. Durrand (1796-1886). The school also included some second generation painters and some luminists. Luminism is a particular style of the school which flourished from 1850 to 1875. Its roots can be traced to seventeenth century Dutch seascapes.

Although the major museum collections of the Hudson River School are in New York, Washington, D.C., and Boston, smaller collections can be seen in the Albany area at the Albany Institute of History and Art, the Canajoharie Library and Art Gallery, the Munson-William-Proctor Institute, and the New York Historical Association.

THE HUDSON RIVER SCHOOL

Ian Porter

Some moderately civilized people still look upon nineteenth century painting, particularly American landscape painting from the Hudson River School, as "candy box art." So the 1984 exhibition, *A New World: Masterpieces of American Painting (1760-1910)*, came at a good time. Many who saw this exhibition in Boston, Washington, or Paris found American art as good as the best and as bad as the worst European art. And many could for the first time compare masterpieces by our leading artists: Thomas Cole's *The Voyage of Life* (1840), Frederic Church's *Niagara Falls* (1857), Martin Johnson Heade's *Thunderstorm Over Naragansett Bay* (1857), John Frederick Kensett's *Narragansett Bay* (1861), and Fitz Hugh Lane's *Owl's Head, Penobscot Bay, Maine* (1862). The magnificent exhibition catalog contains color plates of every work, lucid and exquisitely written essays by Theodore E. Stebbins; John Moors Cabot, curator of painting at the Museum of Fine Arts in Boston; Pierre Rosenberg, conservateur en chef au Departement des Peintures, Musee du Louvre in Paris; and

other scholars. These entries were widely and enthusiastically received. Grace Glueck described it as a "smashing show" in the *New York Times*, and Hughes Roberts wrote in *Time:* "It may be the best survey show of its kind ever held. Certainly it will be the first time that this era of American art has been seen in proper concentration and strength in Europe." No praise seemed too lavish.

Keats' noble phrase: "A thing of beauty is a joy forever," used in his sense that a thing of beauty is a joy forever because it retains its beauty forever, is clearly wrong. Beauty is as transitory as everything else in this world. Beauty depends on the climate of sensibility, and this changes with passing years. A different generation has different needs and demands a different satisfaction. A truer interpretation of Keats' line would be that what has once been considered a thing of beauty will one day be enjoyed again. No tract of history exemplifies this better than nineteenth century American landscape painting, namely, the Hudson River School. Thomas Cole (1801-1848) and his contemporaries and, later, Frederic Edwin Church (1828-1900) and his generation, were much admired in their day. Yet, by the end of the nineteenth century the school had become completely discredited and, until the 1960s, its paintings were considered triumphs of kitsch over camp. The name itself originated contemptuously at the end of the nineteenth century as a critic in the *New York Tribune* implied the parochialism of these painters by condescendingly associating the school with the Hudson River.

In 1874, thirty-eight of Kensett's paintings, known as the *Last Summer's Work*, were deeded to the Metropolitan Museum of Art in New York. By the 1920s, they were relegated to storage, and in 1956 and 1957, eighteen of these stunning landscapes were sold at auction. In 1965, John K. Howat, one of Kensett's few admirers, who later became Chairman of the Department of American Art at the Metropolitan Museum, bought a Kensett seascape for $150. In 1983, another of his seascapes fetched $594,000 at auction.

Between 1890 and 1910, the Metropolitan acquired some fine Coles, Durands, and Doughtys from donors who wanted to unburden themselves of these, by then, unfashionable canvasses. In 1962, James Thomas Flexner noted, in *That Wilder Image, The Native School from Thomas Cole to Winslow Homer*, that some of "the pictures obscured with grime hang unloved on the walls of the Metropolitan Museum." In the 1960s, the Board of the Metropolitan turned down an offer to acquire Cole's *The Voyage of Life* (1841) for $10,000, as they already had six Coles! And as recently as 1970, as distinguished a critic as Hilton Kramer wrote in the *New York Times* that the centennial exhibition of the Metropolitan Museum, *Nineteenth Century America: Paintings and Sculpture*, "is at once an elaborate exercise in cultural nostalgia, a demonstration of museological acquisitiveness, and a celebration of the social class that founded the museum one hundred years ago and still presides over its fortunes today. It is only incidentally an art exhibition."

The Whitney Museum of American Art in New York sold its nineteenth century collection in the 1960s only to launch an expensive campaign to buy another collection some years later. At about the same time, Harvard's Fogg Museum sold Church's *Twilight in the Wilderness* (1860) to Sherman Lee, the recently retired and much admired director of the Cleveland Museum, for a mere $20,000. It is now estimated to be worth three million dollars.

The revival of interest in nineteenth century American art is not unrelated to the acceptance of America as the center of modern art after the second World War. This led to a greater interest in American art in general, as it moved people to look at our artistic past with fresher and more sympathetic eyes. Scholars and connoisseurs found works of hitherto unimagined intellectual and artistic challenges, and the public found an outlet for its reaction against modernism in a style which was perceived as embodying peculiarly American values.

As Hudson River School paintings remained inexpensive until the 1970s, new collectors could stake out a substantial claim. The most influential of them, Martha and Maxim Karolik, unveiled their collection in Boston at the Museum of Fine Arts in 1951. This was followed by John D. Rockefeller III's distinguished collection at the Fine Arts Museum of San Francisco in 1974, Jo Ann and Julian Ganze's collection at Los Angeles County Museum in 1982, and the Thyllen-Bornemisza collection in the IBM Gallery of Science and Art, New York, in 1985.

In 1954, the late Edgar P. Richardson, then Director of the Detroit Institute of Arts (1954-1962), founded the Archives of American Art, which now has a repository of ten million primary documents. In 1970, the Smithsonian Institution's National Museum of American Art in Washington, D.C. began to register all American paintings in public and private collections which were executed before 1914. The Museum now has data on 250,000 paintings and 22,000 artists. These resources have supported the outpouring of doctoral dissertations and other scholarly publications on American art, among which the more popular are Edgar P. Richardson's *Paintings in America* (1956), John Wilmerding's *American Art* (1967), Barbara Novak's *American Painting of the Nineteenth Century* (1969), John K. Howat's *The Hudson River and Its Painters* (1972), and Theodore E. Stebbins, Jr.'s *American Master Drawings and Watercolors* (1976).

The change of interest which took place in the 1960s is also reflected in the increasing number of chairs of American art established across the country at Columbia University, City University of New York, University of Delaware, and University of Michigan. The first occupant of the chair in Michigan is David C. Huntington, the reigning Church scholar, whose reputation is based on his book, *Landscapes of Frederic Edwin Church: Vision of an American Era* (1966). This pioneering work re-established interest in Church and an admiration for his work, which ultimately contributed to Huntington's successful efforts to preserve Church's estate, Olana, which had been closed for over fifty years. After the death of Church's daughter-in-law, Sally, age 96, Olana was in danger of being destroyed, the property divided, its contents scattered. Huntington's collection includes nearly 200 Church paintings, 150 Church oil sketches, many works of art by his friends, and a group of "old masters" catalogued by Gerald L. Carr while on sabbatical from the Dallas Museum of Arts in 1984.

Thomas Cole and His Generation

In 1967, the New York State Office of Parks and Recreation took over Olana from Olana Preservation, Inc. A Victorian mansion built in 1870 by Calvert Vaux near the eastern end of the Rip Van Winkle Bridge, it offers a marvelous view of the Hudson River Valley. Frederic Edwin Church (1828-1900) lived here from 1860 until he died.

In 1979, Edith Cole Silberstein, great granddaughter of Thomas Cole (1801-1848), sold her house to the Catskill Center for Conservation and Development for $125,000. It is a Federal style house built in 1812 by Thomas T. Thompson near the

western end of the Rip Van Winkle Bridge. Looking east one can see Olana, and looking west one sees the 3,945 foot Thomas Cole peak in the Blockhead Range of the Catskill Mountains. Cole lived here from 1836 until his death in 1848.

Cole was the founder of the Hudson River School of American landscape painters, and Church, his pupil, was the leader of the second generation. Olana, the center of Church's world, is the symbol of that school, with its dramatic view of the river and mountains and its eclectic architecture. After Church moved to Olana, his popularity declined, and, at his death, he, who once enjoyed the encomium "Michelangelo of landscape painting," was almost forgotten.

The start of the school, as all the world now knows, is ascribed to the occasion in 1825, when artists John Trumbull, William Dunlap, and Asher B. Durand saw three of Cole's views of the Hudson River in George W. Bruen's shop in New York City and were so captivated by them that they each bought one for $25.

Those artists, whom we now call Hudson River School painters, never applied such a term to themselves or to their work. Although many of them were susceptible to current theories and doctrines, they did not constitute a "school" or work to a common plan. They did, however, paint along the shores of the Hudson River, in the Catskills, around Lake George, and further into the Adirondacks. They ventured into the wilderness of Maine, visited Niagara Falls, (Niagara [exhibition catalog], Corcoran Gallery of Art Washington, D.C., 1985), summered in the White Mountains, and sketched off the shore of Newport. They also traveled to Paris and Rome, where they came under the influence of such seventeenth century painters as Nicolas Poussin, Claude Gellee (Lorraine) and Salvatore Rosa:

"Whate'er Lorraine light--touch'd with
    softening hue,
Or savage Rosa dashe'd, or learned
    Poussin drew."
        The Castle of Indolence
        Canto XXXVIII lines 8-9
            James Thomson

Claude's softly rolling landscapes populated by mythological figures were, in the vernacular of the day, considered "beautiful"; Rosa's harsher and more emotional works were thought "sublime."

They also went to Duesseldorf and London to visit their comtemporaries, Casper David Friedrich, Joseph Mallord William Turner, and John Constable. Turner described Claude's paintings as "pure as Italian air, calm, beautiful and serene," and Constable thought Claude's *Narcissus and Echo* "far surpassing any other landscape one has ever beheld." This aspect of the Hudson River School painting was the focus of *Americans Abroad: The European Experience in the 19th Century* (1985) at the Nassau County Museum of Fine Arts in Roslyn Harbor, Long Island. Holly Pinto Savinetti, curator and chairman of academic affairs, organized the exhibit to document the extent and duration of European exposure and to establish its effect on the synthesis of a unique American art.

The painters traveled during the summer to sketch, but completed their work in the Tenth Street Studio Building in New York City during the winter. (Paint, as you will recall, was not sold in tubes until later in the century.) A painting for an exhibition might start from a *plein aire* sketch, which served as the compositional and color guide, or a *croquis*--a thumbnail sketch accompanied by *etudes* (studies of details)--which was developed into an *ebauche* (or preliminary) painted lay-in on a large canvas which then served as the basis for the finished painting.

In the paintings, stylized trees are used as a framing device to achieve a coulisse-like effect for the dark brown foreground, the body of water in the middle (Cole said a landscape without water was not a landscape at all), and the misty, bluish mountains in the distance. Small figures are often present in the middle to establish the scale and emphasize the loneliness and vastness of the scene. An unsurpassed example is Cole's *In The Catskills* (1837) in the Metropolitan Museum of Art. This is Cole's most Italianate painting. America is seen as a garden with a quiet stream and gracefully rolling countryside in the Claudian manner. In this idealized version of rural life, nobody is working. The view of the mountains and sunset, as seen from his favorite walks along the road leading westward from the village and following the Catskill Creek, demonstrates so well his sense of the Golden Age, Manifest Destiny, and images of perfect harmony between man and nature, touched by a Mozartian wistfulness. Cole and his generation believed, in the words of Wordsworth, that "there was something in trees, flowers, meadows, and mountains which was so full of the divine that if it were contemplated with sufficient devotion it would reveal a moral and spiritual quality of its own."

Cole was born in England and came to America when he was 17. Although his family settled in Steubenville, Cole later moved to Philadelphia to receive instruction at the Pennsylvania Academy of Fine Arts before finally settling in New York City. It was then that he started his forays into the Catskills to make outdoor sketches for his romantic landscape compositions, many of which hang in the Detroit Institute of Arts. Later he matched these scenic motifs with elegiac and Biblical subjects, and after his first journey to Europe (1829-1832), he went on to paint his monumental allegorical scenes. *The Last of the Mohicans* (1827) in the New York State Historical Association, Cooperstown, New York, was painted from James Fennimore Cooper's book: Little Stocking and his companions, prisoners in the Delaware camp, watch Cora begging for mercy from Tanemunt, the tribal leader. This was the first major American painting to illustrate a scene from an American novel in a landscape considered typically American.

In 1836, Cole painted *The Course of the Empire*, now in the New York Historical Society, in five scenes, for Luman Reed, a grocer from Coxsackie, New York, who paid him $2,500. He painted two sets of *The Voyage of Life, Childhood, Youth, Manhood*, and *Old Age*, an allegory of Everyman's passage through life. The first set (1840) was for the banker, Samuel Ward, and now is in the Munson-Williams-Proctor Institute in

Utica, New York. The other set (1841-42) was offered to the Pennsylvania Academy of Fine Arts for $1,200 in 1844, but the Academy Board turned it down. George K. Schoenberger acquired the set in 1857, but when his mansion outside Cincinnati, Ohio, was converted into an old age home, it was forgotten until it was re-discovered in 1962 and sold to the National Gallery of Art in Washington, D.C., in 1971. Sketches for *The Voyage of Life* are in the Albany Institute of History and Art.

The metaphor, of course, is a voyager on the river of life. The first scene represents *Childhood*. A small boat emerges from a cave into the softly lit landscape. At the boat's masthead are personified Hours. The Guardian Spirit is at the rudder, and the infant is nestled in a bed of flowers. *Youth* was the best known picture in the series. It shows the youth holding the rudder, his Guardian Spirit bidding him farewell from the shore, as he heads downstream towards the aberration of a Moorish castle in the sky. This particular scene is laden with images; at the public exhibitions of the *Voyage of Life*, audiences were given a written guide to their interpretation. The third painting shows a blackened landscape and rudderless boat taking its apprehensive passenger toward a cataract. The explanatory text emphasizes the anguish of manhood, which only faith could save from its metaphorical sea of trouble. In the final scene, *Old Age*, the sky is dark but the water is calm, and the voyager has reached the mouth of the river. His Guardian Spirit has returned, beckoning him towards his epiphany. The series is at once a landscape, a religious painting, and a popular panorama which can be read for its storyline. Although these epic paintings are not among those which most appeal to us today, the moral idealism, the brooding on the mystery of time, and the image of life as a dream were deep currents in the mental life of the nineteenth century.

After Cole's memorial exhibition in 1848, his work was ignored until 1940, when the Albany Institute of History and Art put together a retrospective exhibition, *The Works of Thomas Cole, 1801-1848* with a modest catalogue by Director John Davis Hatch, Jr., followed eight years later by *Thomas Cole, 1801-1848, One Hundred Years Later* at the Wadsworth Atheneum in Hartford, Connecticut, and the Whitney Museum of American Art in New York City, with a larger and better documented catalogue by Esther I. Seaver. The 1967 *Studies on Thomas Cole: An American Romanticist* was mounted in the Baltimore Museum of Art to celebrate the rediscovery of *A Wild Scene* (1831-32). It was the climax of an inspired gamble, some exciting detective work, and meticulous scholarship. The painting appeared in an unrecognizable state in a Baltimore auction house in 1953, and on the recommendation of Gertrude Rosenthal and James Breckenridge, Curator of Decorative Arts, the Accessions Committee bought it for $500. Oliver W. Larkin, author of *Art and Life in America* (1949), suggested its identity, and Howard S. Merritt of the University of Rochester, the reigning Cole scholar, confirmed it as Cole's preliminary version of *The Savage State*, the first painting of *The Course of the Empire*, which he had sent to Robert Gilmore, Jr., in Baltimore in payment for a $300 debt. *A Wild Scene* is an important painting because it signals the change from the young Cole's elegiac works to his allegorical compositions. It is also the subject of a fascinating correspondence between an artist and his patron.

The most recent Cole exhibition was held in 1969 at the Munson-Williams-Proctor Institute, Whitney Museum of American Art, Memorial Art Gallery of the University of Rochester, and the Albany Institute of History and Art. The moving spirit was Merritt, who at the time was preparing a *catalogue raisonne* of Cole's work, which, unfortunately, has not yet been published. Merritt also wrote an essay in the catalogue, *To Walk with Nature: The Drawings of Thomas Cole*, for an exhibition at the Hudson River Museum in Yonkers, New York, 1982.

When Cole died in 1848, his patron Jonathan Sturgess commissioned a picture from Asher B. Durand, which he presented to William Cullen Bryant in appreciation of the funeral oration he delivered for their friend. It hung in his home, Cedamere, in Roslyn, Long Island, until his daughter gave it to the New York Public Library. *Kindred Spirits* (1849) is Durand's best known work. It shows Cole, sketchbook in hand, standing with Bryant on a cliff over a stream in the Catskills. Their names are carved into a tree on the left. The work suggests that landscapes promise spiritual sustenance and renewal of life, and is dense with detail suffused with a warm haze. The title is taken from a sonnet by Keats which opens with: "O Solitude! If I must with thee dwell" and ends with "When do they haunt two kindred spirits."

The best biography of Cole is Reverend Louis L. Noble's *The Life and Works of Thomas Cole* (1853). Noble traveled widely and served in many churches. In 1840, he was assistant minister at St. Peter's in Albany, and after a brief time in North Carolina, he became pastor of the Episcopalian church in Catskill, New York, in 1844, where Cole was a vestryman. The book was edited in 1954 by Elliot S. Vessel, M.D., (professor and chairman of the Department of Pharmacology at the Milton S. Hershey Medical Center in Pennsylvania), while he was an undergraduate at Harvard.

While president of the National Academy of Design, Durand published the aims of the Hudson River School in *Letters on Landscape* (1855). His *View Towards Hudson Valley* (1851) in the Wadsworth Atheneum is a product of his philosophy at its best, and shows Durand's considerable gift for the effects of atmosphere and muted harmonies. *View of Troy* in the Albany Institute of History and Art and *Sunday Morning* in the New Britain Museum of American Art, Connecticut, are excellent examples of Durand's pastoral idyll.

In 1911, J. Pierpont Morgan gave the Metropolitan Museum of Art an imposing landscape signed and dated 1850 by Durand. In place of its original title, which had been forgotten, the Museum supplied the title *Imaginary Landscape*. And so it remained until about fifteen years ago, when it was identified as the long lost *Scene from Thanatopsis*, a painting inspired by Bryant's poem (1821). (Thanatopsis is a word coined by the publisher and means "contemplation of death"):

> So live, that when thy summons comes to join
> The innumerable caravan, that moves
> To that mysterious realm, where each shall take
> His chamber in the silent halls of death,
> Thou go not, like the quarry-slave at night
> Scourged to his dungeon, but, sustain'd and soothed
> By an unfaltering trust, approach thy grave
> Like one who draws the drapery of his couch
> About him, and lies down to pleasant dreams.

In 1971, an exhibition of Durand's work was held at the Monclair Art Museum in New Jersey under the direction of Durand scholar David Lawall of the University of Virginia. In 1978, Lawall published *A Documentary Catalogue of the Narrative and Landscape Paintings of Durand's Works*.

The Brooklyn Museum has an interesting painting by Thomas Doughty entitled *Landscape After Ruisdael* (1846). It is a copy of Jacob van Ruisdael's *Le Coup de Soleil* (on view at the Fogg Art Museum, Harvard University in Cambridge, Massachusetts, in the 1982 Ruisdael Exhibition), which Doughty painted in Paris during his second visit to Europe. Doughty learned to paint by copying paintings in Gilmore's collection, notably those of Claude Lorraine and Albert Cuyp. One of his finest arcadian landscapes, *Fanciful Landscape* (1934), now in the National Gallery of Art, depicts the standard jagged mountain peaks, ruins, cascading waterfalls and dark pools; one of his best natural landscapes, *In The Catskills* (1826), belongs to the Addison Gallery of American Art, Philips Academy, Andover, Massachusetts.

In 1973-1974, we had the opportunity to see a collection of Doughty's paintings in the Pennsylvania Academy of Fine Art, the Corcoran Gallery of Art, and the Albany Institute of History and Art, with an tion catalogue by Frank H. Goodyear, Jr. Doughty did not, and still does not, enjoy the same high reputation as Cole and Durand; neither did he have the respect granted the former nor the popularity of the latter, though his best work reveals an uncommon sensitivity to the particular qualities of the American landscape. He died paranoid and poor in 1856.

Frederic Edwin Church and His Generation

Church served his apprenticeship with Cole in Catskill from 1844-1846. He subsequently attained immense prestige and enjoyed unanimous critical and popular acclaim both here and in Europe. He was exuberant and energetic, constantly drawing and painting. His walls were festooned with paintings, his drawers crammed with sketches. Huge numbers of people saw his paintings, for which he demanded enormous prices. *Niagara Falls* (1857), now in the Corcoran Gallery, was bought by his exhibitors for $2,500, with an additional $2,000 for the copyright to reproduce it as chromolithographs. In 1864, it was sold to the financier, John Taylor Johnston, for $5,000, and when his estate went up for auction in 1875, the banker, William Wilson Corcoran, bought it at an auction in Chickering Hall at Fifth Avenue and 18th Street, New York, for $12,500. Exhibited several times in New York, it toured the United States and was sent to London, and then to the Paris Universal Exposition in 1867, where it was awarded a gold medal. A critic in New York called it "perhaps the finest picture yet done by an American." It was greeted with equal enthusiasm in London. It was a momentous occasion for Church when the London Times wrote: "We note with particular pleasure the arrival in this country of a remarkable picture by an American landscape painter of an American subject." And in 1984, the picture was back in Paris as part of *A New World: Masterpieces of American Art 1760-1910*, again receiving favorable reviews.

Heart of the Andes (1859), in the Metropolitan Museum of Art (a sketch of which is in Olana), was bought by the manufacturer William T. Blodgett, a founder of the Metropolitan Museum, for $10,000. It was seen by nearly 13,000 people when first exhibited in the Tenth Street Studio building. It was then sent to London and Edinburgh, before being sent on tour in this country.

Twilight in the Wilderness (1860) is a particularly important painting in Church's *oeuvre*, as it combines his exploration of nature with his experimentation of new pigments. Earth and vegetable pigments were being supplanted by a rainbow of new chemical paints. The first coal tar color, mauve, was discovered by the English chemist, W. H. Perkin, founder of the coal tar industry. Next followed a series of new cobalt greens and blues, zinc white (instead of lead white), chrome green and yellow, then emerald green and artificial ultramarine to replace the expensive pigments made of crushed *lapis lazuli* from China or Tibet. Later still (1859), a series of new reds and purples appeared. In the next few years, most of the ancient, and practically all the organic, colors gave way to synthetic products. Paintings of the 1860s were more highly keyed than those of the 1840s. The problem was to find new harmony, balance, and economy among so many novel and confusing possibilities. Not only did new pigments appear, but they could now also be preserved in tubes. This made it possible to paint outdoors. The ability to paint outdoors with an increased range of colors was a significant factor in the evolution of late nineteenth century landscape painting.

Twilight in the Wilderness is Church's most powerful twilight scene. It is a metaphor for America's promise. He wrote in *Essay on American Scenery:* "Look at the heavens when the thundershower has passed, and the sun stops behind the western mountains--there the low purple clouds hang in festoons around the steeps--in the higher heaven are crimson bands interwoven with feathers of gold, fit for the wings of angels."

The uniquely American style which developed *pari passu* with these technical advances reached its fullest expression between 1850 and 1875. It had its roots in primitive American painting and was influenced by seventeenth century Dutch seascapes. Just as Claude Lorraine was the main pictorial source of Cole's generation, so the seventeenth century Dutch painters, Jan van Goyen and Albert Cuyp, were important sources for Church's generation. This style, known as luminism, is analogous to tonalism in seventeenth century Dutch paintings. It is characterized by meticulously polished realism with no signs of brush work, atmospheric effects achieved with imperceptible gradations of tone, scenes of considerable depth and long horizontal lines, and a serene poetic quality--a kind of sacramental hush. Light and atmosphere, rather than topography, and the recently developed cadmium-based pinks and oranges of the sky, rather than browns and greens of the land, distinguish this style from that of Cole's generation.

Sunset (1856), in the Munson-Williams-Proctor Institute, reflects Church's exploration of the effects of light as reflected off clouds and water. Here he combined his interest in nature with his transcendental concern for nature.

Icebergs (1861) sometimes called *The North*, in the Dallas Museum of Fine Arts, was bought in 1863 by Sir Edward Watkin, Member of Parliament, then "disappeared" until 1979, when the headmaster of Rose Hill, a boys home in Northenden, near Manchester, England, became curious about the huge landscape on the main staircase. An appraiser from Sotheby's identified it as the long lost *Icebergs* from a chromolithograph in Olana. On October 25, 1979, it was put up for auction by Sotheby's in Manhattan. The bidding opened at $500,000 and advanced at $50,000 increments. After three minutes and forty-five seconds, John L. Marion, Chairman and Chief Auctioneer of Sotheby Parke Bernet, let his hammer fall on Lot 34 at $2.5 million amidst the cheers of the 800 people present. Church had been the highest paid living painter in America, and this price was the highest ever paid for an American painting. The buyer, Lamar Hunt of Dallas, Texas, donated the painting to the Dallas Museum of Fine Arts. *Icebergs* is now again, as it was in its day, one of the most famous American paintings. Its

history has been described by Gerald L. Carr in *Frederic Edwin Church: The Icebergs* (1980).

Church was given a handsome memorial exhibition in the spring of 1900 at the Metropolitan Museum of Art. The next exhibition, however, was not held until 1966 at the National Collection of Fine Arts, The Albany Institute of History and Art, and at M. Knoedler and Company in New York City, formerly Goupil's gallery and Church's original dealer. The introduction to the catalogue for the exhibition was written by David C. Huntington, then on the faculty of Smith College in Northampton, Massachusetts.

The most magnificent Frederic Church exhibition, *Close Observation: Selected Oil Sketches* (1978) was made possible by the Smithsonian Institution Travelling Exhibition Service (SITES), a loan from the Cooper-Hewitt Museum of Decorative Arts and Design in New York City, and by Theodore E. Stebbins, Jr. from the Museum of Fine Arts in Boston, who was the guest curator for the exhibition. One hundred twelve works, astonishing in their variety and power, were selected from the group of more than 500 oil sketches given to the then Cooper Union Museum for the Arts of Decoration in 1917 by Church's youngest son Louis. And in 1984, we had the opportunity to see an exhibition, *To Embrace the Universe: Drawings by Frederic Edwin Church*, put together by Elaine Evans Dee, Curator of Drawings and Prints at the Cooper-Hewitt Museum in New York City.

One of the great favorites of Church's generation of Hudson River School painters was John Frederick Kensett (1816-1872). Kensett was almost as popular and successful as Church; he was as much in demand by his patrons as he was respected by his colleagues. An interesting painting by Tomas P. Rossiter in the Albany Institute of History and Art, *A Studio Reception* (1841), shows Kensett in the company of Cole, Durand, Huntington, and other artists, enjoying an evening of music and painting. In the summer, he traveled to sketch and socialize, and in the winter he returned to New York City to paint for his patrons and attend to his many administrative responsibilities. Kensett met Cole in Paris in 1842, summered with John W. Calilear in North Conway, Maine in 1850, hiked with Church in Maine in 1855, and toured the Rockies with Sanford Robinson Gifford and T. Worthington Whittredge in 1870. He was a founding Trustee of the Metropolitan Museum of Art, and a member of the National Academy and the U.S. Capital Art Commission.

In 1968 John K. Howat selected paintings for a Kensett exhibition and wrote an excellent catalogue for the show. Given Kensett's popularity--both then and now--surprisingly little has been written about him. The New York State Library in Albany owns the Edwin D. Morgan Collection of Kensett correspondence, amounting to more than 600 letters.

In 1985, a spectacular exhibition, *John Frederick Kensett, An American Artist*, with an especially well written catalogue by John Paul Driscoll and John K. Howat, opened at the Worcester Art Museum, and later was seen at the Los Angeles County Museum of Art and the Metropolitan Museum of Art. Of particular interest was the obvious development in Kensett's style, from one derived from Cole and Durand to one which incorporated the elements of luminism. His affinity for Claude's warm light and Cuyp's smooth surface is readily apparent. In the five paintings of the Shrewsbury River (1856-1860), the subject is light and atmosphere and the mood is calm and evocative. His seven paintings of the Beacon Rock at the entrance to Newport Harbor (1855-1870) possess an abstract quality typical of his vision of American scenery. These lyrical seascapes from Newport are imbued with a haunting stillness created by a subtle balance between space and atmosphere, and enhanced by a stunning use of silvery blues and rich browns. In his glorious *Lake George* (1869), Kensett reached the culmination of his exploration of color, light, design, and mood with subtle modulations of greys and greens rather than the use of a variety of colors. In Kensett's *Last Summer's Work*, a collection of paintings from Contentment Island, Darien, Connecticut, Lake George and Newport, the symbolic

simplicity was enhanced, a wider range of colors was used, and scumbling gives his work a more painterly quality. The abstract quality is quite pronounced and forms a link with the works of Mark Rothko and Milton Avery.

William Rutherford Mean, an 1867 graduate of Amherst College and later a partner of the architectural firm of McKim, Mead and White, was a collector of Kensett's works and the works of his contemporaries. His collection in the Mead Art Museum at Amherst was on view in New York City at the IBM Gallery of Science and Art in 1985.

Kensett's generosity was reciprocated by his fellow members of the Century Association, who commissioned him to paint a scene of his choice for $5,000. The result was *Mount Chocorna* (1865). At his death in 1872, more than 600 of his works found in his studio were auctioned for the then staggering sum of $136,000, some going for as high as $1,600.

Barbara Novak chose Fitz Hugh Lane's *Owl's Head, Penobscot Bay, Maine* (1862) for the cover of her *American Painting of the Nineteenth Century* (1969), and devoted whole chapters to him and Martin Johnson Heade, with hardly a paragraph, let alone a chapter, on Church--a curious lapse of judgment. In her more recent book, *Nature and Culture* (1980), which examines the iconography of American painting and demonstrates the link between art and culture, Novak's judgments are both more sound and more original. Unfortunately, it is written in that willfully obscure, teutonic style which emanates from the Institute of Fine Arts of New York University.

Lane was the first to evolve the style which encompassed the formal characteristics of luminism, and among the first to use the higher intensity cadmium paints and orange colors which became available in the 1840s. Born in Gloucester, Massachusetts, Lane eventually devoted his full attention to marine painting and returned to Gloucester, making annual visits to Maine. Though Lane enjoyed a good local reputation and regular patronage, his work never reached the attention of the major collectors and critics of his time. He was quickly forgotten after his death, and interest in him revived only in the 1940s. The traits which make his paintings distinctive are the limited color range, the barely noticeable brush work, and the horizontal organization into banks of sky, water and land. His special concern was the nuances which lend character to a scene: a faint change of tint in a clear sky rather than stormy seas under turbulent clouds, subtleties enhanced by simplified compositions characteristic of seventeenth century Dutch painting.

Just as Huntington was responsible for reviving interest in Church and for preserving Olana, so Professor Alfred M. Brooks, President of the Cape Ann Historical Association in Gloucester, Massachusetts from 1939-1951, and John Wilmerding, author of *Fitz Hugh Lane 1804-1865: American Marine Painter* (1964), were responsible for reviving interest in Lane and for gathering 31 of his paintings and 106 of his drawings in the Cape Ann Scientific, Literary, and Historical Association in Gloucester.

In 1833, Martin Johnson Heade (1819-1904), a close friend of Church's, married and moved to St. Augustine, Florida, and disappeared from the public's consciousness until *Thunderstorm Over Naragansett* (1868) appeared in the exhibition *Romantic Painting in America* (1943) at the Museum of Modern Art. It caused a sensation which led Robert MacIntyre, head of Macbeth Gallery (the oldest dealership in New York City to specialize in American art), to write the first Heade biography. At the same time, Martha and Maxim Karolik began collecting Heade's works.

Heade, the son of a prosperous farmer, was born in a small village north of Philadelphia. After several trips to Europe, Heade settled in New York City in 1859, where he earned a modest reputation. His specialty became stormy marsh scenes with haystacks from Newbury, Massachusetts, Rhode Island, and New Jersey. These scenes have been compared to Monet's haystack paintings of the early 1890s.

After the Karoliks "re-discovered" Heade, they bought about fifty paintings from every phase of his career: early portraits, marsh scenes, seascapes, exotic South American landscapes, and, later, sensual still lifes, most of which are now in the Museum of Fine Arts.

Landmarks in Heade's growing reputation were the exhibition of works by him and David G. Blythe at the Harry Show Newman Gallery in New York (1947) and the *Commemorative Exhibition* of Heade and Lane from the Karolik Collection at M. Knoedler and Company Gallery in 1954. On the occasion of his 150th anniversary (1969), Heade was given a one-man show at the Museum of Fine Arts, the University of Maryland Art Department, and the Whitney Museum of American Art, with a catalogue by Stebbins, then an Associate Curator at Yale University. When gathering material for the catalogue, Stebbins found that the famous *Harbor at Rio de Janeiro* in the City Art Museum of St. Louis was a copy of a colored wood engraving published in *Frank Leslie's Popular Monthly* in April 1876, and that the original painting lay hidden in the Lippit Mansion in Providence, Rhode Island, where Governor Henry Lippitt had tucked it away with three other Heades he bought from the artist in 1866. The most recent Heade exhibition (1981) in the Cummer Gallery of Art in Jacksonville, Florida, emphasized his exotic flower paintings.

Stebbin's superb *The Life and Works of Martin Johnson Heade* (1975) is one of the few monographs on American painters which compares favorably with those exemplary studies by Jules D. Proun, *John Singleton*, 1966 and E. Maurice Block, *George Caleb Bingham, The Evolution of an Artist, a Catalogue Raisonne*, 1967. In the preface Stebbins wrote: "I was first introduced to the work of Martin Johnson Heade in the spring of 1965 when Stuart Cary Welch of the Fogg Art Museum told me he had found two impressive landscapes by an American painter at the Vose Galleries in Boston, and asked whether I would like to go and see them. We went together and found that the pictures were by Heade, who was unknown to both of us; he bought one and I the other. Cary Welch then returned to his own scholarly field, and I have been studying Heade ever since."

Luminism disintegrated after the Civil War. Winslow Homer tried a limited form of impressionism which culminated in his majestic seascapes; Jasper F. Cropsey and his followers began to experiment with freer handling of paint and aimed at catching the brilliance of sunlight as it obliterates detail and forces an impression rather than a description on the eye. And yet a third group, which included William Morris Hunt, Ralph A. Blakelock, and George Inness, followed the French influence of the Barbizon school.

Collections and Exhibitions

The signal event in the resurrection of nineteenth century American art was the unveiling of the Karolik collection. In collaboration with William G. Constable, the Curator of Paintings at the Museum of Fine Arts and author of *Art Collecting in the USA*, the Karoliks assembled a collection of 233 paintings for about $250,000 from 1945 to 1951. The earliest dated painting in the collection is Washington Allston's *Landscape with a Lake* (1804), and the latest is Whittredge's *Old Homestead by the Sea* (1883). In the 1950s and 1960s, numerous traveling exhibitions of the Karolik collection were seen throughout the country. Bauer, then Curator of American Painting at the Brooklyn Museum, now Director Emeritus of the Whitney Museum of American Art, wrote a magisterial introduction, *Trends in American Painting: 1815-1865*, to the catalogue. The magnificence of the catalogue matched the collection itself, and first drew attention to the characteristics of the style he later named in his widely quoted paper in Perspective USA, *American Luminism: A Neglected Aspect of the Realist Movement in Nineteenth Century American Painting* (1954).

Maxim Karolik's special attribute was his "eye," the ability to recognize quality in paintings from what he called the "barren period." Only dealers Victor Spark and Robert McIntyre in New York and Charles Childs and the Vose family in Boston, and curators John Baur at the Brooklyn Museum, James Soby and Dorothy Miller at the Museum of Modern Art, and William

Constable at the Museum of Fine Arts, shared his enthusiasm for paintings from this period. Containing works by painters underrated or misjudged in their time, the Karolik collection is not a representative survey of nineteenth century American paintings. The Karoliks, for example, had a particular interest in Lane and Heade, who, though now considered the mandarins of luminism, were not even mentioned in textbooks on American art for a long period, from S. F. W. Benjamin's *Art in America* (1880) to Richardson's *American Romantic Painting* (1944).

In spite of the importance of the Karolik collection, it was, until recently, poorly hung and incompletely represented in the public galleries. This was rectified by former Director Jan Fontein's five year plan, which began with the opening of I. M. Pei's 1981 pristine, suavely sophisticated addition, and continued with *The Great Boston Collections: Paintings from the Museum of Fine Arts* (1985) and the reinstallation of the permanent collection in the refurbished rooms of Guy Lowell's 1909 elegant Beaux Arts building.

Owing to the influence of such early trustees as Church himself, Eastman Johnson, and Kensett, the Metropolitan Museum has had an exceptionally fine collection of nineteenth century American paintings since its founding in 1870. In 1924, the first American wing of the Metropolitan Museum was opened. This had a major impact on the spread of interest in American art of the Colonial and Federal periods. It was a particular pleasure, therefore, to see the Metropolitan's collection cleaned, restored, and expertly hung by Howat in its resplendent new quarters in 1980. In the John Whitney Payson Galleries on the second floor, we can now see the surprisingly high-keyed paintings of the early Hudson River School painters--Cole, Durand, and Doughty--in Gallery 220, and the commanding collection of the later painters--Church, Kensett, Heade, Lane, Gifford, Inness, Bierstadt, Wynant, and Whittredge--in Gallery 221. With the opening appeared Boreen Bolger Burke's long anticipated catalogue, *American Paintings in the Metropolitan Museum of*

Art, which replaces the late Albert Ten Eyck Gardner's much quoted, but outdated, *A Concise Catalogue of the Collection of the Metropolitan Museum of Art* (1965).

The New York Historical Society on Central Park West and 77th Street was founded in 1804. This museum is "the best-kept secret in New York City," according to Director James B. Bell. Few people go there and many have never even heard of it. Among its many wonderful collections, the paintings of the Hudson River School, beautifully displayed on the fourth floor, rank among the society's best; its holdings of Durands are the largest and most representative. Included are several of Durand's presidential portraits, *James Madison* (1833), *John Quincy Adams* (1834), and *Andrew Jackson* (1835), which represent part of a commission from Reed to paint all seven presidents. Also featured are Durand's wonderful *Self Portrait* (1835) and about 20 landscapes, among them several of his famous studies of trees painted in the 1840s.

Reed donated his collection of paintings, including some Coles, Durands, and William Sidney Mounts, to the Society in 1858. "The first American collector and connoisseur," Thomas Jefferson Bryan gave his impressive collection to the Society ten years later, and this was followed by Louis Durr's bequest in 1882. The Society received its most important collection in 1944, however, when the New York Public Library placed the Robert L. Stuart collection of nineteenth century European and American paintings on permanent loan. These collections are interesting not only because of the fine examples of nineteenth century American landscape paintings, but because they illustrate the taste of early American collectors before Joseph Duveen told them what to buy and how much to pay. They also make an interesting comparison with the modern collections of the Karoliks, Rockefellers, and Ganzes. The Society's magnificent collection of nineteenth century American landscape paintings, genre art and drawings was exhibited in 1983 along with a three volume catalogue produced by Curator Richard Koke over a ten year period at a cost of over $300.

Across Central Park from the New York Historical Society, on Fifth Avenue and 91st Street, the Cooper-Hewitt Museum has a collection of nineteenth century American drawings and water colors remarkable for its size, quality, and depth. In 1982, Elaine Evans Dee, the Curator of Drawings and Prints, put on an exhibition entitled *Nineteenth Century American Landscape Drawings*. This exhibition exposed the essence of nineteenth century American art and dispelled any doubt about the distinction and charm of Hudson River School paintings and about the genius and pre-eminence of Church, points which are particularly well defined and illustrated in Stebbin's *American Master Drawings and Watercolors* (1976). These works of art, together with Stebbin's book, serve to remind us of what human beings can accomplish in their better moments. A drawing is a pithy comment, a spontaneous response, a first thought in contrast to the fully deliberated, carefully phrased and balanced statement made by the artist in a painting. In a drawing we look for the essential light, whereas in a painting we look for the characteristic light. In both we look for a focal point around which the action revolves, for resonance and mystery.

The National Academy of Design, just south of the Cooper-Hewitt Museum on 5th Avenue and 89th Street, was founded in 1835 for the purpose of instruction and exhibition, with Samuel F. B. Morse as its first President. Until recently he was perhaps more generally known for his code, but in 1982, Daniel J. Terra, founder of the Terra Museum of American Art in Evanston, Illinois, bought his painting, *The Gallery of the Louvre* (1832), for 3.25 million dollars from the University of Syracuse in New York, the highest price paid for an American painting (a distinction of modest consequence) since Church's *Icebergs* in 1979.

The National Academy of Design is an honorary society which imposes one obligation on its members. At the time of election, an associate must present the Academy with a self portrait or a portrait painted by a colleague; when the associate becomes an academician, he or she must present an example of his work. The academy also has a large collection which is virtually unknown to the public. In the 1980s Barbara Novak, Professor of Art History at Columbia University and Barnard College, together with her graduate students, organized *Next to Nature*, accompanied by a fine catalogue, to draw attention to this fine collection.

The Brooklyn Museum is the seventh largest art museum in the country and one of the most neglected in proportion to what it has to offer. As Michael Botwinick, the former Director, put it: "The Brooklyn Bridge is the longest in the world." The board made an early commitment to assembling an American collection of art; the uniqueness of the collection lies in its holdings of those who were once considered lesser known artists. We owe this collection, on the one hand, to the scholastic range of the first Curator of the Department of Fine Arts, William Henry Goodyear, and to his successors Herbert B. Tshudy and John Bauer. On the other hand, we are indebted to those who donated funds in memory of General and Mrs. John B. Woodward (1902), Charles A. Schieren (1915), and Dick S. Ramsay (1932), which were more or less limited to the purchase of American art. The early commitment of the Museum Board to American art is exemplified by the organization in 1917 of the first serious attempt at a survey of American painting. *Exhibition of Early American Painting* covered the period 1750 to 1850, and an exhibition held later that year to celebrate the opening of the Catskill Aqueduct covered the period 1860 to 1885. The commitment of the Museum Board to the scholarly examination of forgotten American artists whose known works gave promise of quality resulted in a series of one-man retrospectives such as *Eastman Johnson* (1940), *William Sidney Mount* (1942), and *Theodore Robinson* (1946). The Brooklyn Museum was also the first to acquire paintings by such luminists as Lane and Heade during the 1930s and 1940s, generally for less than $5,000 apiece.

In 1967, the Brooklyn Museum acquired Cole's *Pic-Nic* for the then staggering price of $100,000. It had been painted on commission for $1,000 in 1846. Noble wrote of it, "*Pic-Nic*--a sylvan scene, all American, wide, bright, polished waters, manifold woods, over all the sweet glad light and quiet air, and everywhere the sense of beauty with wildness." It includes a self portrait and a portrait of his wife, Maria.

The Corcoran Gallery of Art, founded the same year as the Metropolitan Museum of Art and the Museum of Fine Arts for "the encouragement of American Genius," is now directed by Michael Botwinick and has a pleasing and instructive survey of the Hudson River School in recently refurbished rooms. Church's *Niagara Falls* is the best known painting in the collection. The water pouring over the escarpment, the rising mist, and the sheltering sky are brought into focus by the rainbow. When John Ruskin, the English critic, first saw the painting in London, he assumed that the rainbow was a prismatic effect of the gallery's beveled window glass. Now that the picture has been cleaned and restored, we can again catch that evanescent quality of the rainbow perceived by Ruskin. Bierstadt's *Mount Corcoran* is a portrait of a peak in the Sierra Nevadas named by him for the founder of the gallery. As the catalogue rather melodramatically points out, "It is all at the Corcoran. If you are an American, you have to go there to begin to understand yourself. But whatever you are, the Corcoran's collection is the best readily available summary of a new country, a new mind, a new vision."

By contrast, the distinguished American collection in the National Gallery of Art is relatively new. In the 1960s, William P. Campbell, Curator of American Painting, acquired Cole's *The Notch of the White Mountains (Crawford Notch)* (1839), Church's *Morning in the Tropics* (1877), and Cropsey's *Autumn On The Hudson River* (1860). In the 1970s, his successor, John Wilmerding, acquired Cole's *The Voyage of Life*, Cropsey's *The Spirit of War* (1851), Kensett's *Beach at Newport* (1850/1860), Durand's *Forest in the Morning Light* (1855) and *A Pastoral Scene* (1858), and Casilear's *View of Lake George* (1857). Wilmerding, a former Leon E. Williams Professor of Art at Dartmouth College, is the great-grandson of Harvey Osborn Haver-meyer, the sugar baron and one of the Met-ropolitan Museum of Art's greatest benefac-tors.

The Wadsworth Atheneum, America's first public community art museum, opened in 1844. Daniel Wadsworth bequeathed his collection to the gallery after his death in 1848. One of Cole's early patrons, he intro-duced the young Church to Cole. Wads-worth's first acquisition was Cole's *Land-scape, Composition, St. John in the Wilder-ness* (1827), illustrating the divine presence in the unspoiled wilderness. Next he bought *Scene from The Last of the Mohi-cans, Cora Kneeling at the Feet of Tane-mund* (1827) a replica of which is in the New York Historical Association, Coopers-town, New York, and two of Cole's most picturesque views of the White Mountains, *View of Lake Winnepiewoqee* (1828) and *View in the White Mountains* (1828). Cole painted Wadsworth's neo-gothic country house in Farmington, Connecticut, *View from the Mountain Monte Video, The Seat of Daniel Wadsworth, Esq.* (1828), and his last acquisition was the huge *Mount Etna from Taormina* (1843) for $400. These paintings were on view in 1981 at the Wadsworth Atheneum in an exhibition enti-tled *Daniel Wadsworth, Patron of the Arts* with a superb catalogue by Richard Saunders, Curator of American Paintings.

In 1846, the Wadsworth Atheneum acquired Church's *Hooker and Company Journeying Through the Wildness from Plymouth to Hartford in 1636* for $130. It is an especially interesting painting in that it shows the strong influence of Cole's atti-tude to the relationship between human drama and nature in Church's first full-scale landscape painting.

Interest in Cole, Church, and other members of the Hudson River School con-tinued at the Atheneum during the years 1880-1960, when the school was ignored by most critics, collectors, and curators. The collection was expanded, notably through bequests of Mrs. Elizabeth Hart Jarvis Cole in the 1870s, including Church's *Vale of St. Thomas, Jamaica* (1867), and Mrs. Fred-erick Saltonstall Gould in 1948, including

Mountains of Ecuador (1855). Two oth-er fine Churches and funds were left by Frank C. Sumner in 1927. The collection now offers twelve Coles, eleven Churches, and excellent examples of Casilear, Heade, Kensett, Blakelock, Inness, Wyant, and Homer Martin. Unfortunately, they are poorly hung and seldom are all on view. Neither catalogue nor slides are available.

Mr. and Mrs. John D. Rockefeller III own a magnificent collection of American paintings which will be bequeathed to the Fine Art Museums of San Francisco. The Rockefellers became concerned about enter-taining their foreign guests and friends in a home decorated only with oriental and French art, so they bought Church's *Twi-light* (c. 1856) and Lane's *Ships and An Ap-proaching Storm Off Owl's Head, Maine* (1860). With the help of Edgard P. Richardson, they later acquired a little gem of a sketch by Church, *Snow Scene, Olana* (1871), which recreates in the simplest way a vast sweep of air, sun, and frost, "a stroke of nature," and splendid examples of paint-ings by Johnson, Heade, Bingham, and Bierstadt.

An American Perspective: Nineteenth Century Art, the collection of Jo Ann and Julian Ganz, Jr. (1982) with a catalogue by John Wilmerding, Linda Ayers, and Early A. Powell, was seen at the National Gallery of Art, Amon Carter Museum, Fort Worth, Texas, and Los Angeles County Museum, where it will probably eventually be housed. Wilmerding noted that this is the finest pri-vate collection of nineteenth century Ameri-can art. This is reassuring, as the best paintings must now be in museums. It is a remarkable, though undistinguished, collec-tion assembled since 1964--half of it since 1976. It does contain eight good Giffords, including one of his favorite views, *The Art-ist Sketching at Mount Desert, Maine* (1865), which contains a wonderful conceit: the scene on the open cover of the paintbox is also the view shown in the painting. Gif-ford is a luminist painter of particular in-terest because of his use of the new cadmium colors to the point of fascinating exaggeration.

New Britain Museum of American Art has one of the largest, finest, and most representative collections of American paintings outside a few major city museums, and Church's *Haying Near New Haven* (1849) is one of the finest pictures in that museum. There are modest collections with single superb examples of paintings from the Hudson River School in the Albany Institute of History and Art, the Munson-Williams-Proctor Institute, the New York Historical Association, Worcester Art Museum, Massachusetts, the Yale University Art Gallery, New Haven, Connecticut, and in, of all places, the Canajoharie Library and Art Gallery in Canajoharie, New York, the smallest village in the United States to own an independent art gallery which "is worthy to take its place among the outstanding institutions of the nation." Bartlett Arkell, President of the Beechnut Packing Company, presented his collection to the Gallery in 1927.

The first and one of the most famous modern exhibitions of Hudson River School painters opened at the Art Institute of Chicago and the Whitney Museum of American Art in 1945. Frederick A. Sweet produced the excellent and subsequently much quoted catalogue. At the New York World's Fair in 1964, *Art in New York State* was on view in the State Pavilion, and in 1968, Agnes Haley Jones, Assistant in Art Research at the New York State Historical Association, organized a superb exhibition at the Fine Arts Center of the State University College of New York at Geneseo. This was followed by the centennial exhibition, *Nineteenth Century American: Paintings and Sculpture*, at the Metropolitan Museum of Art in 1970 by John Howat, John Wilmerdings, and Natalie Spassky. A symposium entitled *The Shaping of Art and Architecture in Nineteenth Century America*--one of the first on the subject--was held in association with the exhibition, the proceedings of which were edited by Howat (1972).

Then, in 1973, the R.W. Norton Art Gallery, Shreveport, Louisiana, held an exhibition, *The Hudson River School: American Landscape Paintings from 1821 to 1907*, followed by a plethora of bicentennial exhibitions in 1976, the most splendid of which

was *The Natural Paradise: Painting in America* 1800-1950 at the Museum of Modern Art, accompanied by a spectacular catalogue containing essays by Barbara Novak, Robert Rosenblum, and John Wilmerding. Another noteworthy commemorative exhibition was *The Hudson River School: Nineteenth Century American Landscapes* in the Wadsworth Atheneum with a scholarly introduction by Stebbins. In many of the bicentennial exhibitions, however, critical discrimination was supplanted by a carnival atmosphere fueled by unbridled chauvinistic piety.

An unusual and valuable exhibition with a catalogue edited by Donald D. Keys, *The White Mountains--Place and Perceptions*, was held at the University Art Galleries, Durham, New Hampshire, the New York Historical Society, and Dartmouth College Museum and Galleries, Hanover, New Hampshire in 1980 and 1981. A charming and instructive exhibition, *William Cullen Bryant and The Hudson River School of Landscape Painting* (1981), was held at the Nassau County Museum of Fine Arts in Roslyn, New York, with an excellent catalogue by Holly Joan Pinto. Bryant was buried in Roslyn Cemetery, which abuts the Nassau County Museum of Fine Arts. The exhibition drew attention to Bryant's role as promoter and patron of the Hudson River School painters and to his close friendship with Cole and Durand.

Bryant supported Cole and other young artists in the foundation of the National Academy of Design and was a member of the Bread and Cheese Club, a meeting place for writers and artists as well as scientists, lawyers, physicians, and merchants. The Club evolved into the Sketch Club, which lasted from about 1827 to 1869, and then became the Century Association. On Bryant's seventieth birthday, many of the Hudson River School painters--Bierstadt, Church, Cropsey, Durand, Gifford, and Kensett among others--gave him one of their works as an expression of their respect and gratitude for having espoused their cause for over fifty years. These so-called *Birthday Pictures* were bequeathed to the Century Association after Bryant's death.

For the 1982-1983 season, the six upstate New York museums--Herbert F. Johnson Museum of Art, Cornell University, Ithaca; Munson-Williams-Proctor Institute, Utica; Memorial Art Gallery of the University of Rochester; Albany Institute of History and Art; Everson Museum of Art, Syracuse; and Albright-Knox Art Gallery, Buffalo, collaborated to produce *Golden Day Silver Night Perceptions of Nature in American Art 1850-1920*. The exhibition was organized by Gwendolyn Owens, Associate Curator of the Herbert F. Johnson Museum of Art, who, together with John Peters-Campbell, produced an excellent and inexpensive catalogue. The inspiration for the title of the exhibition came from William Butler Yeats' poem *The Song of the Wandering Aergus*, which ends with the lines:

"The silver apples of the moon,
The golden apples of the sun."

The size of the exhibition--56 works-- gave it a sense of intimacy; it was human in scale and perfused with charm, qualities reflected particularly in Alfred Bricker's *Lake George*, Church's *Sunset*, Durand's *Genessee Valley*, Gifford's *Sunset of New York Bay*, and Kensett's *Coast Scene*.

The first exhibition devoted to luminists was held at the Fogg Art Museum in 1966. It was a modest undertaking, but in the catalogue *Luminous Landscape: The American Study of Light, 1850-1875*, Stebbins made a valuable assessment of Church's contributions to the movement. By contrast, the second and most recent exhibition of luminists, in 1980, was a spectacular event at the National Gallery of Art, *American Light: The Luminist Movement, 1850-1875*. Each of the chief luminists--Church, Gifford, Heade, Kensett, and Lane--was given his own room, but Church took the place of honor both in the exhibition and in the catalogue. Interestingly enough, however, the editor, Wilmerding, now the Deputy Director of the National Gallery, chose Lane's *Ships and Approaching Storm off Owl's Head, Maine* for the cover and his *Lumber Schooners at Evening on Penobscot Bay* (1860) for the frontispiece. An indispensable reference work, it is one of the most

readable of scholarly works on American Nineteenth century painting, luminism, and Church, with essays by leading scholars Novak, Stebbins, and Huntington.

Exhibition catalogues have added enormously to the material available about American art. Government and private sources--the Ford Foundation in particular-- have sponsored the publication of these magnificent and scholarly productions. They have become the place to go for the latest research, representing the most intelligent summation and the best choice of works under review. *A New World: Masterpieces of American Painting (1760-1910)*, for example, is bound to remain a standard reference work for years to come.

Olana

It is neither the size of the exhibitions, nor the magnificence of the catalogues, nor yet the current prices of the Hudson River School paintings, which truly signifies the resurrection of this uniquely American style. (As Jasper Johns said: "One million dollars has a rather neat sound, but it has nothing to do with painting.") It is rather that, since 1980, long lines await admission for the forty-five minute tour of Olana. Twenty-seven thousand people tour the building each year and many more are turned away. Olana is open Wednesday through Sunday, 9 AM to 5 PM, from Memorial Day to October, with an admission charge of $.50 per person.

After Church completed his apprenticeship with Cole in Catskill, he returned briefly to Hartford before moving to New York City. During the 1850s, he traveled widely in the arctic and tropics, and exhibited regularly at the National Academy Exhibitions. In 1860, he took his wife, Isabel, to Mount Marino, which later became Olana, and built Cozy Cottage. In 1867, the Churches went to Europe with Kensett and Bierstadt for the Paris Universal Exposition and then on to the Middle East whence they brought back ideas for their dream house Olana, which is a variation of the Arabic "Al'ana," meaning "our place on high."

The first design for Olana, *A Country Villa for F.E. Church, Esq.*, was signed by Richard Morris Hunt (William's brother), architect of the Metropolitan Museum of Art. After Church's return from the Middle East and their conversion to the "Persian" style, however, the Churches employed Calvert Vaux, architect (with Frederick Law Olmstead) of Central Park in New York City. Church's theme in landscaping his three hundred acre estate was to develop a series of vistas--paintings carved out of nature--of the rolling countryside, the Hudson River, and the Catskill Mountains.

Olana is a five story, thirty-seven room mansion built between 1870 and 1874. The architecture is a mixture of Middle Eastern, Latin and North American, and Mexican design. The house is a fantasy of colors and embellishments--arched Persian style windows outlined with red, yellow and black brick in mosaic patterns, tiles from Iran, Mexico and the United States, and fancy stenciled cornices. Its square towers are crowned with soaring, multicolor slate roofs, and the main entrance on the east facade is framed in glazed tiles.

The central court hall stretches across the entire house, with a brass-railed grand staircase ascending at the back. The formal parlor has tall windows to the east and south; beyond it is the *ombra* which provides a comfortable sitting area with a magnificent view of the twelve acre lake. The room is furnished with European tables and chairs, mother-of-pearl inlaid taborets from Egypt and Morocco, and a fireplace framed with East Indian carvings. Some of the furniture was made in America, the rugs are Persian, and there are Colombian artifacts, Mexican pottery, Waterford crystal and Canton china. Mrs. Church's cousin, Lockwood de Forest, designed some of the mantelpieces, mouldings, and furniture. From the studio, and, even better, from the tower, we get a splendid view of the Hudson River, the town of Catskill, and the Catskill Mountains.

Church lived here with Isabel, his four children, and fifteen servants. Cole's son, Theodore, was his manager. Church also had a house on Park Avenue in New York City and camps in Maine and North Carolina. Not only did the Churches live comfortably, they also lived well. *Olana Custom and Receipts* is an engaging book of selected menus, recipes, and guide to affairs of the table selected from material found at Olana. In 1977, Richard Slavin, then Associate Curator, New York State Historical Association, put on an exhibition, *The Hidden Treasures of Olana*, in the Columbia-Greene Community College. Slavin wrote an interesting but brief catalogue. A reasonable description of Olana is Peter Gross's *An Investigation of Olana: The Home of Frederic Edwin Church, Painter,* a Ph.D. dissertation from Ohio University (1973), which is both difficult to find and to read. For more general reading, two beautifully illustrated articles, which appeared in the English publication *Country Life*, in September 1983, are best. Reprints are available at Olana.

By 1883, Church was so severely crippled by rheumatoid arthritis that he had to escape from the upstate winters. From then until he died, he wintered in Mexico. He died in New York City on April 7, 1900, in the home of his friend and patron, William Osborn, on his way home to Olana. Born into a wealthy family, he died a rich man.

In nature, as in art, grace and exhilaration remain thankfully unexplained, for if explained, they might seem trivial and lacking in wonder. A knowledge of aesthetic theory and iconographic research may be important; it is obviously impossible to comment sensibly about Hudson River School paintings without knowing something about the ideas which shaped their creation. But to ask what a painting "means" in every case is no more appropriate than to ask the same question of a piece of music or a three-course meal. In the last analysis, it is artistic quality rather than content which counts, even though knowledge of the latter adds to the appreciation of the former. In Horace Walpole's words: "Knowledge of pictures is only to be learnt from pictures themselves. The volumes wrote on this art only serve to perplex it. No science has so much jargon introduced into it as painting . . . ." So it is seeing the paintings that is important: the Coles and Churches in the neogothic Wadsworth Atheneum, the Durands in the scholarly environment of the New York Historical Society, the Heades in the elegant Museum of Fine Arts, the Lanes in the intimacy of the Cape Ann Scientific, Literary and Historical Association, and the comprehensive collections of the Hudson River School paintings in the splendor of the Metropolitan and Brooklyn Museums in New York, and the National and Corcoran Galleries in Washington. The point is that we look at a picture with our eyes, but see it with our experience of life, our likes and dislikes, our habits and feelings, our associations, indeed with our whole personality. And the richer our personality, the richer the vision.

And what thousands of visitors find so enthralling at Olana is the natural surroundings of the Hudson River School, the grandeur of the Catskill Mountains, the majesty of the great river, and the mystery of the hemlocks and birches through which the Hudson's tributaries flow--from the room where Church entertained his colleagues and friends, or from the studio where he tried to capture the lead gray morning light and the vermillion evening sky.

Ian Porter, physician and professor of pediatrics, holds positions at the Albany Medical College and Hospital. Dr. Porter was educated in England and has practiced in that country and America. Long a student of art history, Ian Porter developed a keen interest in Dutch painters, English landscape painters, and the Hudson River School. He has a particular interest in Dutch painting and its connections to Albany. Dr. Porter serves on the board of many cultural organizations of Albany, including the Albany Institute of History and Art.

Further Readings

Brown, M. W., *American Art to 1900*. Harry N. Abrams, Inc., New York, 1977.

Flexner, J. T., *History of American Painting, Vol. III. That Wilder Image. The Native School from Thomas Cole to Winslow Homer*. Dover Publications, Inc., New York, 1970.

Howat, J. K., *The Hudson River and its Painters*. The Viking Press, New York, 1976.

Howat, J. K., ed., *The Shaping of Art and Architecture in Nineteenth Century America*, The Metropolitan Museum of Art, New York, 1972.

Huntington, D. C., *The Landscapes of Frederic Edwin Church*, New York, 1966.

Lassiter, B. B., *American Wilderness, The Hudson River School of Painting*. Doubleday and Company, Inc., New York, 1978.

Thomas Cole, Troy c.1830, drawing at Albany Institute of History and Art.

Thomas Cole, <u>Sandy Hill, North River</u>, drawing at Albany Institute of History and Art.

Thomas Cole, <u>Lake Winnipesaukee, New Hampshire</u>, oil on canvas at Albany Institute of History and Art.

Asher Brown Durand, <u>An Old Man's Reminiscences</u>, 1845, oil on canvas at Albany Institute History and Art.

Jasper F. Cropsey, <u>Lake George</u>, 1868, oil on canvas at Albany Institute of History and Art.

Frederic E. Church, <u>Morning, Looking East over the Hudson Valley from the Catskill Mountains</u>, 1848, oil on canvas at Albany Institute of History and Art.

We have seen two great ages in the history of stained glass. The first was during the medieval period. The second was the period from 1870-1920. In the second period, America occupied a position of importance and produced an artist who towered above all others. Indeed, Louis Comfort Tiffany made stained glass windows of unsurpassed beauty. Some of his finest are in Albany and Troy. The Sea of Galilee window in The First Presbyterian Church is exceptional among the 3,000 windows made by the Tiffany studios. In fact, this window was selected to illustrate the frontispiece in the standard reference work on Tiffany windows.

Tiffany belonged to a generation of artists that wished to re-establish the primacy of beauty and that considered crafts an important vehicle for achieving this objective. These artists reacted against the mechanization of life that resulted from the industrial revolution. More specifically, they rejected the accoutrements of daily life, the furniture, rugs, glassware, and pottery that were mass produced by machines. They sought to restore hand-made goods to a position of prominence, and to bring arts and crafts together. Stained glass represented such a unification. And Louis Tiffany became the most famous and the greatest practitioner of this craft, which he elevated to a serious art form.

To do this, he developed new techniques in the manufacture of glass and kept abreast of techniques introduced by other glass makers. His result was a virtuosity of technique that allowed windows of highly varied textures and opacities and infinite shadings and nuances as well as brilliance and vibrancy of color. Tiffany put these techniques to the service of his aesthetic goals, resulting in windows both opulent and mysterious, dazzling and spiritual. Such Tiffany windows can be seen around Albany and Troy.

TIFFANY WINDOWS

Warren Roberts

The Louis Tiffany stained glass windows in the First Presbyterian Church of Albany are of great artistic importance. The William and Sarah Strong Memorial Window, for example, consists of five panels on the lower level, surmounted by three large medallion rose windows, and is one of the finest examples of Tiffany windows anywhere. Note that this is not merely my judgment. Opening to the frontispiece of Alistair Duncan's standard reference work on Tiffany windows, we find a handsome display of the two lower right panels of the ensemble, a glimpse of the dazzling nature scene glowing before us in a way possible only through the medium of stained glass. Perhaps the world's leading expert on Tiffany windows, Duncan singled out this glass as one of the finest examples of Tiffany's art. Indeed, this is Tiffany glass at its grandest. At the rear of the church are three smaller windows, also signed by Tiffany, and the Assembly Room boasts three more, one of which is particularly beautiful.

Tiffany windows number three thousand or better and represent the pinnacle of the second of two great ages of stained glass. The first age dates back to the Middle Ages, from the twelfth through the fifteenth centuries, followed by a long period of stagnation. The second age lasted from 1870 to 1920 and included the career of Louis Tiffany (1848-1933). Tiffany opened his shop in New York in the 1870s, where it remained in operation until the 1920s. Although he employed different techniques from those of the medieval period, it was largely through Tiffany's genius that stained glass was restored to its former greatness.

The second great age of stained glass windows had its beginnings in the pre-Raphaelite circle, consisting of a group of English artists including William Morris, Edward Burne-Jones, and Dante Gabriel Rossetti. These artists were also publicists concerned with the meaning of art. William Morris was the first to take up the cudgels against his adversaries, arguing that design had undergone a long period of degradation and the decorative arts had declined. It was his contention that the machine, which introduced mass-production of furniture and all the decorative arts in the nineteenth century, had deprived those arts of their beauty. Prior to this, the decorative arts had been handmade. With industrialization, however, machines took over; decorative arts were stamped out efficiently and uniformly.

When Morris moved into his own studio in 1857 and set about to furnish it, he found nothing for sale that he wished to have as part of his daily surroundings. That being the case, he decided to make his own furniture. He proceeded to design and make draperies. Ultimately, Morris did much in the way of the decorative arts, giving rise to the arts and crafts movement.

Morris wrote that "as a condition of life, production by machine is altogether an evil." He aimed to dignify the decorative arts, and to remove the barrier between those arts and the fine arts produced by painters and sculptors. He further maintained that "the constructive and decorative arts are the real backbone of any artistic culture." The importance of these words should not be overlooked. Morris stands back from all the arts and looks at them from a particular perspective. Viewing the decorative arts (furniture, pottery, glass, wallpaper, draperies and rugs) alongside painting and sculpture, he contends that the decorative arts are not merely important; they are the backbone of *any* artistic culture.

Morris tried to re-define the position of the artist. In the nineteenth century, the artist was sometimes equated with the genius. The artist first became a godlike or divine figure, a self-styled genius, during the Renaissance. After Michelangelo had completed the sculptures for the Medici Chapel, a fellow Florentine observed that two figures did not at all resemble his models. Michelangelo assured him that while there would be no memory of those living beings a thousand years later, his likenesses would be immortal. He saw himself as a genius and, hence, re-defined the way others perceived the artist. Leonardo, Raphael, and Michelangelo, indeed all of the great figures of Renaissance painting, made a

conscious effort to separate themselves from artisans. The distinction between artists and artisans, so clear in our own minds, had not been fully coalesced until this period. From that time on, the differences between the two became even more pronounced, particularly in the nineteenth century. It was precisely these differences which William Morris wanted to eliminate.

According to Morris, "that talk of inspiration," or Michelangelesque flights of creativity, "is sheer nonsense. There is no such thing. It is a mere matter of craftsmanship." Skill is the essence of art. The French writer, Riviere, wrote, at the same time, "a nice table is just as interesting as a piece of sculpture or a painting." The ideas which grew out of the arts and crafts movement in the 1860s and 1870s took hold. These writers had remarkable success persuading large numbers of the art public of the importance and authenticity of their views. Consider for a moment some of the major artists and artistic movements which came under the influence of these new doctrines. Gauguin, for instance, a leading painter of the Impressionist and post-Impressionist movements, made pottery. Picasso produced an enormous amount of pottery. This was no accident; he also made textiles. He worked not only as a painter, but in the decorative arts. Frank Lloyd Wright did all decoration himself, including the ornamentation in many of his homes. Louis Sullivan did the same and, among the next generation of architects, Mies Van der Rohe and Walter Gropius followed suit. New artistic movements, such as the Secessionist movement in Austria, helped kick open the doors of Modern Art. Leading artists in this movement, Gustav Klimt and Oskar Kokoschka, moved back and forth between the fine and artisan arts, the latter having a considerable effect on the former.

The arts and crafts movement played an important role in the Modernist breakthrough, which, in turn, had a very large impact on America. In my own judgment, no country played a more important role in furthering the decorative arts in the period 1870-1920 than did America. Out of our arts and crafts movement came art, glass, and pottery of striking beauty. Many potteries from the 1870s made daily utensils which recreated the eye and made the interiors of homes pleasant and agreeable. Among American art potteries was the Rookwood firm, founded in the 1870s along with the Tiffany studio. This and other pottery firms, such as Weller, Gruby, and Van Briggle, acted as catalysts, contributing to the fertilization of the decorative arts in America. Glass makers, of course, made a similar contribution, helping to elevate life by creating everyday objects which adorned household interiors.

This movement acted as one of the leavening forces leading to the second great age of stained glass. The significance of stained glass was appreciated by the aforementioned group of artists and writers, the pre-Raphaelites. It was none other than William Morris who first began to design stained glass windows. Edward Burne-Jones later did the same. One can see the stained glass windows of these artists and their pupils just a short distance away at St. Peter's Episcopal Church on State Street in Albany. They very much warrant a special visit. Comparing them with these and other Tiffany windows in Albany and Troy, one can trace the development of the art form.

Although Louis Tiffany was a member of the great Tiffany family, he chose to develop his talent as an artist rather than enter the family jewelry firm on Fifth Avenue. He went to Paris, where he was trained as a painter. Upon returning to America, he built a house in New York, for which, not surprisingly in light of his awareness of the arts and crafts movement, he decided to make his own stained glass windows. He was so enchanted with the results that he began to make windows commercially. Out of this came his studio, the center of the most important part of his artistic life. He built up a shop which, in time, employed perhaps as many as 100 artists. It was a large establishment attracting the very best talent. While Tiffany designed many of his own windows, he hired designers to assist him in the production of these art objects. Some of the artists employed by Tiffany worked for other studios, among them the Lamb Studio, which made the windows on

the far wall of this church [First Presbyterian]. Nevertheless, all of the 3,000 or so windows which came from the Tiffany studio had to be approved by Tiffany himself; most bear his signature.

With his studio well established and the commissions rolling in, Tiffany used vast quantities of glass. Initially he bought glass from other makers, but, by the 1890s, he made all his own glass. Ultimately, Tiffany produced a surplus of glass which he then used in an ancillary studio, where he manufactured the art glass and lamps for which, much to his chagrin, he is now best known. Four years ago, his lamps fetched as much as $250,000 on the market, and undoubtedly sell for more today. New York's Lillian Nassau Tiffany Shop carries a variety of Tiffany's wonders in glass, as well as brilliant examples of the arts and crafts movement by other makers, both American and European.

As sensational as Tiffany's art glass and lamps were, it was his stained glass windows which he valued most. Toward the end of his career, when interest in stained glass as an art form had waned, Tiffany's lamp shop subsidized his main shop, where he continued to make stained glass windows. Besides being an artist of major status and a genius at the medium in which he had chosen to specialize, Tiffany was an astute businessman. An important factor contributing to his success was the construction of churches in America, on a scale dizzying by today's standards. If you will recall, it was in the year 1870 that Tiffany made his first stained glass window. That year saw the construction of some 4,000 churches in America. Church construction continued at that rate over the next several decades, providing a good source of potential commissions for Tiffany. Competition, however, was stiff. Tiffany was forced to compete with numerous manufacturers of stained glass windows and did so with stunning success.

Tiffany was a patrician to the manor born. As one might well imagine, this by no means hurt him when he met with ministers, elders, and deacons of affluent churches. Not only did he have a fabulous reputation; he had a personal charm which he turned on at will. Thus he secured commission after commission, encouraging a healthy competition between churches for Tiffany windows. As one church installed Tiffany windows, members of another would initiate recruiting drives and solicit large sums of money to commission even grander windows. In many cases, Tiffany managed to persuade church officials to install new windows to replace old, outdated windows. One cannot help but wonder about the conditions under which the windows of a church were made. Although First Presbyterian was built in the 1880s, the windows date back to the year 1915. The implication is obvious: Tiffany's windows were not the originals here.

Tiffany was not only a highly successful businessman; he was--how might one put it?--a hard-headed business man. When some of his workers decided to go on strike, Tiffany hired women who, ostensibly, filled most of the menial positions in the shop. The advantages here were numerous. Although they were highly skilled, women worked for forty percent less wages than men and were more tractable, (i.e., not a threat to strike for more pay). Wages for skilled artisans in the Tiffany shop ran about $3 a day. It is estimated that a small window cost as much as $700 and the more extravagant windows between $3,500 and $5,000. A multiplier of 25 to 30 would be appropriate to establish contemporary economic equivalents for these expenditures. In short, the windows were tremendously expensive. From a church's point of view, this was a phenomenal investment.

Contemporary critics concur with those of Tiffany's day as to which windows were most artistically successful. In the main, the windows fall into two quite separate categories. First, there are nature scenes, exemplified by the William and Sarah Strong Memorial Window, in which the Sea of Galilee is represented in glass with a star spangled firmament overhead. To the second category belong Biblical scenes depicting angels and Old and New Testament figures, such as those in the three windows at the rear of the First Presbyterian. The critics of Tiffany's day considered his nature scenes

the glory of his art, and the summit of his genius, but sharp criticisms were directed at windows within the other category.

The Biblical scenes depicted in the latter type of window were often paraphrased or copied paintings from the Renaissance or Baroque periods. Frequently one finds Tiffany scenes taken straight from Raphael's paintings. A number of windows in Troy, particularly at St. Joseph's Catholic Church, are derived from Raphael.

Critics claimed it was in the more abstract and naturalistic forms that Tiffany was at his best. The nature scene of the William and Sarah Strong Memorial Window provides a splendid example of Tiffany's style at its finest. In order to fully appreciate Tiffany's achievement, one must know something about the techniques he employed. The glass made in his shop, including some 500 varieties, all carefully catalogued, was the result of years of refined technique. Various pieces of glass were selected and incorporated into a window only after a careful inventory had been taken of all that was available.

The William and Sarah Strong Memorial Window contains the most characteristic form of Tiffany glass, known as mottled glass. Mottled glass was extraordinarily difficult to make, requiring a technique perfected over thirty years: flourine was introduced to molten glass at carefully controlled temperatures, creating the famous mottled effect. One color blends into another--blue and green in this case. Varying opacities and textures inherent in the technique heighten vibrancy, express richness, and create a wide range of coloristic effects.

One of Tiffany's most spectacular types of glass was fractured glass--or confetti glass, as it is sometimes called. Fragments of glass were scattered on a table onto which molten glass was poured. In this way, the fragments were impregnated into the sheet of glass. Tremendous variation of color is characteristic of confetti glass; reds, pinks and blues appear painted on. Obviously, this technique allowed Tiffany to portray scenes of startling naturalism without painting the glass.

Plating was another extraordinarily difficult technique mastered by Tiffany. Plating occurs when sheets of glass are bounded together to produce different textures. Tiffany sometimes bonded as many as six sheets of glass. In the memorial window there are cracks in the center of a panel. A few years ago, part of the glass was broken when a protective translucent sheet was being installed outside the window. Upon examination, the glass proved to consist of six sheets securely bonded in a prodigy of technique. Plating alters the luminosity of glass: light passing through up to six sheets of glass produces a different effect than light passing through only one sheet. Moreover, plating allows the artist to create a design or designs within the interior sheets, producing various images which appear lost in a nebulous distance, intangible and mysterious. The magic of the window's flowers, for instance, is the result of this plated glass technique. The brilliant reds and the combination of strong primary colors stand out from the darkness.

Another technique characteristic of Tiffany's work is etched glass. Wax was rubbed onto the glass and acids poured over it, and it was possible to control forms which were part of or etched onto the glass. Whenever one sees a Tiffany sky, he is almost invariably looking at etched glass. (In the Galilee scene, in the mountain between the sky and sea, one sees an example of etched glass.) Wax was applied to the glass and the pattern resulted from acid poured over the sheet. In the rear of the Presbyterian church, we find more examples of Tiffany's techniques. Drapery glass was used specifically for angels and Biblical figures. This type of glass has folds simulating clothing, a texture achieved by pouring viscous glass onto a table and rolling and manipulating it with tongs. When it solidified, sheets of drapery glass would be catalogued and stored until used as needed.

Jeweled glass was made by pouring molten glass into molds. Behind the heads of angels in a church window, are pieces of jeweled glass, creating brilliant diadems of blue and red. Some molds were oval, others

had prisms. Light is transmitted brilliantly through the various configurations.

In all these techniques, Tiffany combined craftsmanship with an aesthetic objective which gave rise to a form of high art. These windows are not the work of an artisan, but an artist--perhaps one of America's greatest in any medium. Although America boasts some very fine painters, they hardly rank with such great European painters as Leonardo, Raphael, Rembrandt, Goya, or Van Gogh. In the medium of stained glass, however, Louis Tiffany reigns supreme. Those who made windows in the first great age of stained glass were artisans whose names are unknown to us. By contrast, Tiffany signed his windows; he elevated an art form once considered the domain of the artisan to the level of high art.

In conclusion, I should like to bring to your attention additional churches in Albany and Troy having Tiffany windows. First, the windows of St. Peter's Episcopal Church, on State Street in Albany, are significant both from an artistic and historic point of view. A number of these windows were made by key figures of the arts and crafts movement, which, as we have seen, paved the way for the second great age of stained glass. St. Peter's also has a fine Tiffany rose window. From St. Peter's, it is but a short distance to the First Reformed Church on North Pearl Street, the home of yet another sensational Tiffany window. Actually, the window is not in the church itself, but in a building off a side street on the north side of the church. Unfortunately, the window stands behind a stairway obscuring much of the glass. Nevertheless, it is more visible than any other Tiffany window of its size and quality, as the same stairway which cuts a path through the window and obstructs a full view also makes it possible for the viewer to see the glass at point-blank range. The stairway is just inches from the window, allowing the viewer to analyze the glass with microscopic attention to detail. By doing so, one can appreciate uniquely the virtuosity of Tiffany's technique.

After a visit to St. Peter's, First Presbyterian, and First Reformed in Albany,

I would recommend a drive to Troy. Of the ten buildings in Troy having Tiffany windows, the three most worth viewing are St. Joseph's Roman Catholic Church, St. Paul's Episcopal Church, and St. John's Episcopal Church. St. Joseph's contains more Tiffany glass than I have seen in any other building. In addition to the sanctuary windows, there is a complete set of windows in a semicircular room adjacent to the choir. A separate chapel with mosaics, light fixtures, and windows was also designed by Tiffany. St. Paul's is worth seeing for its wonderful windows, timbered ceiling, and mosaics, all designed by Tiffany. Actually the entire interior of this church was designed by Tiffany, making it a must for all interested in the work of this great American artist. Finally, St. John's and its remarkable window, *St. John's Vision of the Holy City*, has to be seen to be believed. Like the Strong Memorial Window in First Presbyterian Church of Albany, it represents a pinnacle in the work of Louis Tiffany and ranks among the finest stained glass windows anywhere. All of these windows in Albany and Troy contain treasures, indeed.

Warren Roberts is distinguished professor of history at SUNY, Albany. His field of research is cultural history, with a particular focus on the relationship between art and society, on which he has published two books. He has long been interested in the Louis Tiffany windows in Albany and Troy, which he regards as among the finest examples anywhere of the stained glass art form. He received his B.A., M.A., and Ph.D. degrees from University of California, Berkeley.

Further Readings

The standard work is Alistair Duncan, *Tiffany Windows* (New York, 1980). Since this book contains an extensive bibliography, what is listed below is not recommended titles but something more useful, the other local churches that have Tiffany windows.

Albany

St. Peter's Episcopal Church
   The Rose Window

St. Paul's Episcopal Church
   The "Good Shepherd Window" (in an office, not the sanctuary).

First Reformed Church
   Landscape (in a room adjacent to the church, and not to be missed).

Beth Emeth Synagogue
   Several windows, "Moses" and others.

Troy

St. Paul's Episcopal Church
   Many, many windows. Also, the entire interior design is by Tiffany.

First Presbyterian Church
   "Angels and Christ" window.

St. John's Episcopal Church
   The "St. John's Vision" window is one of the best Tiffany windows anywhere.

Earl Memorial Chapel
   Various windows.

St. Joseph's Roman Catholic Church
   One of the fullest sets of Tiffany windows in any church.

Detail of Strong window at First Presbyterian Church, State and Willett Streets.

Much of Albany's rich history can be traced through its cultural heritage. Supported by its economic strength, Albany has fostered awareness and appreciation of the arts since its earliest settlement. The city's prosperity in fur trading, transportation, and finance contributed to its cultural development as certainly as did its Hudson Valley location. Albany's tastes, while rarely high style, represent American middle class tastes.

The Dutch settlers brought an appreciation of comfort and quality. The prosperity of their fur trade enabled them to decorate their homes with quality furnishings, colorful pictures and objects. In the eighteenth century, area artists were commissioned by wealthy merchants and landowners to paint their portraits. While lacking formal training, these anonymous "limners" were talented and clearly aware of European portrait styles. Scripture paintings, copied from engravings in Dutch bibles, were also popular.

With the elegance of the Georgian period came a mastery of painting technique, and portraits remained the most common form of art. Following the colonial wars, landscape painting emerged as a distinctly American style developed from the sense of newly-found freedom and an appreciation of America's beauty. The picturesque landscapes of the Hudson Valley inspired many artists and inspired the Hudson River School of artists.

Folk artists and craftspersons were attracted by the wealth and beauty of the Albany area. As the middle class prospered and grew, the demand for the decorative works of these largely untrained artists increased. Young girls learned needlework and produced popular mourning art; the favorite sport of the day, horse racing, was depicted in paintings; nautical art, especially of that fascinating new invention, the steamboat, was common; and genre and street scenes recorded everyday life in the burgeoning city.

The expressive sculptures of Erastus Dow Palmer (1817-1904) were the distinctively American products of a self-taught artist, one of America's finest. Albany produced many significant artists during the late nineteenth century, including William and James Hart, Homer Dodge Martin, and George Boughton.

The artistic tradition continues in Albany. Numerous galleries, public buildings, and exhibitions display the work of prominent American artists as well as the works of contemporary Albany artists.

ART IN AND ABOUT ALBANY

Roberta Bernstein

This survey of art in and about Albany will link early periods of Albany art with the present by focusing on themes of portraiture and landscape in painting.[1] I intend to demonstrate the existence of a vital contemporary art scene in Albany, where a number of artists are producing work which could be of equal or greater historical importance than that produced in the Albany area during the eighteenth and nineteenth centuries. Although many more artists could have been selected for discussion, this paper is not meant to be comprehensive; rather it is intended to give a sense of the range of art produced in the Capital District.

Albany's museums and galleries provide exposure for local art works from colonial times to the present. The Albany Institute of History and Art has one of the finest collections of early American art, and most of the eighteenth and nineteenth century works referred to are from its collection. The Institute also exhibits works of contemporary Capital District artists in both the Gallery and the Harmanus Bleeker Center.

These two galleries add to the growing number of places where the work of local artists can be viewed by the public.

Another important resource for Albany's art community is the Nelson A. Rockefeller Empire State Plaza Art Collection, consisting of 92 paintings and sculptures selected by an art commission appointed by Governor Rockefeller in 1966. The collection includes works by some of the major artists of the New York School, most of which are representative of the genres of abstract expressionism, color field, and hard-edge abstraction. Since its installation, the plaza collection has provided Albany with an accessible assemblage of contemporary art. While some have cherished this controversial collection, others have bemoaned it. With the recent defacing of paintings in the collection, much discussion has centered around these works and the public's reaction to them.[2] The majority of the works in the plaza collection are signed by artists who established a national reputation in New York City. Three of the artists represented in the collection--David Smith,

George Rickey, and Ellsworth Kelly--have at one time or another lived and worked in the Albany area: Smith in Bolton Landing, Rickey in East Chatham, and Kelly in Chatham. However, because artists of national stature have enjoyed greater representation than local artists, the plaza collection has underscored the perception of Albany as a provincial art center stifled in the shadow of New York City. With the increased visibility and energy of the Albany art scene, though, this collection can be seen more as a historical backdrop for local contemporary art than a reminder of its national invisibility during the 1960s and 1970s.

Portraits produced in the Albany area during the Colonial and Post-Revolutionary periods rank among the finest examples of early American portraiture. By the first half of the eighteenth century, artists were painting portraits of wealthy landowners, and of merchants and their families. To this period belong *Ariaantye Coeymans* (c. 1717), attributed to Nehemiah Partridge, and *Abraham Wendell* (c. 1737), attributed to John Heaton. Until recently most of the artists who painted portraits of this period were unidentified. These limners were largely self-taught, and strongly influenced by European art. Generally quite realistic, the faces in these portraits were done from observation. By contrast, the poses, costumes, and backgrounds were often copied from prints.

These portraits provide a vivid depiction of Albany area settlers. *Ariaantye Coeymans*, daughter of a Dutchman, depicts an exceptional woman for her time. As a 51 year-old landowner, she married a 28 year-old man. In *Elsie Rutger Schuyler* (1723), attributed to Gerardus Duyckinck, the emphasis on the sitter's hands gives us a sense of her personality. Also emphasized is the headdress, typical of portraits of women, which served to frame and accentuate the face. In *Abraham Wendell*, one of seven portraits of members of the Wendell family, the artist has chosen to show the sitter in a very self-confident pose. The background is a local site, the family mill which Abraham inherited upon his fa-

ther's death. Although it was intended to play a secondary role as backdrop for the figure, the background is considered one of the earliest American landscapes.

Albany's most renowned portrait painter was Ezra Ames. Born in Massachusetts, Ames was working in Albany by 1793 and was very successful, both as a portraitist and a banker. Ames initially earned a living doing a variety of crafts, with a home and shop at 41 Pearl Street. Before long he found a market for his portraits. *The Fondey Family* (1803), a formal group portrait, portrays the Fondey parents proudly showing off their children, who range in age from eight to 19. A touching detail in the background is the tombstone of a child who died at age 21 months. This painting demonstrates Ames' ability to capture a sitter's likeness, although at this point he had not yet developed his mature style. A certain stiffness links this work to the earlier limner tradition, but as he developed his own style, the stiffness disappeared. With improved technique, partly the result of copying works by John Singleton Copley and Gilbert Stuart, his figures became genuine and lifelike.

Among Ames' portraits of well-known individuals in the area is *Governor De-Witt Clinton* (1817), taken from his series of *Portraits of Seven Governors of New York*. Clinton, who sat for this portrait soon after he was elected governor in 1817, had previously commissioned several portraits of himself by other artists while running for office, in an attempt to keep his image before the public. This points out an interesting function of portraiture during this time, not only as a document of an individual's appearance and social stature, but as a means of promoting a political candidate's visibility, a function similar to that of television in our own time.

After Ames, a number of talented and successful Albany portraitists made their mark, most notably Charles Loring Elliott (1812-1868).

While most contemporary portraits preserve their function as documents of individual appearance, they reveal a range of concerns not found in the portraits discussed above. Gayle Johnson, who lived in the Albany area for almost ten years, has recently turned to portraiture from still life painting. In 1985, she did a series of untitled self-portraits in pencil and gouache which are not unlike Ames' works in their detailed realism. Done on a small scale, between two and four inches, they are directly linked to the tradition of miniaturist portraits represented by Ames' miniature of his niece, *Mrs. John Hills* (1831). In several of Johnson's miniatures the headdress is an important feature, relating her work to earlier portraits using the same device. Her miniatures, however, reflect an interest in self-scrutiny which is atypical of early American portraiture. She portrays herself in a variety of moods and temperaments, self-consciously adopting a broad range of expressions and using contrasts of light and shadow to enhance sometimes comic, sometimes theatrical effects. In this way, her work is close in spirit to Rembrandt's early self-portraits.

Lori Lawrence has done self-portraits, figurative scenes, and landscapes. She graduated from the State University of New York at Albany's Master of Arts program and has remained in the Albany area for the past ten years. For Lawrence, doing self-portraits involves a process of self-confrontation and self-examination. She distorts and exaggerates her features on a larger-than-life scale to achieve an expressive effect. In *Self Portrait Wait Out the North* (1977), her curls become a headdress, framing her face and adding an element of electrical vitality to the image. In *Good-Bye to Cigarettes* (1981), her expression is serious and somber; the artist has made an important resolution and captures the feeling of her commitment to breaking a deeply ingrained habit. *Face Into the Future* (1983) represents another facet of self-confrontation, as the artist looks past the viewer into the future and, at the same time, within herself.

Another direction in contemporary portraiture is revealed in two portraits entitled *Ray* (both 1985) by June Beneson, a 1985 graduate of the SUNYA's Master of Fine Arts program. All of Beneson's portraits are either self-portraits or portraits of her husband, Ray, and thus involve an intimate, personal relationship with the sitter. Portraits such as these, along with Johnson's and Lawrence's, are different in mood from the more formal, emotionally detached early-American portraits. In one of Beneson's portraits, we see her husband standing shirtless against an ambiguous landscape. In another, an oversized head fills the entire canvas. Both convey an expressionistic sense of isolation, and an awareness of the human dilemma, which link Beneson's portraits to modern and contemporary styles more than to early American portraiture.

Carol (1984) is a portrait by Scott Brodie (who presently lives in Albany and teaches at Skidmore College) of his wife. Brodie recently turned to portraiture and figure painting after painting still life subjects for several years. His work reflects a tension between abstraction and realism. Without question he rejects the tradition of descriptive realism which was characteristic of early American portraiture. Although a recognizable likeness of the woman is portrayed, Brodie's preoccupation with color and composition as independent elements is readily apparent. His strident, unusual colors have a life of their own, and his placement of facial features contributes to a sense of overall composition, as the same features would on a realistic face. Furthermore, an interest in space and texture predominate over image realism. Brodie adds a strong conceptual dimension by juxtaposing the human figure with still life objects which appear to float in a vertical line above the field of brushstrokes. There is a sharp, unexpected break between the figures and objects, not only in subject, but in scale. The break is also seen in the various modes of representation used as the artist plays the relatively flat, amorphous figure against the solidly modeled, three-dimensional objects. In another of Brodie's large oil paintings, *Bill*, (1984), the features of the full-length figure are generalized to the point where its reading as a portrait of a specific individual is almost totally undermined. The figure is again juxtaposed with still life objects (cups, pitchers, and other pieces of pottery), although this time they divide horizontally, balancing the figure's vertical placement.

Allen Grindle, another SUNYA graduate who has remained in the Albany area, produces generalized representations of the human figure, rather than portraits of specific individuals. His figures, depicted as abstracted, emblematic heads in profile, represent all of humanity, as an "everyperson." Grindle, like Brodie, works in large scale and is interested in the effect of juxtaposing seemingly unrelated objects within the same work, as in *Head And Figure With Glove* (1984), and *Lesions* (1984), which shows a head with gaping wounds in one section and a fish in another. Most of Grindle's paintings project an unsettling image of the confusion and pain suffered by humanity in contemporary society. Although Grindle began his career as a figurative artist, he moved away from the figure during a formalist phase and only returned to it a few years ago.

Jason Stewart's figures represent a new subject, marking a major break from his earlier commitment to nonrepresentational, constructivist images. In his paper reliefs, *A Burning Man, A Man Off Balance,* and *A Man Falling Upward* (1983-84), Stewart uses a constructivist vocabulary to create images of gesticulating figures conveying states of the human condition with which the artist personally identifies. More recently, Stewart completed a series of over life-sized heads in cardboard and gouache which, like his earlier constructions, attempt to resolve the tension between formalist and expressionist concerns.

Lillian Mulero depicts anonymous figures realistically in *Falling Woman* (1984) and *My Way* (1985), creating images reflecting the inextricable connection between the personal and the political. Her images of male and female nudes and portrait-like faces, set against decorative, patterned backdrops, focus specifically on the relationships of gender, race, and power.

Over the past five years, the resurgence of the visibility of figurative art has been a major development in which Albany area artists have played a significant part. An exhibition entitled *The Use of the Figure in Contemporary Art*, guest curated by Julie Wyatt, was held in 1985 at the Rensselaer County Council on the Arts, in Troy. Spotlighting the lively work in figurative art of the Albany area, the exhibition featured the works of Stewart, Grindle, Brodie, and Johnson, along with that of Marta Jaremko, Corinna Ripps, and Wendy Williams.

The work of Mark Greenwold, a Professor of Art at the State University of New York at Albany, has had a decisive influence on many area artists. Dealing with the dynamics of intimate human relationships and the powerful forces of the psyche in a uniquely contemporary manner, such works as *Divorce Drawing #3* (1982), *Broken Home* (1982-83), and *A Family Tragedy* (1984-85) present a striking contrast to early family portraiture represented by Ames' *Fondey Family*, and to nineteenth century Albany interiors, represented by Walter Launt Palmer's *Interior at Arbor Hill* (1878).[3] Greenwold's three works show Greenwold and members of his family acting out violent emotional and physical confrontations. Rage, pain, and guilt are portrayed as concrete actions. While the autobiographical nature of these images is a crucial source of inspiration for Greenwold, these works are not meant to be personal documents; rather, according to Greenwold, they are to be seen as "morality plays." Greenwold works in small scale and in a meticulous, obsessive, realistic style; every detail is important, every object precisely rendered. The acts of family violence occur in "idealized" bourgeois, domestic interiors where everything is up-to-the-moment, dust free, and perfectly in place, creating a chilling contrast between action and setting.

Although the contemporary portraits and figure paintings discussed demonstrate continuity of theme with early Albany art, continuity of content is lacking. In the case of landscape painting, however, a direct link in both subject and content can be seen between many contemporary Albany artists and landscape artists of the past. Many local artists feel a strong bond with the painters of the Hudson River School who worked in the Albany area during the nineteenth century, including Thomas Cole, Asher B. Durand, John F. Kensett, and Frederick E. Church. Cole, the leading artist of the first generation of Hudson River School painters, made his first trip up the Hudson River from New York City in 1825. He subsequently spent summers in Catskill, New York, painting scenes of local landscapes, including some of Albany. Best known of these paintings is *The Van Rensselaer Manor House* (1814), highlighting the Van Rensselaer home which stood in North Albany from 1797 until 1873, when it was moved to Williams College in Williamstown, Massachusetts. Across the river from Catskill, Cole's pupil, Church, set up an ideal summer residence, Olana, with spectacular views of the Hudson River and of the distant Catskill Mountain range.

William M. Hart and his brother, James, were Albany-based artists specializing in landscape. William Hart's *Albany From Bath* (1846) (Figure 1), provides a record of the city as it looked from directly across the Hudson in the midnineteenth century. (Cole did a drawing of a similar view of Albany at approximately the same time). Painted from the same vantage point, David Coughtry's 1979 watercolor, titled *Albany* (Figure 2), documents the city a century and a quarter later. The serenity and openness of Hart's painting contrasts vividly with Coughtry's crowded buildings and highway ramps, evidence of the congestion and bustle of a contemporary urban center.

As a Contemporary Realist, Coughtry has produced scenes of Albany since the mid-1970s. His drawings and watercolors of Albany's South End, known as The Pastures, offer a poetic, poignant interpretation of urban decay, and record the dilapidated face of this section of the city before its recent gentrification. His cityscapes can be compared to those of earlier artists, namely James Eights and John Wilson. Eights did a series of at least 15 watercolors in the 1840s and 1850s depicting the streets of downtown Albany as they appeared

around 1805. The nostalgic quality of these watercolors, popularized through lithographs, relates them to Coughtry's interest in the changing face of the city, brought on by decay and development. Wilson's watercolor, *View of State Street* (1848), is a straightforward documentary scene, providing a vivid glimpse of the architecture and street life of the day.

While Coughtry's works serve as documents, not unlike Eights' and Wilson's, an awareness of contemporary sociopolitical issues distinguishes his work from theirs. This is also true of his recent Adirondack landscapes, which are close in spirit to the wilderness scenes of the Hudson River School artists with whom he closely identifies. Many nineteenth century landscape artists were preoccupied with America's shrinking wilderness, an issue which is also of central concern in Coughtry's landscapes. What distinguishes his works from theirs is his position as an artist working in an advanced technological/nuclear age rather than during the rise of the Industrial Revolution.

Tom Nelson has been doing panoramic views of Albany and its surroundings since his move to the area in the early 1980s. *View South Over Albany*, *View Toward Cohoes*, and *View of Dunn Memorial Bridge* are characteristic in their horizontal format and relatively small scale. Nelson views his work as a continuation of the naturalistic landscape tradition represented by seventeenth century Dutch landscapists, by Hudson River School artists such as Kensett and by John Constable. Rather than idealized or exotic landscapes, Nelson is committed to painting landscapes of the places where he lives. Like Coughtry, Nelson paints in his studio, working from sketches and photographs made at the site.

Carol Luce, who has been doing landscapes for the past three years, feels a strong connection with Hudson River School artists, and has made pilgrimages to Church's Olana and Cole's Catskill residence. Unlike Nelson and Coughtry, whose landscapes are sweeping panoramic views, Luce focuses on a small segment of nature, as in *Park Landscape* (1985), painted in

Albany's Washington Park, and *Peeble's Island* (1984), painted where the Hudson and Mohawk Rivers converge. A recent exhibition at the Gallery, entitled *Spaces Within/Without*, included works by 15 local artists and demonstrated the diversity of contemporary approaches toward a very broadly defined concept of landscape.

In the past, Albany's proximity to New York City has been a liability for local artists, as they found themselves in the shadow of the major contemporary art center. At present, however, this liability is more an asset for artists in the Albany area because Albany is more affordable (and in other ways more liveable) than New York or other urban centers. Albany artists now benefit from the ready accessibility to New York City by keeping abreast of the cultural activity there and making contacts for exhibiting work in the city. Not all artists in the Albany area desire or need this type of contact with a major art center, but it is an advantage for those who do. Unlike other cities further removed from New York City, Albany no longer has to establish itself as a viable art center vis-a-vis New York. Furthermore, the growing number of artists who have chosen to live and work in Albany are creating a sense of community and a

lively art scene which has become more visible to the public over the past few years. This is reflected in the growing number of Capital District museums and galleries showing and selling the work of local artists. Critics, such as Ken Johnson, provide intelligent, informative analyses of local artits' work. Among the most exciting exhibists of recent years are those organized by the artists themselves: *Under the Bridge* (1981), a weekend-long event held outdoors in downtown Albany; *WaterWorks* (1982), held in Bath House #2, in the South End; and the *Portrait Gallery* show (1984), at the EBA Dance Studio off Lark Street.

While Albany has yet to develop an interested public willing to collect works by local artists, one can already see the emergence of a sense of Albany as a place where art is nurtured. This sense of place is reflected not only in the local landscapes discussed today, but also in Lori Lawrence's *Sheridan Ave. Two-Step* (1982) (Figure 3), a scene of street activity outside the loft building on Sheridan Avenue which she shares with several other artists, and Jason Stewart's *Ironweed* (1985) (Figure 4), named for William Kennedy's award-winning novel.

Roberta Bernstein, an art historian specializing in modern art and American portraitures, received her B.A. from the University of Massachusetts, Amherst, and her M.A., and Ph.D. from Columbia University. She is currently an assistant professor in art history at SUNY Albany. She has published and lectured widely on such artists as Jasper Johns, Rene Magritt, Andy Warhol, Frank Stella, and on such topics as <u>Images of Women in 20th-Century Art</u>, <u>The Circus in Modern Art</u>, and <u>The Hudson River and Its Artists</u>.

Endnotes

Among the sources used for this paper were: Allison P. Bennett's *The People's Choice: A History of Albany County in Art and Architecture* (Albany, NY: Lane Press, 1980) and Tammis K. Groft's *The Folk Spirit of Albany* (Albany, NY: Albany Institute of History and Art, 1978). I also want to acknowledge Ken Johnson's unpublished manuscript, *Serving Room: Mark Greenwold's Theater of Psychological and Moral Conflict.*

1   Notable Albany area sculptors discussed were: David Smith, George Rickey, Ellsworth Kelly, Erastus Dow Palmer, Alice Morgan Wright, Richard Stanckiewicz, Larry Kagan, David Formanek, and Edward Mayer.

2   At the time this paper was written, the first defacing of works in the plaza collection had just occurred; shortly thereafter, a second defacing involved even more extensive damage.

3   Greenwold was discussed in a section on interiors. Also discussed were William Launt Palmer's nineteenth century interiors, Patricia Loonan Testo's interior scenes of the Menands apartment where she grew up, Greenwold's works, and JoAnne Carson's complex constructions merging interior and exterior spaces.

Further Readings

Albany Institute of History and Art. *Hudson Valley Paintings 1700-1750.* Albany: 1959.

Bennett, Allison P. *The People's Choice: A History of Albany County in Art and Architecture.* Albany: Albany County Historical Association, 1980.

Bolton, Theodore, and Irwin F. Cortelyou. *Ezra Ames of Albany.* New York: the New York Historical Society, 1955.

Dilliard, Maud E. *An Album of New Netherland.* New York: Bramhall House, 1963.

Groft, Tammis K. *The Folk Spirit of Albany.* Albany: Albany Institute of History and Art, 1978.

Peluso, A.J., Jr. *J. & J. Bard, Picture Painters.* New York: Hudson River Press, 1977.

Webster, J. Carson. *Erastus D. Palmer.* Newark: University of Delaware Press, 1983.

David Coughtry, _Albany_, watercolor, 1979.

William H. Hart, _Albany from Bath_, oil on canvas, 1846.

Jason Steward, _Ironweed_, mixed media, 1985.

Lori Lawrence, _Sheridan Avenue Two-Step_, oil and encaustic on canvas, 1982.

POPULAR CULTURE

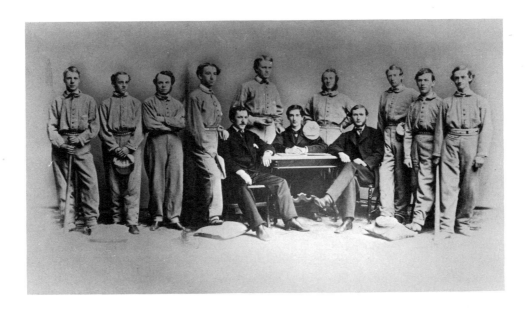

Baseball has captured the hearts and imaginations of America for well over a century. America's national game developed in this country out of the traditional British sports of rounders and cricket. Similar games were played with sticks and balls since colonial times. Alexander Joy Cartwright is credited with the establishment of rules for baseball in 1845, and the game caught on with urban gentlemen's clubs. This new game demanded accurate throwing and catching as well as swift running, and its appeal grew rapidly during the Civil War.

Baseball soon lost the reputation of a gentleman's sport. In its early days, it was a rough, loosely structured game played for blood and money. While baseball appeared a players' amateur game for some time, in reality, players were often recruited and paid with either cash or no-show jobs. In the late 1860s teams were acknowledged as professional, though this did little to change the game at first. It did set the course for the commercialization of baseball, though. Like horse racing, the most popular sport of the day, baseball appealed to gamblers.

Spectators were few and fickle, and more than one professional team was dissolved after a few losses. To insure wins, the umpires were chosen from among the spectators or the ranks of former players. The clubs paid and fed these umpires. These amateur umpires were greatly abused and insulted. Not until the formation of the American League in 1900 were umpires professionalized and respected.

Baseball provided opportunities for most anyone, even those at the bottom of society. Sports often mirror their times, however, and the exclusion of blacks from the major leagues until 1946 paralleled the Jim Crow restrictions of the age.

Baseball has been an important part of Albany's heritage since before the Civil War. Albany is credited with certain innovations in the game such as the 'fly game' and the use of the curve ball. Michael J. Kelly, born in Lansingburgh, perfected the slide in the 1880s and was one of the highest paid players of his day. Later, Babe Ruth played exhibition games in Albany, home of a Yankee farm team. Albany has produced championship teams, most notable the Albany Senators, winners of the Eastern League pennant in 1949. Today Albany once again boasts a Yankee farm team in the Eastern League's Albany-Colonie Yankees.

LET'S PLAY BALL

Stephen Hirsch

Ask a fan about the founding cities of baseball and you are likely to get one or two predictable responses. Cincinnati will be mentioned, of course, as will Chicago and Brooklyn. The more scholarly respondents may possibly mention Louisville, and those who know no better are sure to mention Cooperstown. Few, however, are likely to mention Albany or Troy, New York--two cities usually dismissed by baseball mavens as "bush league." Yet these two Hudson River towns are among the pioneers of the great American game. Troy, in fact, even rose to national prominence. If baseball cities have a starting team, Troy and Albany are certainly players.

As all but the most tenuous believers are willing to admit, the idea of baseball originating through some immaculate conception of Abner Doubleday is part of the Myth America Pageant. Baseball evolved from British games like cricket or rounders, and the first identifiable game took place in New Jersey in 1846. In a New Jersey park aptly named the Elysian Fields, the New York Nine beat the Knickerbockers 23-1, and

only a decade later--very early compared to other cities--Albany newspapers were making references to the popular game. According to the premiere sporting paper of the time, *The New York Clipper*, there was only one organized club in all of Pennsylvania in 1859, while at the same time there were organized clubs in Albany, Hudson, Troy, and other upstate cities.

Indeed, on 18 June 1859 the *Clipper* announced senior and junior members of the Albany club played each other on "the island opposite this city," and in a testimony to youth, the juniors won 40-36 in the tenth inning after a ninth inning 36-36 tie.

Incidentally, there was a rematch on 25 August, and the kids got their comeuppance, the seniors won 67-53.

Don't be surprised by the scores and by ante-bellum standards--they don't indicate poor play. Despite popular mythology, John McGraw-style one-run-games were not representative of early baseball, at least not in the nineteenth century. Games with blowout football scores were not uncommon: there were no gloves; there were many wild pitches and passed balls when a ball goes past the catcher; and there were fewer "fly catches"--though a ball caught on the first bounce was an out.

We can tell from the reports of the early games that Albany and Troy played what came to be known as the New York game rather than the New England game. In the New England game, according to *A Manual of Cricket and Baseball* published in Boston in 1858, a "feeder" called "Play!" and threw a ball at the bat of a "striker," 30 feet away.

If the striker hit it, he ran from home to first, second, third, or fourth base (not the same as home)--all marked by "stones or a small plug." He was out if he had three strikes, if his ball was caught on the fly or first bounce, or if he was hit by a thrown ball while running the bases. Only one out was allowed per side.

To score, the striker had to cross fourth base and yell "Tally!" The game was played to a predetermined number of tallies--and the book recommends 50.

By the way, the book states "when two players get on one base, either by accident or otherwise, the player who arrives first is entitled to the base."

The rules needed to be codified and in 1858 the National Association of Base-Ball Players established the modern diamond with canvas bag bases, nine innings, and a generally disregarded prohibition of betting.

Both Troy and Albany were represented at the second convention in 1860. The convention decided to keep the "out-on-first-bounce" rule (the Albany delegates split on this vote). Along with formalizing the rules, the convention designated "champion teams"--sort of an informal league--including New York and Brooklyn clubs, Washington, Baltimore, Syracuse, Rochester, Buffalo, Troy, and Albany.

The 1861 season began with the Charlestown Confederates throwing out the first ball at Fort Sumter. As might be expected, baseball activity diminished considerably at home, though most historians would agree that the spread of the game in the Union Army was one of the major reasons for its later popularity.

Albany papers barely mention baseball in the first years of the war, but by 1864, with Union teams leading in the late innings, hometown activity seems to have picked up considerably. The *Albany Evening Journal* contains references to 16 local clubs for that year--the Star Club, the Rival Club, an Eckford club, a Holyoke Club (each of the latter with two nines each), a Knickerbocker Club, and a newly organized club called the Nationals which would later become the number one team in the city. A Knickerbockers vs. Eckfords game on the parade grounds on 16 June was considered important enough to make the lead story in the next day's paper, even if it was only a one sentence report that the Knicks won. Incidentally, the Rivals had two Lawlor brothers on the team, at second and third base. It's tempting to believe they were the older brothers of future major leaguer Mike Lawlor. Born in Troy, Mike was ten in 1864 and years later would have a major league career in which he batted a lifetime .063.

By baseball season 1865, the war was over. On 6 June, nearly two months after Lincoln's assassination, the unfortunate Dr. Mudd was being questioned for his assumed part in the conspiracy. The "Skating Park Base Ball Ground" opened in Albany, and members of the Knicks, Nationals, and Eckfords played the opening game. J. C. Cuyler was president of the Base-Ball Association of Albany, and the *Evening Journal* rhapsodized "the new ground will soon be one of the best in the state; and the association intends to make ample accommodation for the ladies who shall attend the matches."

The Knicks practiced Monday and Thursday, the Ecks Tuesday and Friday, and the Nats Wednesday and Saturday. The Eagle club of Albany had two nines and a sergeant-at-arms. There was a Pioneer Club, an Empire and a Resolute club, and an Indianola club. The Hiawatha and Live Oak clubs also played out of Albany, and the Minnesotas played in Watervliet. The Washington, Conqueror, and Roanoke clubs played out of Troy, as did the Enterprise, Neptune, and Mohawk clubs. And in

Lansingburgh lurked the Union Club--later known as the feared Troy Haymakers.

It was a fun season. Albany players took regular excursions to New York City to watch games between the famed Atlantics and Mutuals. Steele of the Nationals hit an inside-the-park home run in a 53-15 loss to the Knickerbockers--they couldn't find the ball; and the married men of the Charles Van Benthuvsen company beat their single counterparts, 29-19. The Nationals played against Utica on the fourth of July and got creamed 75-17, and a rain delayed game between the Eckfords and Nationals ended with an argument when the umpire couldn't remember what inning it was.

By 1866, with the armies at home and disbanded, baseball was everywhere. William Kyle's of Albany one dollar fine for playing ball on Sunday seemed not to have discouraged others from taking up the game. The Tivoli Hose Company challenged the Post Office clerks and won 67-32, and Truck Two of the Fire Department challenged any other hose company. Engine Co. 12 accepted and won. The Beaverwyck club had a well publicized game between the "Heavies" and the "Lights" of the team--squad assignment by poundage--and the *Evening Journal* said "rare sport may be expected." Indeed, the game turned out to be "a most amusing affair. There was all manner of muffing and considerable good playing," said the *Journal*. The Lights won 28-26 with a visiting delegation from the Utica Fossils present at the game.

The larger teams also continued to flourish. A 19 July game between the Nationals and the Victory club of Troy was important enough for the *Journal* to print an entire box score--a rarity at the time. The Nats won 42-27, even considering Victory had an 11-run first inning--the Nationals came back with ten in the sixth and 12 in the eighth. On 27 July, the *Journal* reported "a large number of spectators witnessed the game yesterday between the Knicks and Live Oaks. The Knicks appeared in a new and tasty white flannel uniform." The *Journal* noted the Live Oaks also wore uniforms. The Knicks won, 43-11.

The local championship game that year was between the Knicks and the Nationals, which was played on 2 August. The *Journal* reported, with its usual and frustrating reluctance to give numbers, that "a large number of spectators were present." The Knicks won, 22-17, never falling behind, and the unusually complete newspaper report gives some idea of how the game was played:

> The Knicks had 6 fly catches to the Nats 10. The Knicks missed 3 fly-catches; the Nats missed 6. The Knicks had 10 outs on bases, the Nats 11. Outs on fouls, Knicks 4, Nats 9. Home runs, Knicks 1, Nats none. The game took a very normal two hours and 10 minutes.

Meanwhile, over in Troy, the Lansingburgh Unions were continuing to show uncanny strength. On 28 August, they beat New York's mighty Mutuals 32-18. Imagine what they were like playing more mundane local teams--for example, on that day in June when they met some poor lambs from Cohoes and beat them 110-35. The great days of the Unions, however, were yet to come.

By 1867, the *Evening Journal*, in a curious change of attitude, began to ignore local baseball almost entirely. Reports on "national" games like the Boston Lowells vs. the Philadelphia Athletics appeared occasionally, but the paper printed practically nothing on local games. In fact the *Journal* ignored local games entirely until 7 July, when it reported on a game between the Nationals and a Newburgh club. It did come out with the following admonition, however:

> The merchants of Boston refuse to employ persons connected with baseball clubs, the sport having been carried to such an excess there as to render those who engage in it unfit for steady labor. So take warning, young men. It's a glorious sport, but may be carried to excess.

Baseball was getting bigger, and in the minds of the average fan--or "krank" as he was called in those days--local teams were fading in importance, while nationally known teams were beginning to attract more and more attention. One of them was in Troy. Troy's Haymakers continually met and matched the best teams in the nation. By 1869, *The New York Clipper* was calling the Haymakers famous, and what's more, gentlemanly. "They always look after the wants of their visitors," the *Clipper* reported, mentioning a picnic between the Troy team and the equally famous and gentlemanly Brooklyn Atlantics. Indeed, 1869 saw the climax of the Trojan rise to power. But its fall was not gentlemanly at all.

A digression: In 1867, another Nationals team--this one from Washington, D.C.--had soundly defeated the local team from Cincinnati. Cincinnati got even by creating the first professional club: the great Red Stockings. The names are part of baseball legend--manager Harry Wright; pitcher Asa Brainard; left fielder Cal McVey. By 1869, they were awesome.

As they came east, the *Evening Journal* reported their progress with mounting fear, recording kill after kill by the invading barbarians. They reached Troy on 7 June 1869. The *Albany Argus* recorded a crowd of 6,000 at the game, mentioning that the road to the field was crowded with citizens from the early morning hours. The game took three and a half hours, and the *Troy Times* called the result "a first class muff game. The great expectations that had been aroused by the former achievements of the two clubs were grievously disappointed by the result." In essence, Troy lost 37-31--a close game for Cincinnati--and the *Troy Times* blamed the loss on the "execrable playing" of two of its starters.

The next day, the Reds mounted their attack against Albany's Nationals. The result was humiliating--Reds 49, Nats 8. But even that wasn't as bad a pasting as that suffered by the next victims of the original Big Red Machine. The Springfield team lost 80-5. Oddly enough, the *Evening Journal* ran no report at all of the Albany--Cincinnati game. Instead it ran a totally unrelated story called "How It Feels to be Hanged."

The Reds went south, eating up every team they faced. Meanwhile, the Haymakers continued to disdainfully tromp all their other opponents. The *Troy Times* dismissed a game with Albany's Nationals as "utterly devoid of interest" and pronounced the Ancient City Club of Schenectady "the poorest baseball club we ever saw."

The Haymakers wanted big game. On 2 August they beat Brooklyn's famous Atlantics 17-10, and the *Times* reported that betting was heavily in favor of the Troy team--one citizen had bet $6,000 on them. On 9 August they left on a western road trip. They beat club after club, preparing for the big rematch with Cincinnati on the 25th.

In Troy, arrangements had been made at the telegraph office to keep track of the game. At the end of each inning, scores were telegraphed back to the anxious crowds at half a dozen different sites in the city. Excitement ran high as Troy opened with a six-run first inning and the Reds were blanked out. In the second, Troy scored seven more, but the Reds came back with ten. What was worse, the umpirical decisions seemed to increasingly go against them. Troy was shut out in the third and fourth innings, while Cincinnati added two and then one more. In the fifth, sparked by a home run by Troy left fielder Steve King, our boys scored four more. Unfortunately, Cincinnati scored four as well. At the bottom of the fifth, the score was a 17-17 tie, and the 10,000 Cincinnati kranks were getting louder, while Troy was growing increasingly upset with the umpire.

In the top of the sixth, Cal McVey, the Cincinnati left fielder who would later go on to a .328 lifetime average in the National league, got up to bat. Fisher, the Troy pitcher, delivered the ball, and McVey hit a foul tip. Bill Craver, the Troy catcher, caught it, or so he claimed. But the umpire said no, and Troy was furious. This had gone too far. Craver called his team together on the field and demanded a new umpire--they would go no further with this obvious fraud. Cincinnati refused, and Troy left the field, followed, as the *Times* put it, "by the roughs of Cincinnati, who heaped all sorts of abuse and imprecations upon their heads. Even the hotel where they stopped had to be guarded by the police-- which shows how intense the feeling was that if they had beat the Red Stockings they would have scarcely got out of town with their lives."

The game was a tie. Cincinnati, never in danger from another ball club, ended their season with the remarkable record of 56 wins, no losses, and one tie--to the Troy Haymakers. Troy canceled the next day's game with the Cincinnati Buckeyes, unwilling to face an Ohio umpire again.

Whether or not we can believe Bill Craver's story is open to question. Bill, a sterling son of Troy, began his career with the Troy Enterprise club in '65 and the Victory club in '66, and had been Haymaker catcher since '67. In June 1869, the *New York Clipper* said he had "few equals as a catcher." Local baseball authority Warren Broderick credits Craver with many firsts in the game--the first player to slide; the first catcher to play directly behind the batter rather than the usual ten feet away. But twice in his career Craver was in big trouble. He was expelled from the White Stockings in 1870 on what the ever faithful *Troy Times* called a "trumped up charge" and thrown out of the National League in 1877 as a player implicated in the Louisville Browns game-throwing scandal. He joined the Troy police force in 1882, and lived comfortably by making dubious claims on his Civil War pension. Did he catch that ball? We'll never know.

The first professional baseball league, as we understand the term, was founded on Saint Patrick's Day in 1871. It was the National Association of Professional Baseball Players, usually referred to as the National Association. Troy was a member team of the league, which also included the Boston Red Stockings, Chicago White Stockings (the Reds had finally lost and folded in 1870), Cleveland Forest Citys, Fort Wayne Kekiongas, New York Mutuals, Rockford Forest Citys, Washington Nationals, Philadelphia Athletics, and Brooklyn Eckfords. Managed by none other than Bill Craver--

until he left in mid-season to be replaced by Lip Pike, the first Jewish major leaguer--the Haymakers finished fourth with a 15-15 record. The team also included Steve Bellan, an infielder with the distinction of being the first Cuban in the major leagues. Craver did pretty well as a player himself, hitting .303 and switching to the infield from his customary catching position.

The next year, however, Craver was gone (as were all but one of the members of the 1871 club), managing and playing for the Lord Baltimores of Maryland. Troy itself, however, looked strong at the beginning of the 1872 season. The stockholders had procured a charter with capital stock at $30,000. New uniforms arrived, so sartorially splendid that one newspaperman seriously suggested calling the team "the chocolate creams." The *Baltimore Advertiser* called the team "one of the best clubs in the country--second to none," and the season began with a seven-game winning streak during which they outscored their opponents 126-35. By early July, however, fortunes had changed, and one newspaper reported, "The Haymaker Club wants the rules changed so that the club losing the greatest number of games shall be champions. They are confident of winning under these circumstances." To make matters worse, the old financial problems of the previous season resurfaced, and on 23 July, the stockholders, upset at the team's financial status, dissolved the club after 25 games. The players were informed of this disconcerting fact while on a road trip. They were not paid their back salaries. According to *The Troy Press*, team assets were enough to pay all indebtedness, but the management did not live up to its written engagement with the players.

That was the sort of thing that killed the National Association. Teams were always dropping out and in--teams like the Fort Wayne Kekiongas or the Middletown Mansfields or the much lamented Elizabeth Resolutes who went 2-21 in 1873. Some teams played more games than others. Gamblers played havoc with the moral standards of the game, and odds and bets were frequently reported in the newspapers.

The association, minus Troy, lasted until 1875. Bill Craver lasted the duration, playing another season with the Lord Baltimores and spending 1874-1875 with three Philadelphia teams, including the original Athletics. Various unaffiliated clubs bearing the Haymaker name continued along in Troy until 1878, but they were not remarkable.

The greatest years of Troy baseball came a few years later, when Troy, New York, joined the infant National League. Most Trojans are entirely unaware of this team, and are apt to identify them with the Haymakers. They were not, nor were they ever a Haymaker organization. They were, however, one of the most remarkable teams of the early days of the league.

Troy was not a founding city of the NL. The original circuit was formed in 1876 and included Chicago, St. Louis, Hartford, Boston, Louisville, New York, Philadelphia, and Cincinnati. The new league was supposed to control the abuses of the old National Association--gambling was out, as were Sunday games. Rules for team conduct were strict--any team not finishing its season would be drummed out. And indeed, in the initial league season, both Philadelphia and New York were expelled from the league for exactly that reason. A year later, the Louisville team disbanded after a gambling scandal (and Bill Craver was permanently blackballed from the league even though no charges against him were proven). By 1878 the league was struggling along with only six teams, only three of which were originals. In 1879, after the additional default of 1878 teams in Milwaukee and Indianapolis, the National League added franchises in Buffalo, Cleveland, Syracuse, and Troy. There was now a lovely league railway route from Providence to Boston and then West.

On 21 March 1879, *The Troy Times* reported "arrangements for the base ball season are completed. The surgeons are fully prepared and the makers of false noses and glass eyes will reap their usual bounteous harvest." Troy was indeed excited about returning to the big time. Every detail of the arriving ball club was chronicled to the readers--when individual players arrived, where they stayed, where and when they practiced. After reporting on the inaugural league meeting for the season, the *Times* confidently reported that "the Troy club was regarded as one of the strongest of the number recently admitted to the league, and the opinion was freely expressed that it would occupy at least an honorable position at the close of the contest."

The *Times* had reason to be excited. Some of the new players were interesting. The rookies, for instance, included Herm Doscher, distinguished by moral standards similar to Craver's (he would be an umpire in later years and be thrown out of the league for cheating) and a 28-game veteran in the National Association. There were elderly 26-year-old rookies like Eddie Caskins and Thorny Hawkes, both from Danvers, Massachusetts. In later years, Herm Doscher would credit Thorny's "lightning plays" around second base as a primary cause for the league's placing an umpire behind the pitching box.

There was also at least one major star coming to Troy--Grin Bradley. George Washington "Grin" Bradley, known as "Grin" for the odd smile he always wore, was one of the more interesting pitchers in early NL baseball. Bradley has the honor of having pitched the first recorded no-hitter in the National League--for St. Louis vs. Hartford, 15 July 1876, one of three successive G. W. Bradley shutouts. Bradley arrived in Troy the week of 24 March 1879 and set up in rooms at the Bull's Head Hotel. He had played an exhibition game in Philadelphia before arriving, and the *Troy Times* happily reported he had made no errors in the game, not that he was more susceptible to errors than other pitchers of his day. The *Times* also reported that Bradley was named captain of the new team and put under oath to report any violation of the rules.

And then there was the manager, Horace Phillips. Before the organization of the National League, Horace had tried to set up an association including St. Louis, Cincinnati, Louisville, Pittsburgh, Baltimore, and Philadelphia. He organized a meeting of team representatives and then forgot about it and failed to show up. Troy was his first managerial assignment and later he died in an insane asylum.

Practice began on 7 April, and the team uniform, called "the handsomest ever worn by a team in this city," went on display to the admiration of all. In an event recalling the great days of the Haymakers, a stockholder's meeting was canceled for lack of a quorum. Nevertheless, a confident ad appeared in the paper:

BASE-BALL
Grand Opening of the Season. On Troy City Grounds. Tuesday, Troy Citys vs. Capital Citys of Albany. Thursday, Troy Citys vs. Capital Citys of Albany. No ladies admitted unless accompanied by a gentleman. Ladies to grand stand free. Game called at 3:15 pm. Admission 25¢, Children 15¢.

The game, actually illegal under league rules forbidding contests with nearby non-league teams in season, drew about 1,500 spectators. Troy won 2-1, with Bradley providing some real histrionics. He was hit by a line drive, and, as the *Troy Times* reported it, "he staggered, then picked up the ball and threw it to first base, putting out the runner, immediately after which he fell to the ground and fainted." Old Grin seems to have recovered rather rapidly, though, as he stayed in the game and struck out Albany's best hitter with two outs and a man on third in the ninth.

On 24 April the team was photographed before starting west on the regular season. *H.M.S. Pinafore* was playing in town, and Bill Craver was around talking about restarting the Haymakers. The *Troy Times* quoted the *New York World* as reporting "in what few games the clubs of Troy, Syracuse, and Cleveland have thus far been seen, that of Troy has shown itself in the best form for successful work." That morning the team left on their road trip.

They got creamed. Bradley ran into trouble immediately. Wild pitches were far more common then than now, but Bradley had collected six of them by the fifth game of the season. Though he was leading the team with ten hits, he also had ten errors (poor Charlie Reily, his catcher, had 16). On 5 May, club president Gardner Earl reported the team was in good spirits despite the defeats. On 6 May, *The Buffalo Express* reported that left fielder Tom Mansell ran into Cincinnati shortstop Ross Barnes and deliberately injured him. The *Express* suggested "if some baseman will kill one or two of the fellows who resort to such tricks the practice will soon be abandoned." By 10 May, the *Troy Times* reported that newspapers all over the league--even at equally winless Syracuse-- were picking on the Troys. By 12 May, the *Times* was archly reporting the Troy Citys were "beaten as usual." On 13 May, after six straight league losses, the team gave Bradley a day off and played him at shortstop while Pete McManus pitched a non-league game against Detroit. McManus won. But Bradley at least contributed with a two-run homer.

The first league victory, a 1-0 decision over Buffalo on 17 May, did go to Bradley, who moved the winning run into scoring position when he reached first on an error. Back in Troy, each inning's score was reported by telegraph and posted at the club's headquarters. Said the 17 May 1879 *Times*, "it was greatly amusing to watch the facial expressions of the persons who went in to see the score." Said the 19 May 1879 *Buffalo Courier*, "hereafter the Troy Citys will command some respect."

There was some small satisfaction for Bradley here and there in the season--such as when Eden, the Cleveland right fielder, who boasted he could homer off Bradley in every game, went hitless in a three game series; or when the *Times* reported him, the seventh hitter in the order, as second on the team with an average of .308; or on the 17 June loss to Buffalo when he struck out nine batters; or the day in July when the *Providence Journal* called him the best pitcher in the league. But the best pitcher in the league had no one to support him, and his record for the season was a dismal 13 and 40, the worst loss record in the circuit. To make matters worse, his child was seriously ill throughout the season. The story has no Tommy John ending. Two weeks after Bradley received a telegram saying the youngster was improving, the child died.

Bradley pitched two remarkable games that season--the first is most interesting for devotees of baseball strategy. It was 14 June, at home, the game after the league champion Chicagoes had slaughtered Troy 13-3. With Chicago ahead 8-7 in the eighth inning, Chicago catcher Frank Flint knocked a huge shot over the center field fence. To the amazement of everyone, Chicago manager Cap Anson held Flint at third. The strategy, as best as we can reconstruct it, was as follows. In nineteenth century ball, the catcher played ten feet behind the plate except when a man was on third, at which point he played in the contemporary spot. With the catcher behind the batter, however, more pressure was on the pitcher, who did not have his customary target. Anson seems to have gambled that Bradley would have trouble and deliver a fat pitch, yielding a base hit, scoring the man from third anyway, and putting a new runner on base.

It didn't work. Bradley got the next batter and Troy scored three runs in the ninth to win 10-9. As the *Troy Times* reported, "the Troy directors could scarcely contain themselves with joy at having beaten the champions." In the next day's issue, a long forgotten Trojan bard contributed the following:

> Chicago sent her stalwart nine
>   All petted up with fame,
> Down to the iron clad city
>   To gobble up some game.
> They came with varied castors,
>   But left much wiser boys,
> To Syracuse to get some salt,
>   Being peppered by the Troys.

Late in June, Troy acquired a first baseman inaccurately identified by the *Times* as "Broedders." He was Dan Brouthers of Wappingers Falls, New York. Brouthers had played for the Eastern League's Springfield Ponies before coming to Troy. There were stories that in a game against a Fishkill, New York, club, he slid into second base, colliding with a player named McGlynn and killing him. Brouthers' obituary in the 11 December 1911 *New York Journal* claims he killed a catcher named Quilty in a similar collision. Even if the stories are not true, at 6'2" and 207 pounds, Brouthers must have been a fearsome baserunner. He was let go by the Troy Club after the season and spent the winter laying sewer pipe between Troy and Lansingburgh. He signed with Buffalo the next season, and went on to a 19-year career, a .343 lifetime batting average (still ninth overall) and a place in Valhalla at Cooperstown. Troy, however, had not been impressed with his pitching.

It was a difficult season and there were charges of drunkenness and disorder against the players--all denied. There were long apologies for poor play. There was a switch in managers--veteran Bob "Death to Flying Things" Ferguson, the man who preceded Cap Anson in Chicago, took over for Phillips for the last 17 games. There was a nasty debate over the contract rights to a sickly but talented minor leaguer named Alex McKinnon--a debate that led to him being blackballed from the league over what appears to be a misunderstanding. There was the game at Syracuse on 30 June with only 211 fans in attendance (Syracuse folded later in the season). There was the strange home game against Chicago on 17 September where two of the Chicago players were sick, so Doscher played for the visitors, driving in a run for them. And there was the absolute nadir--when on 21 August, the Troy Citys committed 27 errors in a 16-0 loss to Boston. Headlined the *Boston Herald*, "Helen of Troy Will Weep."

The 1880 season was a welcome change, even if it did begin with a 13-1 pasting at the hands of the new team from Worcester. This year, Troy won its third time out--on 8 May, it shut out the Boston team 7-0. The *Boston Herald*, considerably upset, lamented that "the knowledge that the powerful Boston team had been entirely put to rout by a little country club was not pleasant to contemplate and will not soon be forgotten." The team went on to finish a very respectable fourth place that year--two places ahead of "the powerful Boston team."

When trouble came this year it was not because of the way the team played--it was due to the way it didn't. During a series with Providence towards the end of May, one of the games had been postponed by rain. Providence demanded Troy stay in town two days after the series was over to finish the game. The Troy team, afraid of missing rail connections back home, refused to play. Providence fielded a team nevertheless, and the umpire declared the game a forfeit. H. T. Root, president of the Providence club, demanded that Troy be expelled from the league. Root's demand was soundly--if vindictively--based on the league Constitution, but the league board of directors refused to expel the Troy club, perhaps remembering the chaos that followed the expulsion of New York and Philadelphia in 1876. Troy received an official censure instead. This time, they escaped.

By June, both Troy catchers had been disabled by injuries (not unusual for un-armored catchers in those days), and the team had to struggle two and a half weeks with amateurs in that position. One Troy native got his start in the majors this way--Charles "Fatty" Briody filled in for a while, and then began a respectable eight year National League career. During the off season he traveled as a faith healer. By 25 September, however, the catcher problems were solved. Troy called on a minor leaguer from Rochester who went on to become one of the greatest catchers of early baseball. His name was Buck Ewing (not the Buck Ewing of the Schenectady Mohawks--that Buck was named for this one), and he batted a lifetime .303 over an 18-year career. Ewing, also a successful manager, was one of the first players honored with immortality in the Hall of Fame.

Ewing arrived too late in the season to make a difference, but other newcomers made quite an impact and also went on to remarkable careers. There was pitcher Tim Keefe, who won his major league debut with a 4-2 win over Cincinnati and hit a double in the process. Though he was only 42-59 in his three years with Troy, he went on to

be the eighth highest pitcher on the lifetime wins list. Keefe is also third in lifetime complete games, and the first pitcher in baseball history to win 19 straight. In 1887, pitching for the Giants, he became the inspiration for the pitcher in Edward Thayer's "Casey at the Bat." Keefe was elected to the Hall of Fame in 1964. He shared pitching duties with "Smiling Mickey" Welch, one of the few men in the league without a mustache. Mickey, the Dale Murphy of his day, never touched liquor or tobacco. Even though he had a remarkable, league-leading 0.86 ERA his first year, he had three only so-so seasons with Troy. But Welch went on to a lifetime record of 311-207 and election to the hall. Then there was Roger Conner, who hit .329 his first year with Troy. Conner hit 138 home runs before he retired in 1897, and home runs were a rarity in his day. His achievement as a slugger was so overwhelming that it stood unmatched until 1921, when his record was broken by none other than Babe Ruth. Conner is also with the gods in Cooperstown--even though he did have 60 errors in 1880.

Like any expansion club, however, Troy also had its share of mediocrities. There were men like Terry Larkin, a four-year veteran utility player when he came to Troy. Terry was, like so many other players then and now, undistinguished. In 1883, while playing for Baltimore, he shot his wife and cut his own throat. Both of them recovered, and she didn't press charges. Fifteen years later he attacked himself again. This time he succeeded.

The 1881 season saw a slip to fifth place, a respectable, if unimpressive, standing. The usual pattern held--Troy lost its first six games, but finally beat Cap Anson's Chicago White Sox 6-5. There were some excellent moments that season which masked the fact that Troy was the worst hitting team in the league. There was the 4 July double header in Buffalo where Welch pitched and won both games in front of a crowd of three thousand. There was the wonderful game played in Albany on 10 September. It was a game against Worcester, which was leading 7-4 in the ninth inning. Ewing led off the ninth with a single. Frank Hankinson, the poorest hitter on the team, followed with another. Keefe, playing right field that day, walked. Worcester pitcher John Lee Richmond found himself facing Roger Conner. Conner won the game with a single swing--the first recorded major league grand slam.

Nine days after Conner's grand slam, President James Garfield died from an assassin's bullet. There's no connection between the events except by way of transition. Alas, the next season was to be the last for Troy. The season began well, with only three consecutive losses, and in the first win Ewing pulled off a triple play on a dropped third strike. The owners had moved the club to newer, snazzier grounds, and the future looked pretty good. By 13 June, Troy was riding a four-game winning streak and gaining on second place.

But there was a problem--the perennial problem of small franchises--attendance. Even in those days, a big game in a major city could pull in excellent crowds. For example, the 4 July double header in Chicago attracted over eight thousand. But a 20 July game in Troy pulled only two hundred and eighty. What was worse, the League Alliance Clubs had begun to look menacing.

According to the National League Constitution:

> In case a club forfeits its membership during the season, the directors are empowered to elect a League Alliance Club to temporary membership, to replace it so the scheduled games will be completed, the membership terminating at the close of the season, the games not counting in the membership record.

Troy had no intention of forfeiting anything, but it couldn't pull in the money like the big city clubs--or even like the two League Alliance clubs, New York and Philadelphia. And the league wanted money.

On 24 September, the National League announced that Troy and Worcester had voluntarily resigned. They hadn't. What had occurred was that the mayor of Detroit,

also owner of the city's NL franchise, had introduced a resolution at the league meeting to expel the two clubs. The large city teams did not make any money playing in Worcester and Troy. The gate receipts were small enough even without being divided between host and visitor. The expulsion move was in complete violation of the league constitution. Its resolution passed, 6-2.

Troy and Worcester protested vehemently. There were threats of lawsuits, and Worcester threatened to stop playing immediately and foul up the standings. The Troy players swore they'd remain loyal to the club and secretly began making deals with other franchises. While this was going on, team president Gardner Earl accepted the inevitable. After being promised two exhibition games from each league club for the next year (never played: Troy's own fault), he gave up the struggle.

The Troy City National League Baseball Club won all its remaining games, all of them away, and three of the four against fellow cripple Worcester. On 28 September, the gate receipts were three dollars. On 29 September, the team played its last game, beating Worcester 10-7. Attendance: 25.

The League was as polite as pie to Troy and Worcester at the December meeting. The teams' representatives were allowed to stay, and perhaps out of a bad conscience, the delegates voted Troy and Worcester "honorary members" of the National League. The rights and privileges thereof were never clearly enumerated, nor were they ever revoked. Today, 103 years later, Troy, New York, is still an honorary member of the National League.

As might be expected, Philadelphia and New York were quickly elected league members. Most of the Troy team was bought by New York industrialist John B. Day, owner of the American Association Mets. Some of the players went to the Mets, but the better ones went to his new National League franchise. Both teams played, sometimes simultaneously, at the Polo Grounds. While watching his new NL team play, Day rose with excitement and exclaimed "My Giants!" The name stuck.

The great New York Giants had their roots in Troy.

Major league baseball is gone for good in the Capital District. We're a minor league area now. Even if Troy still is an "honorary member" of the National League, no one seems to have mentioned that fact over the last century or so. We've become used to our demotion: Most of us don't even know that we were pioneers, major leaguers, Hall of Famers. Avarice--the same kind that bullied Troy from the majors--is now commonplace between owner and player.

But the experiences of a century ago demonstrate that it always was. Baseball thrives on mythology--there never was a pristine, innocent golden age. Many of us are apt to agree with a statement appearing in the *Detroit Free Press* one day in May 1879. "There was a time that base ball was fun," the author wrote. "That time has long since passed away."

Stephen Hirsch, former chair of the Humanities Division of the College of St. Rose, received his doctorate in English from SUNYA. His dissertation was on the popular response to Uncle Tom's Cabin *and he has produced several media presentations (television shows, slide/tapes, videotapes) as well as lectures on this topic. Hirsch has developed a research interest in baseball in the cities of Albany and Troy, which differed considerably. He and David Veeder have been working together to retrieve manuscripts and other primary materials as documents for the study of baseball and its impact on the cultural life of the area. He is currently working in the computer field.*

Further Readings

Coffin, Tristram P. *The Old Ball Game: Baseball in Folklore and Fiction.* New York: Herder and Herder, 1971.

Crepeau, Richard C. *Baseball: America's Diamond Mine, 1919-1941.* Gainsville, Florida: University Presses of Florida, 1980.

Dickey, Glenn. *The History of American League Baseball since 1901.* New York: Stein and Day, 1980.

Dickey, Glenn. *The History of National League Baseball since 1876.* New York: Stein and Day, 1976.

Kennedy, William. *O Albany!* New York: Viking Press, 1983.

Okrent, Daniel, and Harris Lewine, eds. *The Ultimate Baseball Book.* Boston: Houghton Mifflin Co., 1979.

Rice, Damon. *Seasons Past: The Story of Baseball's First Century.* New York: Praeger Publishers, 1976.

Smith, Robert. *Baseball.* New York: Simon and Schuster, 1970.

Voight, David Q. *America Through Baseball.* Chicago: Nelson-Hall, 1976.

172

ECHOES OF AN ERA

David Veeder

The modern game of baseball was born in the mid-1840s in the metropolitan New York area. Amateur athletic clubs adopted the new sport and began participating. Very soon, baseball games began to attract large numbers of paying (and non-paying) spectators. By the end of the decade, baseball fever had hit the Albany area. Organized athletic clubs began fielding teams, as did businesses and civic groups. Many of the teams, made up of employees of local businesses, consisted of enthusiastic neophytes. Witness an early score between the clerks of two different banks: State Bank 97 and National Commercial 85.

In spite of some stiff competition from cricket, baseball became our national pastime, and was referred to as such as early as 1858. The Civil War had a great deal to do with increasing baseball's popularity, and not long after the war, in 1869, the first all-professional team was fielded, the Cincinnati Red Stockings. Although professional baseball has been played in Albany on a minor league level since the 1880s, amateur and semi-professional play continued to be popular. Today that tradition is continued by the Albany Twilight League.

Indeed, baseball is our national sport. And Cooperstown, New York, is home to the Baseball Hall of Fame. Less well-known, though, is that Albany was the home of several famous teams and a baseball factory, owned and operated by the deBeer family since 1889. The deBeer baseball and softball company has supplied baseballs and softballs to professional and recreational teams, little leagues, and other groups for nearly a century. J. deBeer & Sons also provided the baseball hit by Robert Redford in the movie, *The Natural.*

David Veeder, *former executive director of the Albany County Historical Association, received his doctorate in history from SUNYA and began an ambitious project on the history of baseball in the Albany area. "Echoes of an Era" is the theme of the baseball hall of fame he has created to document the fact that the Albany area is the "cradle of baseball" as an organized sport, beginning in the 1850s. Veeder is interested in the impact of baseball on the area, especially its effect upon the cultural life of Albany. He contends that the sport was a catalyst for the "melting pot" phenomenon which helped to erase color lines. Veeder is also engaged in an oral history project on baseball in Albany.*

Seldom have the disciplines of art and industry been so successfully linked as in the popular, decorative, yet highly functional cast-iron stove. Albany's contribution to the art and industry of stovemaking cannot be overlooked.

Large-scale production of cast-iron stoves in America did not begin in any quantity until the first quarter of the eighteenth century. Cast-iron stoves were not introduced to the Albany area until the Revolutionary War when General Philip Schuyler ordered a number of them for the army's winter quarters at Saratoga. Albany became one of the largest centers in the world for the production of stoves during the nineteenth century. Albany's convenient location for transportation and high quality raw materials favored the development of an iron industry in the region.

The stoves produced in this area were noted for their superior quality of casting and imaginative design and decoration. Patterns mirrored the tastes and sentiments of the times. Decorations were often quite elaborate. Functionally, early nineteenth century stoves were designed to burn coal or wood. As these fuels became scarcer, stoves were re-designed to burn kerosene and gas.

Advances in stove design and efficiency affected development in the design of domestic architecture. Houses became larger and window sizes increased.

Stove production in the Albany area began to decrease in the last quarter of the nineteenth century. Competition from large western foundries, frequent labor disputes, failure to keep up with new technologies, and dwindling supplies of raw materials contributed to the decline of the industry in Albany. Yet a legacy remains, preserved in museums and private collections, to tell of Albany's important role in the development of the cast-iron stove.

CAST WITH STYLE: NINETEENTH CENTURY CAST-IRON STOVES FROM THE ALBANY AREA

Tammis K. Groft

Nineteenth-century American cast-iron stoves, once prominently displayed in Victorian parlors and kitchens, were relegated to barns and basements as modern central heating systems evolved. Recent increases in fuel costs, however, have restored interest in coal- and wood-burning stoves. As museums, collectors, and the energy-conscious public re-examine cast-iron stoves of the past, they are discovering that those manufactured in Albany and Troy, New York, during the nineteenth century best combine the achievements of American foundry and decorative arts.

Ironically, a wood shortage in the Northeast during the 1820s encouraged the mass production of cast-iron stoves. Small cast-iron stoves capable of containing and radiating more heat with less wood were developed because of the inefficiency of large open fireplaces and the diminishing supply of wood due to growing consumption by factories and steamboats. Albany and Troy, located nine miles apart on opposite banks of the Hudson River near the confluence of the Hudson and Mohawk rivers, had

prospered as centers of trade and transportation since the 1700s. The combination of water and rail transportation, availability of raw materials, and local ingenuity made this area an ideal place for the development of the stove industry.

The strategic locations of Albany and Troy afforded easy and inexpensive transportation for raw materials to the foundries and for finished stoves to worldwide markets. The Hudson River provided a direct route south to New York City; the Erie Canal, which opened in 1826, facilitated movement west along the Mohawk River to the Great Lakes; and the Champlain Canal provided passage north to Canada. By the mid-1850s the area was a hub for rail traffic as well.

All the raw materials needed for making stoves were readily accessible. Iron ore, easily mined and smelted into pig iron, came mainly from Clinton and Essex Counties in the Adirondacks and Columbia and Dutchess Counties south of Albany. The limestone used as flux during the smelting process was also abundant in the surrounding counties. Coke, which fueled the furnaces, was shipped from Pennsylvania by way of the Delaware and Hudson Canal to the Hudson River. The molding sand used in the casting process, known as Albany molding sand, is still considered among the finest molding sand available. This sand, sediment from a glacial lake that covered Albany between 12,000 and 15,000 years ago, has a fine granular quality. When moistened, it retains the exact shape of a pattern, making for well-defined decorative surfaces and tight-fitting seams.

Four area men were responsible for inventions that contributed to the development of the stove industry in Albany and Troy. W. T. James of Lansingburg is credited with designing the earliest cookstove sold, but not made, in Troy in 1815. Eliphalet Nott patented one of the first successful anthracite-burning stoves in 1832. The stove, known as Nott's Patent, revolutionized the industry because it burned anthracite, a source of energy previously untapped for domestic consumption. In 1838, Philo Penfield Stewart of Troy, founder of Oberlin College in Ohio, perfected one of the nineteenth century's best-known cooking stoves, with sides and base shaped so that the wood rolled to the center to facilitate combustion. This Stewart Cookstove was manufactured by the Fuller and Warren Company of Troy. In 1854, D. G. Littlefield, of Albany, patented the first successful base-burning stove, into which fresh fuel is automatically fed from a hopper as the lower layer of fuel is consumed. Base-burners were considered the most powerful heaters available during the late nineteenth century.

The commercial manufacture of stoves began in Albany in about 1820 and in Troy in 1821, although records indicate that stoves made in New Jersey and Pennsylvania were shipped to upstate New York and sold in great quantities by stove dealers in the 1820s and 1830s. Most Albany stove dealers had shops on Green Street near State Street. In Troy, the center for stove merchants was River Street. In 1872, the *New York Times* reported: "A man that cannot suit himself with a stove along River Street, Troy, must be one of those crea-tures . . . too often to be met . . . impossible to please."

The first types of stoves made in Albany and Troy were six-plate box stoves. The bottom, or hearth plate, on these stoves extends at the front end and serves to catch the ashes when the fuel door is opened. Tie-rods connect the top and bottom plates; detachable legs slide into channels under the bottom plate on all stove types. A recessed ash pit with a removeable plate to control the air draft was added to the design of the box stove during the 1820s. Larger box stoves often have secondary chambers within, which prolonged the circulation of hot air and prevented downdrafts. The selling point of these wood-burning stoves was fuel economy and portability. The design was popular throughout the nineteenth century and is still made today.

Franklin-type stoves were also made early on in Albany and Troy. Benjamin Franklin invented a similar type of stove in 1740 and called it the "Pennsylvania Fireplace." Although the technology of his original stove was improved upon during the eighteenth century, the design remained the same. In 1816 James Wilson of Poughkeepsie, New York, patented a stove reminiscent of Franklin's and called it a "Franklin Stove." Thereafter, all similar models carried the original designer's name. In these stoves, heat was conducted by the cast-iron and radiated by the open flames. Franklin-type stoves, though more efficient than fireplaces, were the most inefficient and furnished the least heat of all cast-iron stoves. They were not designed to be air-tight, although doors were eventually included and could be closed to contain the heat. The stove design is still popular today. Indeed, it has always been a pleasure to see the flickering flames of wood-burning fire.

By the mid-1830s stove manufacture was a thriving industry in Albany and Troy. While the early stoves consisted of relatively flat plates decorated with delicate floral or geometric low reliefs, cast-iron stove-making soon reached its highest artistic achievement and technological advancement. During the period from the 1840s through the

1860s, two-sided flask casting and the advent of the cupola furnace, which provided better control than a blast furnace, permitted more convoluted surfaces and finer quality casting. This improved technology accommodated the designs of the period.

The eclectic Victorian tastes are reflected in the designs and names of parlor stoves manufactured since the 1830s. These stoves simulate the architecture of castles, Gothic churches, and Italian villas, and also exhibit the lavish and intricate flora and fauna ornamentation so typical of the period. The intricate stove patterns were cast from carvings in mahogany or pine, executed by skilled craftsmen who borrowed freely from manuals for architects and cabinetmakers. Bowls or urns often topped the stoves and were filled with perfumed or spiced water to counteract the disagreeable smell and dryness caused by the heated iron. Many of these stoves were given romantic names--such as Venetian Parlor, Castle, and Temple Parlor--to enhance their allure and help buyers identify them when ordering from catalogs. Made at the height of cast-iron technology, such stoves display some of the finest examples of casting known today.

Column parlor stoves, made during the 1840s, featured two, four, six, eight, or ten columns rising out of the firebox and connected at the top by a horizontal chamber. Intended to circulate hot air for a longer period and increase heat radiation through additional surfaces, the distinctive form inspired many splendid variations in design.

Many of the cast-iron and sheet-iron parlor stoves manufactured during the 1850s and 1860s were advertised as "airtight." Although most of the stoves allowed a little air to leak through the seams, some individual stoves proved less air-tight than others, depending on the seam quality. The great advantage of an airtight stove was that the rate of combustion was completely controlled by the damper; thereby the fuel burned with the greatest efficiency. Some parlor stoves had hinged or sliding front doors (first patented by Ezra Ripley of Troy) that exposed the fire and decorative grate. They were called "Franklin Parlors" by the manufacturers because their opened doors were reminiscent of Franklin's invention.

By mid-century many new homes were built with central heating systems, making possible more rooms, higher ceilings, larger windows, and often no fireplaces. Parlor stoves were still used in these houses; it was more economical to heat one room with a stove than an entire house. Older homes, however, still used stoves or fireplaces for heat.

Cookstoves and ranges, because they were manufactured over a long period and performed numerous functions, incorporated the widest variety of changes in style and technology of all stove types. They often have between two and eight boiling holes, special reservoirs for boiling water; several ovens; and were made of cast-iron, sheet-iron, and later enameled steel.

Base-burners, probably the most powerful heaters made during the nineteenth century, were self-feeding anthracite-burning stoves. They contain a cast-iron fire pot within a circular firebox with a rotary grate, which was shaken several times a day to free the coal from ashes, thus clearing the shaft for a better fire. Direct draft flues conducted cool air to the base of the stove for efficient burning and hot-air flues circulated the warm air evenly within the stove. Most base-burners have isinglass windows, hence the name "illuminated base-burner." The more elegant base-burners have nickeled turnkeys, hinge pins, railings and legs, copper urns and ornaments, and often a shelf for a kettle.

By the 1860s, Albany and Troy manufacturers were among the largest producers of cast-iron stoves in the world, and the stoves they made were renowned for their quality casting and innovations in design and technology. Demonstrating the importance of the overseas trade, many of the stove catalogs, published annually, were written in English, French, and German. Of Troy stoves it was said that "Llamas have carried them across the Andes to the farthest coasts of South America, camels to the shores of the Black Sea, and ships to Turkey, China, Japan, and Australia."

Fifteen stove companies in Albany were producing over three million dollars worth of cast-iron products in 1875, and 18 companies in Troy were producing over 2.8 million dollars worth of cast-iron products. Together, the two cities produced 450,000 stoves that year, which sold for between four and forty dollars each, including all accessories. However, the large-scale mass production of stoves during the 1870s and 1880s led to simpler designs, routine patternmaking, and increased use of sheet metal. Despite the addition of nickel-plating, the manufacture of stoves became less inspired. Most companies continued to produce an "art stove" line, however, for those willing to pay the price for quality craftsmanship.

Albany and Troy foundries manufactured a multitude of other cast-iron products, such as: hollowware, kettles, pots and pans; stove furniture, implements needed to tend the fires; machine parts; agricultural implements; railroad wheels; and architectural artifacts or entire building facades.

By the 1890s, production had declined sharply because the local supply of raw material, especially coke and iron, had greatly decreased, while keen competition was coming from new midwestern foundries. In addition, union drives for better wages and working conditions resulted in turbulent labor-management conflicts that prevented the companies in Albany and Troy from keeping up with new technological advances in cooking and heating. By 1900, most of the foundries had shut down or moved west. Stoves currently on the market, however, are still modeled after popular nineteenth-century designs, and the same criteria used then--fuel efficiency, proper draft control, and durability--still determine the most desirable stove of today.

Tammis Kane Groft, *curator for the Albany Institute of History and Art, was trained in the Cooperstown Museum program, after studying at Hartwick College in Oneonta. She has worked extensively with Albany area art and has developed expertise on nineteenth century stoves in Albany.*

Further Readings

Adkin, Jan. *The Art and Ingenuity of the Woodstove.* New York: Everest House, 1978.

Curtis, Will and Jane Curtis. *Artistry in Iron.* Ashville, Maine: Cobblesmith, 1974.

Groft, Tammis K. *Cast With Style: Nineteenth Century Cast-Iron Stoves from the Albany Area.* 2nd ed. Albany: Albany Institute of History and Art, 1984.

Mercer, Henry C. *The Bible in Iron.* 2nd. Ed. edited by Horace Mann. Doylestown, Pennsylvania: The Bucks County Historical Society, 1941.

Pierce, Josephine H. *Fire on the Hearth.* Springfield, Massachusetts: The Pond-Ekberg Company, 1951.

Waite, John G. and Diana S. Waite. "Stove Manufacturers of Troy, New York." *Antiques* 103(January 1973):136-144.

Waldowitz, Daniel J. *Worker City, Company Town: Iron and Cotton-Workers Protest in Troy and Cohoes, New York, 1844-1855.* University of Illinois Press, 1978.

White, Frank G. "Stoves in Nineteenth Century New England." *Antiques* 116(September 1979):592-599.

*Two-column parlor stove, J. Rathbone,
Albany, c. 1835.*

*Two-column parlor stove, Ransom & Co.,
Albany, c. 1845.*

*Parlor stove, morning-call, Stow &
White, Troy, c. 1861.*

*Franklin-type stove, sign of gilt, Stafford and
Benedict & Co., Albany, c. 1815*

Gon'na sail my little boat on the river, just like Henry Hudson did in 1609. Gon'na sail my little boat on the

The Hudson River has not been as celebrated in song as have many other bodies of water. A few folk songs set in New York State are familiar whaling songs, and sea shanties abound.

Richard and Lee Wilkie have spent the last twenty years exploring the Hudson River, along its banks and by boat. Richard has collected information about the river and its well-known characters, and turned them into song. He has captured the great inspiration of the Hudson River in several types of song. One is a portrait of a crusty marine captain, called "Captain Adams"; another describes a part of the river which has caused innumerable wrecks, titled "Storm King"; a third is "Hudson River Valley Home," a paean of praise for the valley through which the Hudson River flows.

Lee and Richard sing these songs together, accompanied by folk instruments such as the autoharp, the banjo, the hammered dulcimer, and the guitar. They have done much to bring awareness of the Hudson River's complexity to many people living in New York State.

SONGS OF THE HUDSON

Richard W. and Lee Wilkie

The first "folksong" I ever remember hearing was *Little Joe the Wrangler* sung by a young man, Lindy Wagner, who worked for my father in the machine shop. Lindy lived in the top of one of two shops with which Dad began his Wilkie's Spring and Tool Company. It must have been about 1932 when Lindy came to work. Dad told my brother Pete and me "not to bother the boys." So of course we did, particularly when we heard the guitar and the songs. Toward the end of the depression in 1934 when Dad moved us and the business from Short Street in Independence, Missouri to a new location just north of town, there were other men who came to work for a while and some of them sang songs, too. Pete and I heard a number of cowboy songs from these men, usually in the evening after work.

I heard a lot more music, however, at church. The Mormon Church, in which I grew up, considered music to be about as important as the scripture itself. The hymns were long--that gave me a chance to figure out a part for myself, since I never

learned how to read music well enough to actually sing the notes. It was more fun to make up a part anyway. Roy A. Chaville was the music director for the young people. He was a fine teacher: We learned part singing, lining out, and how to sing rounds, as well. Dad and Mother were fine singers, too. We always sat together at church so that I could hear what they were singing. Singing harmony and learning melodies all seemed very natural. Both Lee and I, however, listened to the Grand Ole Opry on the radio in the late 1930s and early 1940s. I don't recall ever hearing the term folksong, and the folksong revival was unknown to us. We thought of such songs as "cowboy" or "hillbilly" music, or perhaps as social music for the campfire.

The only folk instrument I learned to play back then was a harmonica. I recall having a list in my harmonica box of some 30 songs I knew by heart. Dad played the harmonica very well and showed me how to hold my mouth to play single notes. He bought me my first Marine Band Hohner on the condition that I learn one song that same afternoon. I learned *Where Oh Where Has My Little Dog Gone*. That was the summer of 1937. I longed to play the guitar, and after Dad took us to the "Brush Creek Follies" in Kansas City, a weekly country and western program popular in the late 1930s, I made a two-string "guitar" which sounded about as good as the orange crate slats from which it was made.

At about this same time--late 30s, early 40s--Lee recalls hearing her grandfather play the fiddle on the back porch of the farm near Burden, Kansas. Her mother did "recitations" and sang a bit, too.

The first song Lee and I ever did "in public" was *Sweet Betsy from Pike* for a Library School party at Emporia Kansas Teachers college. She sang; I played the harmonica. Lee and I bought an Oscar Schmidt autoharp in 1952 when we were teaching in Dodge City, Kansas. I was attempting to learn the cello at the time, and we thought those two instruments might work together! The cello was out of my reach, but what I learned there allowed me to develop a system for playing the mountain dulcimer which became the basis for the book, *Playing Lead Dulcimer*, which we published in 1973.

It was not until 1957, however, that Lee and I became part of the folksong revival. We lived in Ames, Iowa, then, and we met a number of local singers interested in American folklore and folksongs. The folksong culture took the form of informal sings at our home and several others in Ames and Des Moines. I learned to play the five-string banjo and the guitar, and Lee and I began to learn new songs from other singers and from records. At the same time we also began to "recall" parts and versions of songs we had first heard years before in Kansas and Missouri.

Awareness of and concern about civil rights and the war in Southeast Asia were growing around the college campuses in those years. Folksongs about hard times, slavery, labor, and peace began to take on new meaning. Lee and I and others began to be invited to share songs concerned with social issues at church meetings and college gatherings. Lee and I, with our dear friend

Bernie Gerstein, took part in an evening of folksong at a church in Ames in late 1957 or early 1958. It was that evening I first fully realized how well Lee could belt out an old blues song like *In the Pines*! Our active work in American traditional music began that evening.

Lee and I and the children, Karl and Kay, moved our home and fortunes to Albany, New York, during the summer of 1961. That fall I found a genuine interest in traditional folksong among my students at the Albany State Teachers College (as SUNY Albany was then known) when I incorporated folksong into my courses. As part of the 1962 summer program at the college I invited some of those students along with several local singers to help me present an evening concert of traditional music. Lee and I were invited to do traditional songs for community groups around Albany that fall, and shortly thereafter we began singing folksongs with the children of Trinity Institution downtown and at their summer camp in the Helderberg Mountains. Partially because of that connection, we were invited to join with several other local singers to organize the C.O.R.E. Singers to raise money through local concerts for the civil rights struggle. The first "protest" song I ever wrote, *The Albany to Dixie Blues*, became a standard number for the group. For a period of four years or more we marched, sang at rallies at churches and synagogues, and then sang and marched some more.

The year 1967 marked an important phase of our work in traditional music. That fall we got a note from Peter Seeger (whom we had first met in Ames after a concert we helped organize for him) asking us to join with him and others for the founding of the Clearwater movement at the Depot Playhouse at Garrison, New York. We subsequently took part in concerts and rallies up and down the valley in the interests of that environmental program. Lee first danced the limberjack at boat and home shows to attract folks to the Clearwater booth. The little dancing man has delighted children we sing for ever since. That same fall we attended the Fox

184

Hollow Festival for the first time, and a bit later helped organize, along with a number of other local singers, the Floating, Picking and Singing Gathering, as the organization was then called. This same fall, in a concert at the Dutch Reformed Church of Albany, Lee included her autoharp in the accompaniment of our songs. The combination of autoharp and five-string banjo shortly became our standard instrumentation, and the following year I added the mountain dulcimer.

In the next decade we met and sang with hundreds of local and touring singers. We swapped songs and stories with folks representing nearly every type of traditional music know to American folksong. We have, of course, been influenced by the many fine artists we have known, and we have come to see our own personal tradition in the broader setting of the later folksong revival. It is my personal conviction that the "folk process" does indeed consist of the creative work of countless poets using and reusing the common stock of melodies and ideas worn smooth by the minds and hands of so many. Authorship in folksong is problematic at best and truly impossible if one fails to acknowledge the tradition. The folksong, mine included, is not that which is printed on the page, but rather that which happens when we sit down to pick and sing.

Richard W. Wilkie, *associate professor of rhetoric and communications at SUNYA, received his Ph.D. at the University of Michigan. Wilkie's fields are rhetorical theory, theory of argument, political rhetoric of left radical movements, and discourse analysis. He and his wife Lee are well-known folk singers in Albany and collectors of Hudson River songs.*

Lee Wilkie *is a well-known folk singer in Albany. She has done extensive research in the tradition of Hudson Valley folk music and has organized music festivals to celebrate this regional music. Lee plays the autoharp and sings with her husband, Richard, who plays the dulcimer. The Wilkies have a collection of early folk musical instruments. Lee holds graduate degrees in English literature and library science, taught English, and was a librarian before her musical interests led to another field.*

Sailing Song

Words and Music by Richard Wilkie

Gon'na sail my little boat on the river,
Just like Henry Hudson did in 1609.
Gon'na sail my little boat on the Hudson
With my family and a good old friend of mine.

Have you seen the oily water 'round Green Island?
Birds and fish will die from there to Tappan Zee.
If we really love the Hudson River Valley,
We will let that water run on clear and free.

You can find us if you know Coxsackie Landing,
Or the pretty hills around New Baltimore.
We will round the light at Rattlesnake Island,
And sail back by the Schodack Valley floor.

Oh the river's wide at Rip Van Winkle Crossing,
And the marsh lands run on down to Saugerties.
And I wish I could have sailed along that valley
With the water clear the way it used to be.

But the waters of the Hudson are still flowing
Past the farms and hills and docks and industry.
Melting snow upon the Adirondack Mountains
Will carry ships from New York Harbor to the sea!

This is the first Hudson River song I wrote. It was in January of 1967 when I was resolved to own a small cruising sailboat on the Hudson, that is, after having sailed some bays of the Hudson on a lateen-rigged wet boat. We had already heard about the beginnings of the Hudson River Sloop Restoration, as the Clearwater organization was then known, and were persuaded to help with that portion of the ecology movement. The political rhetoric of the song arises from those concerns. The song was presented at fund-raising concerts for the restoration at Newburgh, Garrison, and elsewhere in the valley. The song was composed with the autoharp and guitar in mind, indeed as a "rally" type song for the movement.

Storm King

Words and Music by Richard Wilkie

I used to draw near 15 feet, I was 90 on the waterline.
My engines made of brass and iron, my timbers oak & pine.
But they left me here to die, they left me here to die.
They broke my back a-haulin' freight and they left me here to die.

No fancy ladies walked my decks, nor gamblers on the fly,
But horses, sheep, and cattle for the farming men to buy.
(Chorus)

Coxsackie was the northern port, New York the southern run.
Against the tide I could make some knots and with it twenty-one.
(Chorus)

Well all the miles I worked and sailed along that Hudson line
Ended when they hauled me out in 1929.
But maybe down that valley where the blue haze dims the sky.
Someone remembers Storm King when she was sailin' by!
(Chorus)

Storm King was a four-deck freight ship whose "bones," keel, deadwood, frames, and bilge planks, lie rotting just a few feet north of the New York State boat landing at Coxsackie. The late Mr. Youmans of that town, who told me her story, said he had been a deck hand on board in the days when the steam freighters worked the run from New York City to Coxsackie. In my August 1967 conversation with him, he actually used the words which became the chorus in the song, "Yup . . yup, they broke her back haulin' freight and left her here to die." The song was published in *Songs and Sketches of the First Clearwater Crew* in 1970.

I've Seen My Valley Filled With Spring Time

Words and Music by Richard Wilkie

I've seen my valley filled with spring time.
I've seen it filled a-gain with the fall,
And I've walked along the sand with the rushes by my hand,
And I've heard the speckled river bird call.

Some say the river winds are blowing.
Some say they hear the valley cry,
And if the winds prevail, they'll catch a morning sail
And hold a silent wing against the sky.

Have you seen the working in the valley,
The cargo ships bound southward to the sea,
Or how the barges ride with the tugboat by their side
All the way to Troy and Albany.

This song occurred to me in September of 1967 toward the close of our first season sailing the Hudson. Lee and I had an eighteen-foot, two-bunk sloop that year which was rigged with a small hammock for our third child, Paul. He could nap while we sailed, beachcombed, and watched the life in the river valley. It was then that I first realized why nineteenth century European travelers contrasted the Hudson River Valley so favorably to the Rhein and other continental rivers. I thought the modal movement--tonic to the flattened seventh note-- would capture the serenity and the sense of mystery I always feel in the Hudson Valley.

Captain Adams

Words and Music by Richard Wilkie

I'll see you in the springtime in the hills near Albany,
We'll walk along the meadows of the yellow honey bee,
For it's winter on the Hudson and frozen it will be,
But the Edmund waits at anchor just north of Saugerties.

My name is Thomas Adams, a captain I am too,
Upon the Lewis Edmund since 1822.
Its true I've been a rover and love to run so free,
But tell your folks I'll settle down just north of Saugerties.

Remember our first meeting on the dock at Castleton?
I tipped my cap in greeting, I knew you were the one.
But you were with your father who looked so hard at me,
And left me there a-standin' far north of Saugerties.

But how my heart did quicken, Oh how it sang for joy
When you whispered that your father was a merchant up in Troy.
For our sloop she was bound northward with hardware, flour and tea,
And I knew that we would meet again far north of Saugerites.

I can't forget our parting, these letters that I write
Can never fill the longing, or warm the chilly night.
You know we should have married, but your folks would not agree,
And I had work at West Camp just north of Saugerties.

So I'll see you in the spring time in the hills near Albany
We'll walk along the meadows of the yellow honey bee,
And surely we will marry, for let the promise be
We'll make a home together far north of Saugerties.

Through a lead provided by Peter Seeger, I obtained a few fragments of Captain Adams' memoirs from his granddaughter, Miss Beaver of Saratoga. The Captain began his memoirs about 1875 but never finished them. The song here draws upon the events of his life as a sailing captain. The ballad was composed in the spring of 1968, and first presented in concert by my wife Lee and I at St. Rose College, Albany, that same fall.

POPULAR ART OF THE HUDSON

These prints by William H. Bartlett capture the spirit of the Hudson River during the mid-1800s.

A Distant View of Schenectady

Peekskill Landing

Winter

Crownest from Bull Hill

Albany

FINAL RESTING PLACES

Decorative cemetery art has a fine tradition and many artists working in cemeteries were well-known sculptors. For early Americans, gravestone carving, done by highly trained people, was the first serious art. The earliest American cemeteries were filled with carvings of skeletons, skulls and crossbones, and hour glasses running out of time. Later came the winged skulls which evolved into winged heads, a symbol for the soul's journey.

Early burial in Albany's churchyards did not last, as the city became more crowded and congested. Flooding and erosion also took their toll on Albany's church cemeteries. In 1868, the city fathers moved some seventeenth and eighteenth century stones from the old State Street Burial Grounds to the Albany Rural Cemetery. These stones provide the art historian with rich evidence of the early gravestone art that was practiced in New England and Upstate New York in those centuries.

GRAVESTONE IMAGERY

Patricia Clahassey

In Section 49 of the Albany Rural Cemetery, we find an important group of gravestones. These stones are of historical significance for Albany and represent a unique form of folk art dating back to the seventeenth and eighteenth centuries. These stones found their way to Albany Rural Cemetery from the churchyards of at least a dozen churches in the city of Albany.

In 1789, the Common Council of Albany appointed a committee to select a common burying ground, as the burial ground allotted each of the churches had reached capacity and additional land was needed for development. The committee selected a plot bordering Eagle, Lancaster, and State Streets, where the Telephone Building and the Justice Building now stand. Each church was allotted approximately one acre of the land, and the stones and remains were moved from the churchyards to that site. Due to rapid growth in the city, this burial ground was moved farther west to a plot of land between State, Hudson, Snipe, and Robin Streets in 1801. Known as the State Street Burial Grounds, the graveyard

remained intact from 1810 to 1862, at which time the remains were again moved to Plot 49 in the Albany Rural Cemetery, in order to make room for the construction of Washington Park. The stones in this section represent only a small fraction of those which must have existed prior to these moves.

A small number of stones in Section 49 were carved during the eighteenth century and contain a winged head set in an arch. Ten of these stones will be discussed, and are listed at the end of this chapter, but additional winged stones are in the Albany Rural Cemetery and are not discussed here. Although generally designated Puritan or early New England gravestones, these stones are found in graveyards other than those associated with the Puritan or Congregationalist Church. For instance, a number of stones at Albany Rural are carved in Dutch, reflecting an obvious connection with the Dutch Reformed Church. Also relevant is the fact that the stones are found in New York State, not ordinarily considered part of New England. Although some carvers may have moved here from Connecticut or Massachusetts, many were native to this area. The principal characteristic allowing us to group these stones together is the presence of a winged head set in an arch surrounded by foliage. Circa 1800 the winged head disappeared, giving way to the urn and the weeping willow.

These stones are considered a form of folk or vernacular art. Folk art refers to that image-making found among the common people (in Europe among peasants, or in the Colonies among farmers and tradesmen) as opposed to that which is a direct result of education or training in the academies of art. Several characteristics of folk art relate directly to gravestone carving. In formal terms, the carver will use rather abstract forms, organizing them in a symmetrical manner and repeating them to create a pattern. Limited realistic faithfulness to nature and a high degree of stylization of the images are characteristic here.

The winged head symbolizes transformation, i.e., the soul taking flight to the afterlife or the transformation from life on earth to life in heaven. The winged skull, appearing in the earliest gravestones around Boston in the seventeenth and early eighteenth centuries, represents a variation on the same theme. An example of the winged skull at Albany Rural (1728) conveys the idea of transformation with an emphasis on death as an event filled with fear and dread. Some writers suggest the skull evolved into the human head, citing as evidence stones carved by Gershom Bartlett, which depict a human head ending with a saw tooth edge at what should be the chin. That the human head is found on stones carved as early as those with skulls would seem to weaken this argument. We might conclude, instead, that the winged skull and the winged head were two preferred symbols until circa 1730, when the winged skull disappeared. The winged head remained the preferred symbol for the next 60 years or so, when it gave way in the early 1800s to the urn and weeping willow.

Albany Rural's winged skull (1728) is typical of a simple, almost geometric, style. The area surrounding the skull and wings is cut away so that they are in low, but flat, relief. The eyes are mere circles, and the nose is a triangle. By contrast, the border design is more complex and decorative with sweeping curved lines and careful articulation of leaves and blossoms, clearly differentiated one from another. Note the sharp contrast between the style of the border and that of the tympanum, suggesting the possibility that the carver worked from two different models with no intention of integrating the two.

The Harmanus Wendall stone (1756) provides an example of an early winged head. The wings here are merely incised lines; they do not come together at the bottom and enclose the form. Short, curved lines running between the long sweeping lines remotely suggest feathers but remain simple markings, and a spiral appears on each of the finials. Both the head and the crown are treated differently from the wings. The crown takes on a shape which is raised from the surface of the stone. The face, however, is not raised from the surface; rather it is set back into it with a slight modeling of the surface.

The Harmanus Wendall stone demonstrates the early stages in the development of carving, the first being the simple cut into the stone to make a line. Next, that line becomes more decorative, as in the case of the spirals. The line is then joined to itself, creating a shape like that in the crown, and the area around the shape is cut away, creating a simple relief. The surface of the shape is then modeled, rendering a curve that, in a very simple way, begins to represent the surface of forms found in nature. We can see this development in the treatment of the face.

The shape of the head on the David Van der Heyden stone (1770) is quite different. Its sagging jowls give it a bit of a comical look. Bear in mind that this is not an attempt at a realistic portrayal of a person; rather, it is an individual carver's presentation of a symbol. The style employed by a carver is partly his own invention, partly a borrowing of other styles. Note the minimal modeling around the drooping jowls and the nose. The line forming the top of the eye is extended, first to form the nose, and then the other eye. Above the head, a series of spirals may signify hair. A form made up of several spirals may even indicate a crown. It should be pointed out that the spiral is a decorative motif characteristic of a people in an early stage of mark making. Interestingly, it is also found in the early marks made by young children.

The Gertrude Van der Heyden stone (1784) is unique for several reasons. It bears the worn signature T. Brown at the bottom of the stone. Even more unique is the treatment of the winged heads in the tympanum. First, the heads are depicted in profile. Second, they are not mirror images, but are different one from the other. It is as if each were a different person with a different chin structure. The rendering of these heads is more realistic than the stylized heads of the other stones. This does not suggest that these heads were carved from life. It is clear, however, that the models were not those found on other gravestones. Apparently the model was an illustration in a book or print, or on a broadside. Observe that the hair is carefully drawn and gradually changes into the wings. Yet this is a simple relief carving where the images are skillfully drawn and the background is cut away. All forms maintain the flat surface of the stone; there is no modeling of the surfaces. This, combined with the style of lettering, would suggest that T. Brown was trained in drawing or illustration and was not principally a carver.

In the Harriet Roseboom stone (1787), the winged head image is carved in yet a different style. Here the winged head appears with no other decoration. The face is modeled very sensitively with strokes at the top of the head suggesting hair. A greater degree of realism is apparent in the treatment of the mouth and the eyes. The wings are carefully articulated, the shapes and surfaces suggesting an understanding on the part of the carver of what wings actually look like. Acting as a counterpoint to this incipient realism, however, is the organization of the forms. The spherical head fits into the curve created by the wings for the sake of the design. The apparent symmetry here is somewhat misleading; the shapes along the top of the wings do not exactly repeat each other, and the head is turned ever so slightly from an upright position. The slight inconsistencies lend a kind of quirkiness to the image.

In the figure on the Jacob Lansing stone (1791), a similar quirkiness results from the awkward carving of the head and wings. There is no awkwardness, however, in the rosettes of the finials or in the letters. One might question whether all the parts of this stone were carved by the same hand. The simple incised lines suggest the wings are a bit irregular. Despite a slight modeling of the face, most of the figure is rendered with simple lines.

The Sarah Ten Eyck stone (1791) reveals similar treatment of the winged head. Unlike the Lansing stone which has a rosette in the finials, this stone incorporates the sunflower, a common symbol of the period. While the rosette is somewhat generic, the sunflower obviously represents a specific flower. The carving on this stone is more skilled than that on the Lansing stone, as evidenced in the subtle modeling of the surface of the face. Although the wings are more linear than the face, the short horizontal cuts in them form a pleasing pattern. The head, however, is somewhat geometric and stylized and lacks the human presence found in some of the other images.

Although the Elsie Ten Eyck stone is also dated 1791, it marks an interesting development. The wings have disappeared, leaving a disembodied head framed by foliage ending with two rosettes. The rosettes are repeated in the finials. Again the head is geometric and stylized. The modeling of the surface of the cheeks and the chin is very slight, and the head is surrounded by a border of even width. The stem and leaves create an elegant line, running from each finial above the head. A raised border forms an outline of the leaves with no real rendering of their surfaces. Obviously the carver of this stone exhibits a high degree of skill in the use of his tools; the lines are crisp and straight. But there is little understanding of or concern for the carving of convincing surfaces.

The most fascinating stone in this group is the Snyder stone (1789), signed Z. Collins Sculp. Zerubbabel Collins was one of the most productive, highly skilled, and better documented of the early gravestone carvers. Born in 1733 in Columbia, Connecticut, Collins was the son of a stone carver known as the Collins Master. When his father died in 1759, Zerubbabel inherited the Collins Master's "working tools." In her *Gravestones of Early New England*, Harriet Forbes (1927) states that, although Collins learned carving from his father, his designs were his own.

> He seems to have been a carpenter and cabinet maker as well as a stone-cutter and he may have adapted some of his furniture designs to his stone carving. Or possibly some embroidered bed set or curtains or even a gay Chinese or Indian print or tapestry may have pleased his fancy. The sea captains were bringing home many treasures from distant lands--the 'trees of life' bore curious flowers not unlike those he carved.

The young Collins moved to Shaftsbury, Vermont, in 1778, where he carved a large number of stones until his death in 1797.

Collins is credited with reversing the relationship between figure and ground. Whereas in most stones of the period the head was sunken into the stone, Collins carved his forms so they emerged from the surface, as seen in the Joseph Lytell stone (1793), located in the Salem, New York, graveyard. The surfaces are modeled with great sensitivity and are raised from the surface of the stone. Collins developed a style for the winged head which changed very little over time: the eyes protrude, the nose is angled, the mouth is but a faint line, and a band surrounds the top of the head, ending in a small curl at either end. The surface of the face is delicately modeled. He also established a unique shape for his stones, which consist of a large central arch with two or three semicircles protruding from each side. This shape is unique to

Collins; his stones are easily recognized from a distance.

While Collins' stones are consistent in shape and in the carving of the winged head, they exhibit great variety in the decoration around the head and on the borders along the lower portion of the stones. He makes use of a rich array of fantastic fruits and flowers such that no two stones are exactly alike. In the Jane Adams stone in Salem, New York, scroll-like forms under the head end in imaginative blossom-like forms with leaf forms arching over the head. On the David Edger stone (1792) in Salem, New York, a sunflower emerges from a fantastic pod carved under the winged head. The shapes over the head are now more scroll-like. Scroll forms also surround the epitaph in the lower part of the stone. On the Robert Blair stone (1794) at Bennington, Vermont, the form beneath the head becomes a basket containing fantastic foliage.

On the Edward Long stone (1792) in Salem, New York, we see the scroll-like forms beneath the head and smaller scroll-like forms surrounding the epitaph. Of greater interest here is the carving of the price beneath the lower border--12 dollars. Although other carvers would occasionally specify the price, it was generally carved in pence on the back of the stone. In this case, the inscription, Pr. 12 Dollars, is very large, nearly as large as the lettering on the epitaph. Carved below the border, it may have been intended to fall below the ground when the stone was set. The inscription is so close to the border, however, that in order to cover it, the bottom border would have had to be set at ground level.

Another interesting aspect of this inscription is its relationship to the Coinage Act. Passed in 1792, the Coinage Act established the mint and determined which coins were to be in circulation. Curiously, the first dollars were struck in 1794, two years after the date inscribed on the Edward Long stone. This might be explained by the fact that stones were sometimes erected a year or two after the burial.

Another stone carved by Collins is located in the Albany Rural Cemetery. Although it is very worn, those characteristics typical of Collins' carving are still evident: the unique shape of the stone, the style of the winged head, and the rich foliage. The most unusual aspect of this stone is the signature. Unlike the price on the Edward Long stone, which is carved below the lower border, the signature is carved inside the border. Clearly, the signature was meant to be seen by all. More curious than the signature itself is Collins' reference to himself as a sculptor, a term generally reserved for the fine artist. In eighteenth century documents, as well as current writings about early gravestones, these craftsmen are referred to as stone carvers. Indeed, they were engaged in a trade and were producing a product for a buying public. Having learned their craft in their fathers' workshops, they did not belong to that elite group trained in the academies to produce art. This raises a number of interesting questions about the relationship between crafts and art. Certainly the existence of this controversy cannot be denied in the twentieth century world of art. One cannot help but wonder, considering Collins' self-adopted title, if this issue was not also relevant in rural Vermont in 1789.

The last stone we will consider is the William Woods stone (1799). At first glance it would appear to be a Collins stone; the shape of the stone, the style of the head, and the carving of the foliage are all characteristic of Collins' work. The wings, however, are quite different. On all of Collins' stones, the wings are horizontal with slightly upturned edges. On the William Woods stone, the wings are turned down in a vertical direction. Moreover, the stone is dated 1799, two years after Collins' death. In an article published in 1976 in "Puritan Gravestone Art," William Harding reveals that Collins had an apprentice named Benjamin Dyer, who was 19 years old at the time of Collins' death in 1797. Dyer left little in the way of a legacy, as, according to Harding, 1801 marked Dyer's transition from the winged head to the new, more favored urns and willows. Although Dyer continued to carve gravestones until his death in 1856 few can be identified after 1810. With the disappearance of stylistic differences among gravestone carvers, gravestone carving was transformed from a folk craft into an industry.

The eighteenth century winged head gravestones found in the Albany Rural Cemetery represent an important part of our heritage. The Albany Common Councils of 1789 and 1801 are to be commended for ensuring the preservation of these headstones and the remains of our early Albany citizens. Many cities and towns have lost their old burial grounds with the pressures of a growing population. We are fortunate to have retained these remnants of an early American and Albanian folk art. We should do everything possible to see that these stones are preserved.

Patricia Clahassey, *professor of art at the College of St. Rose, has been working in the field of art education for many years. As part of her investigation of the development of imagery, she researched the imagery of gravestones. As an art historian and educator, Ms. Clahassy has given talks on gravestones to many groups in the Albany area.*

Winged Gravestones Cited in Albany Rural Cemetery

Name	Date	Carver
Unnamed	1728	
Harmanus Wendall	1756	
David Van der Heyden	1770	
Gertrude Van der Heyden	1784	T. Brown
Harriet Roseboom	1787	
Jacob Lansing	1791	
Sarah Ten Eyck	1791	
Elsie Ten Eyck	1791	
Mrs. Femmitie(?) Snyder	1789	Zerubbabel Collins
William Woods	1799	Benjamin Dyer

Works Cited and Further Readings

Alden, Timothy. *A Collection of American Epitaphs and Inscriptions.* New York: Arno Press, 1977.

Brown, Raymond Lamont. *A Book of Epitaphs.* New York: Taplinger Publications Company, 1969.

Coffin, Margaret. *Death in Early America.* Nashville, Tennessee: Thomas Nelson, Inc., 1976.

Forbes, Harriette Merrifield. *Gravestones of Early New England.* New York: Da Capo Press, 167.

Ludwig, Allan. *Graven Images: New England Stonecarving and Its Symbols, 1650-1815.* Middletown, Connecticut: Wesleyan University, 1966.

Mann, Thomas Clifford. *Over Their Dead Bodies: Yankee Epitaphs and History.* Brattleboro, VT: S. Greene Press, 1962.

Markers, The Annual Journal of the Association for Gravestone Studies. Vol. 1. 1979-80.

Puritan Gravestone Art. The Dublin Seminar for New England Folklife Annual Proceedings. 1976.

Tashjian, Dickran and Ann. *Memorials for Children of Change: The Art of Early New England Stone Carving.* Middletown, Connecticut: Wesleyan University Press, 1974.

Walcott, John. "Albany's Dutch Stones." *Washington Park Spirit* (29 July 1971).

Wallis, Charles Langworthy. *Stories on Stone: American Epitaphs, Grave and Humorous.* New York: Dover Publications, 1973.

For More Information

Association for Gravestone Studies

Carol Perkins, membership secretary
1233 Cribb Street, Apartment 204
Toledo, OH 43612

Rosalee F. Oakley, executive secretary
46 Plymouth Road
Needham, MA 02192

Gertrude Van der Heyden monument, 1784, Albany Rural Cemetery.

William Woods monument, 1799, Albany Rural Cemetery.

Femmitie Snyder's monument, 1789, Albany Rural Cemetery.

Albany Rural Cemetery (1841) developed from the first wave of interest in a new kind of cemetery that arose after Bostonians established Mount Auburn Cemetery in 1831. Up to that time, Americans had buried their dead in modest, nearby town or church graveyards. With increasing urbanization and burgeoning populations, these burial grounds proved inadequate and unhygienic. Furthermore, Romantic ideas of nature were influencing the thinking and feelings of Americans. As a result, they believed that Nature conveyed God's gifts and messages and could soothe mourners, inspire the disheartened, and teach proper conduct to the young. The new, rural cemetery was inevitable, for such a cemetery would have plantings to cheer the eye, trees to attract the soothing songs of the birds, and hills, valleys, ponds, or streams to provide picturesque views. This new kind of burial ground provided for the emotional and spiritual needs of the living as well as respectful burial of the dead. Although a century and a half have passed, Americans maintain the same expectations for a proper burial place: They still want a lovely landscape and carefully groomed grounds.

Albany played an important role in the Rural Cemetery Movement for reasons that had little to do with cemeteries: It had one of the earliest horticultural societies in the United States; Albany was also important to the Rural Cemetery Movement because it was a publishing center. The Honorable Jesse Buel, incidentally, first president of the horticultural society, printed an agricultural and horticultural magazine that promoted rural cemeteries and encouraged a scientific approach to attractive and productive planting in farms, gardens, and cemeteries. *The Horticulturist*, a magazine that began publishing in 1846, became the medium through which Andrew Jackson Downing, America's first landscape architect, praised rural cemeteries and used their popularity to urge the creation of public parks.

CEMETERIES FOR THE DEAD AND LIVING

Barbara Rotundo

This chapter deals with what historians call the rural cemetery movement. Here, the natural country setting provides beauty for the eye and inspiration for the soul. Of course, many rural cemeteries today are located in built-up areas. A whole new set of ideas about life, death, and nature lay behind this changed setting, and this new attitude toward what a cemetery should be and look like. I want to provide background for the establishment in 1841 of Albany's rural cemetery, which began in what is now Menands. In checking the one fact connecting Albany with the beginning of the rural cemetery movement in 1831, however, I discovered a significant new pattern of information which changed my interpretation of the movement. Therefore, I want to cover the complex group of trends, ideas, and events influencing American thinking in the 1830s and the cemeteries which came about as a result. Then I will retrace with you my recent reading, to share with you the pleasure, even exhilaration, of scholarly humanistic research which leads to new facts or new relationships between old facts.

First, we must consider the relevant conditions and events in the United States in 1830. The population was growing rapidly, and the shift from rural to urban areas had already begun. Surrounded by bustling commerce, old graveyards lacked adequate space, and while conditions in New World cities never reached the extremes of London and Paris, improper burial practices were causing serious public health concerns. The obvious response to crowding was the establishment of new burial grounds on the outskirts of town. Fortunately, other concerns forced people to see beyond this simplistic solution, which, at best, would have been a mere stopgap measure. Americans were learning to think big. Only the United States, they proudly said, could declare itself independent and force its former rulers to sign peace treaties. They knew they would soon have great cities, and they foresaw the need for large spaces out in the country to accommodate a rapidly growing population.

Early cemetery founders were also conscious of another need. As commercial interests pressed for more space, old graves were moved or built over. Thus, the idea of a permanent resting place was on their minds.

Cemetery founders experienced a feeling for family closeness which accompanied the transition from an agricultural society of villages and towns to one in which commerce and industry stimulated the growth of large impersonal cities. Few families still lived on family farms, and none knew the grandparents or married children of their neighbors. These new conditions increased the demand for privacy in the home, glorified the role of the mother as the keeper and shaper of high moral character, and magnified the desire for public identification with other members of the family. If a Victorian father (bear in mind he was the god-like figure who provided for all) could purchase a large cemetery plot where all his descendants, and perhaps his parents and unmarried sisters as well, would be buried together, he could emphasize the closeness of this group in its separation from others, and the community within its structure would be obvious to the passer-by. The developments which ensued came as a surprise to those who had sponsored the rural cemetery movement. After purchasing large family plots (the standard lot was 300 square feet), owners would proceed to erect a central family monument, often before a single burial had taken place. They planted trees, shrubs, and flowers to ornament the grounds, and enclosed the whole with a cast-iron fence; over the fence they trained vines or climbing roses. Although the separation implied privacy, the fact that the fences were only waist high shows that public recognition or observation was important to the family. Owners also placed rustic benches and flower-filled urns on their lots, conveying the idea that their cemetery lots were an extension of the gardens surrounding their homes.

Ultimately, the concept of the cemetery as a garden gave way to one of a landscape filled with hundreds of private gardens. By the Civil War, twenty or thirty years after the founding of these cemeteries, cemetery boards were discouraging the installation of fences and hedges. This was true not only because of the visual impression of clutter and disunity created by fences and hedges, but because, with the passing of time, the maintenance problem in the new type of cemetery had come to light. When families died out or living relatives moved away, fences lost their protective coating of paint, rusted, and fell to the ground. Bushes grew large and shapeless. These maintenance problems led to yet another innovation connected with the rural cemetery movement-- the payment for perpetual care. Originally, cemetery directors had expected lot owners to care for their own plots, while general funds were used for the upkeep of roads and the ornamental grounds surrounding the entrance, and for chapels soon to be built. At first, the boards offered perpetual care contracts only to those who wanted them, though by the end of the century most cemeteries required perpetual care contracts for every new lot sold. These contracts rarely covered the care of stones or special paintings. Furthermore, they were calculated with no expectation of inflation. One might well imagine the havoc inflation has caused to perpetual care funds. Carefully managed cemeteries, such as the Albany Rural Cemetery, see to it that lawns are mowed and roads maintained. Rarely, however, do they have funds for the labor-intensive care of tricky areas, such as the steep banks of the ravines in Albany Rural.

Let us return from this digression to the early days of the rural cemetery movement in the 1830s and 1840s. Actually, the three problems the rural cemetery was expected to solve--overcrowding, the absence of guaranteed permanent burial, and failure to provide lots large enough for burying different generations of the same family--had satisfactorily been addressed by a new cemetery some years before. In 1798 a group of citizens organized the New Haven Cemetery, known today as the Grove Street Cemetery. Standing on the border of the Yale Campus, this cemetery attracted many lot owners, though it attracted no imitators. No other city tried to copy the New Haven plan. Obviously some element was lacking, but was present in Mount Auburn at the inauguration of the rural cemetery movement in 1831. Mount Auburn's example lit a fire of enthusiasm for rural cemeteries which then broke out all over the settled East, as though by spontaneous combustion.

The missing ingredient might be called romanticism, that set of ideas influencing educated men and women all over the western world. Romanticism encompassed several ideas which have a direct connection with the unique aspects of the rural or garden cemetery. For such romantic writers as England's Coleridge and Wordsworth and America's Emerson and Bryant, God appeared to mankind through nature. Nature inspired men and women, teaching them all they needed to know. Although death was natural, those who mourned a loved one found consolation, compensation, and a reminder of happy memories in nature. English poets writing melancholy poems in the eighteenth century about death and burial were so numerous that they are now referred to as the Graveyard School. The best known poem, perhaps, is Thomas Gray's "Elegy in a Country Churchyard."

Certain conventions characteristic of Romantic painters had an influence on the rural cemetery movement. American painters, more specifically the Hudson River School, believed nature was most beautiful when it offered a varied landscape combined with picturesque irregularity. Nature could have nothing to do with the monotony of a straight line or the harsh sharpness of a right angle. Artists might improve on nature, but the feeling was they should not impose on it such manmade geometry. Believing the highest kind of beauty was sublime, they found this beauty in awesome, distant mountains, or in the mystery of what was only half visible in the midst of a storm or under dim moonlight. They liked to incorporate water in nature scenes to reflect the beauty of nature, and they often used the skeleton of a dead tree to frame one side of a scene.

This description of romanticism is no more exhaustive than is the mention of the changing attitude toward family relationships. Entire books have been written on these subjects. I have raised the concept of romanticism as a crucial connection with the rural cemetery movement only to demonstrate what was lacking in the early New Haven Cemetery. Sitting on a level square of land and laid out in a neat, careful pattern of straight roads, paths and plots, with four right angles as corners, the New Haven Cemetery was both clean and efficient. It did nothing, however, to soothe the viewer or raise the spirits. Only the rural cemetery achieved that effect.

The romantic attitude toward nature held that there could be no better place to bury one's dead than in the beauty of the countryside, where the whisper of the leaves, the murmur of the brook, and the melody of the bird would offer encouragement, inspiration, and solace to the disconsolate mourner. (It is difficult to avoid the seductive power of the romanticist's tone and vocabulary, and it is interesting to note that much of the language of the modern funeral director has descended directly from dedication speeches and cemetery guidebooks.)

The words and deeds of the men and women who founded cemeteries in the 1830s and 1840s contain a hidden message. The simple change from graveyard or burying ground, emphasizing the disposal of the corpse, to cemetery, derived from a Greek word meaning to sleep and thus emphasizing a gentle end to life, reflects a new and very different concern for the needs and sensibilities of those left behind. Calvinism--whether the Congregationalism of New England or the Presbyterianism centered in Princeton, New Jersey--taught that men and women prepared themselves for death all their lives. If counted among the elect, one's death represented the attainment of the ineffable state of divine life with God. The alternative was condemnation to the eternal agonies of hell. Convictions about heaven and hell were weakening in the nineteenth century; the majority of social and intellectual leaders who believed in the importance of good moral character, rather than a particular theology, wanted people to remember God's benevolence rather than his awful power. The cemetery was intended not to cover up death, nor to avoid the dead, as some modern writers have suggested. Rather, it was a place to remind us of the divine goodness which gave us nature for the consolation of our inevitable losses.

In preparing the land for cemeteries, founders followed the romantic principle of cooperation with nature, rather than trying to control or subdue it. They dammed brooks, for example, to make ponds with curving shorelines.

Cemetery founders chose sites with varied topography and plant life, seeking a mixture of woods, fields, and flowering hillsides. They laid out paths and roads in accordance with the natural contours of the land. Cemetery planners were interested in creating a flowing landscape with picturesque views and statues, and temples resembling those of the famous estates they had read about or visited in England.

An important influence on these eighteenth century manmade landscapes, as well as on later American romantic painters, was the French artist, Claude Lorraine, who worked in the second half of the seventeenth century. Lorraine painted landscapes which generally provided a glimpse of classical architecture, such as a ruined arch or column. Such continental art, mostly from France and Italy, shaped the vision of eighteenth century Englishmen and nineteenth century cemetery designers. The contrast of nature's greenery with the marble temples of antiquity had tremendous appeal. This combination appears in many cemeteries today.

People enjoyed and continue to enjoy visiting rural cemeteries. Throughout the nineteenth century, transportation companies set up routes that would pass the cemetery gates. They even ran special excursion trips to cemeteries on Sundays. Guidebooks to such cemeteries as Mount Auburn in Cambridge, Massachusetts, Greenwood in New York, and Laurel Hill in Philadelphia went through many editions. Notice both famous cemeteries as well as the myriad small cemeteries usually have names reflecting an interest in nature.

In addition to the beauty of the grounds,

the exuberance of Victorian monuments attracts many people to the old cemeteries today. By the 1850s, purchasers of monuments were reacting against the restraint of the classical willow and urn design. Since the growing network of railroads made the transportation of large blocks of marble feasible, patrons of the new generation of carvers could indulge in any number of towering stones and three-dimensional sculptures. Especially popular was the realistic detail carved in stone: flower petals, folds in drapery, or the feathers of angels' wings.

The broken column, the cut down tree, and even the broken flower stem were popular symbols of death, and a shock of wheat represented the harvest of a full life. Sculptures of human figures, whether portraits or stylized representations, incorporated realistic detail. Although tools of trades and professions were a frequent occurrence, few were incorporated into the design as winningly as the firehose framing a stone at Greenlawn, Columbus, Ohio. A Cave Hill stone offers a pun with the popular streetcar conductor reaching his terminal. Many stones, like one from Newton, Massachusetts, commemorate a literal belief in the gates of heaven.

Albany's connection with the beginning of the rural cemetery movement centers around the Honorable Jesse Buel. Apprentice to a Rutland, Vermont, printer at 14, Buel moved from one town to another along the Hudson River until he finally settled in Albany in 1813, where he started the *Albany Argus*. Because the postal service carried newspapers very cheaply, in the interest of diffusing knowledge essential to a democracy, thousands of small rural newspapers sprang up all over the country. Albany, however, had more than its share of printing offices and newspapers, opening the first printing press outside New York City in 1771. Printing was a major enterprise in the city by 1828, and in 1850 there were 300 employees in nineteen Albany print shops. Buel developed an interest in farming and a missionary-like zeal for the reform of agricultural practices and for the cultivation of fruit trees and attractive gardens. After selling the *Albany Argus*, Buel created a model farm and a commercial nursery on the Great Western Turnpike. In 1834, he began weekly publication of *The Cultivator*. Its motto, "To improve the soil and the mind," was Buel's personal motto as well. Just before his death in 1839, Buel completed a book on modern farming at the request of the Massachusetts Board of Education, of which Horace Mann was executive secretary.

After Buel's death, Luther Tucker moved from Rochester to Albany, where he merged the *Genesee Farmer* (which he had been publishing since 1831) with *The Cultivator*, thereby perpetuating Buel's interests and policies. In 1846 Tucker established a monthly magazine, *The Horticulturist*, with Andrew Jackson Downing as editor. Now, while the names Jesse Buel and Luther Tucker are very likely unfamiliar, Andrew Jackson Downing is known to many as America's first native landscape architect and as a very influential man in all matters pertaining to horticulture and rural taste. Since Downing's home was in Newburgh, I had always assumed that *The Horticulturist*, which was the leading magazine of its kind, was published in New York City, but the lesson is to never underestimate the importance of Albany.

Downing is significant to this discussion because of the praise he offered rural cemeteries in his monthly lead articles. He went so far as to use the popularity of visits to these cemeteries (amounting to thousands of people annually) as the basic argument in his campaign for public parks. After his early death, others successfully completed Downing's campaign for New York's famous Central Park and Albany's Washington Park, leaving millions indebted to the rural cemetery movement.

You might think that Buel, Tucker, and Downing make a rather tenuous connection, but Buel is responsible for yet another source of support to the rural cemetery movement. Buel was the founding president of the Albany Horticultural Society, in January, 1829. Two months after he wrote to Boston friends, urging them to start a similar society, the Massachusetts Horticultural Society was founded. The Massachusetts Society held title to Mount Auburn Cemetery land for four years, standing behind the pioneering experiment as a reassuring guarantee of its performance. In my reading of Jesse Buel's weekly *The Cultivator*, I noticed the frequent recurrence of certain names as officers of agricultural or horticultural organizations, who would write reports of new developments in farming or gardening and of exhibits at Horticultural Society shows. According to Henry Phelps' *History of Albany Rural Cemetery*, these same people accounted for most of the organizing committee. Cemetery historians have always perceived an interest in horticulture, landscaping, and exotic trees of rural cemeteries. This Albany coincidence, however, suggests that Horticultural Societies are of greater importance than earlier suspected.

A charming coat of arms was designed for *The Cultivator* by Alexander Walsh of Lansingburgh, north of Troy. Walsh's 1833 speech has been read before the New York Horticultural Society in an attempt to persuade the society to create a rural cemetery. Research on the Albany Rural Cemetery has demonstrated an unquestionable link between horticulture and the rural cemetery. No doubt the same would prove true of Dalewood Cemetery in Troy.

Barbara Rotundo, associate professor of English at SUNYA, first became interested in cemeteries as an academic pursuit when she was working on her doctoral thesis on Annie Fields. She has published extensively on cemeteries, including studies of the rural cemetery movement, and a history of Mt. Auburn Cemetery, which she visited and studied extensively while writing her doctoral dissertation. She has also visited most of the garden cemeteries east of the Mississippi River and has a vast slide collection from her visits. Dr. Rotundo has degrees from Mount Holyoke, Cornell University, and Syracuse University.

Further Readings

Bender, Thomas. *Toward An Urban Vision: Ideas and Institutions in Nineteenth-Century America.* Lexington: University Press of Kentucky, 1975.

Benson, Albert Emerson. *History of the Massachusetts Horticultural Society.* Boston: Printed for the Society, 1929.

Downing, Andrew Jackson. "Public Cemeteries and Gardens." *The Horticulturist* 4 (1848): 9-12.

Fuller, Wayne E. *The American Mail.* Chicago: University of Chicago Press, 1972.

Hedrick, Ulysses P. *A History of Horticulture in America to 1860.* New York: Oxford University Press, 1950.

Hix, John. *The Glass House.* Cambridge: MIT Press, 1974.

Lancaster, R. Kent. "Green Mount: The Introduction of the Rural Cemetery into Baltimore." *Maryland Historical Magazine.* 74 (1978): 62-79.

Phelps, Henry P. *Albany Rural Cemetery: Its Beauties and Its Memories.* Albany: Phelps and Kellogg, 1893.

Rotundo, Barbara. "Mount Auburn Cemetery: A Proper Boston Institution." *Harvard Library Bulletin* 22 (1974): 268-279.

Schmitt, Peter J. *Back to Nature: The Arcadian Myth in Urban America.* New York: Oxford University Press, 1969.

Stilgoe, John R. *Common Landscapes of America, 1580-1845.* New Haven: Yale University Press, 1982.

"But only God can make a tree." The paper bark maple, Mt. Auburn Cemetery, has long inspired sculptors.

Marketing memories, one gardener's advertisement.

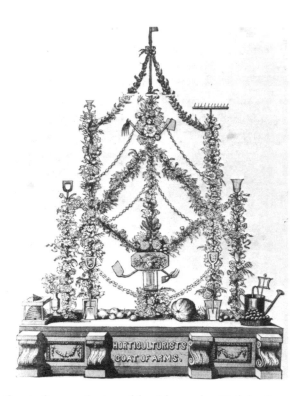

Coat of arms designed by Alexander Walsh of Lansingburgh for The Cultivator.

Inspired by the rustic tree above, sculptor carved naturalistic monument stone.

As the nineteenth century began to sentimentalize death and to recognize hygienic problems associated with death, the rural cemetery replaced that of the family, church, and synagogue. Rather, family and church plots were allotted in pleasantly wooded areas outside of the city limits but close enough for visits by relatives and friends. The rural cemetery movement reflected society's attitudes towards death, and beautiful hills, glades, and valleys became final resting places for loved ones.

The rural cemetery became so popular that civic groups began planning similar "garden parks" in the city for enjoyment and landscape gardening. Thus, many centrally located parks owe their existence to rural cemeteries.

Rural cemeteries were often a showcase for the artist and sculptors of the day, and funerary art became highly developed. The Albany Rural Cemetery epitomized the heights that both landscape gardening and artistic sculptures attained. It's "Angel of the Sepulchre" by Erastus Dow Palmer is a fine example of cemetery art done by one of the outstanding sculptors of the day.

CEMETERIES AS CULTURAL EXPERIENCES

Suzanne Roberson

Burial customs reveal a great deal about the cultural attitudes of a particular society. Despite its everlasting inevitability, death has been alternately exalted or ignored throughout the history of mankind. Funerary art and architecture serve as powerful indicators of social, religious and artistic trends and may form the only existing record of cultural attitudes. Indeed, artifacts of death are important historical sources, particularly for ancient times. While the forms and symbols of funerary architecture have endured throughout the ages, the ideas and sentiments expressed by them have varied.

Many monuments are balanced or geometrical in design, reflecting the eternal repose of the body. The pyramid, drum, cone, rectangular house, tomb, and obelisk date back to ancient times. Many tombs were modeled after the domestic architecture of the period, underlining the concept of the tomb as a permanent resting place, and accounting for the splendor in its creation. In ancient times the dead were provided with great domestic comforts. No subsequent culture has expended as much effort and cost in the construction, upkeep and protection of its mausolea as did the ancient Egyptians. This was practiced both to commemorate the dead and to provide comfortable surroundings which would prevent the dead from troubling the living.

Much of the etymology of funerary architecture originates with the ancients as well. Sarcophagus means "flesh-eater," derived from limestone coffins which quickly dissolved flesh. Mausoleum is derived from the monumental tomb erected for King Mausolos in 353 B.C.

The Christian church later provided the dead with a house of eternal rest. Early Christian tombs were altarlike and, in compliance with Roman law, were placed in underground cemeteries or catacombs. Eminent Christians were subsequently interred under churches, or in churchyards. The church became the guardian of the dead, and burial in consecrated ground became requisite. Eternal rest and interment within the church, however, were privileges reserved for the wealthy, who continually vied with one another in the design and construction of their tombs. The use of sarcophagi and canopies was borrowed from pagan customs. The Christian doctrine of the resurrection of the body led to the encapsulation of the corpse in a coffin, though again, until recent times this was a privilege often denied the poor. Nor were the bones of the common man granted everlasting repose, for burial plots were typically available on a limited lease basis only. Churchyards were regularly cleared of bones, which were then placed in charnel houses.

Funerary art flourished in the Middle Ages. Tombs were elaborately decorated with Christian symbols and Gothic motifs. Serenity, balance, and exquisite detail were the hallmarks of medieval funerary art. Medieval tombs serve both as records of the costume, armor, heraldry, sculpture, metal work, and architecture of the time, and as examples of superb craftmanship. Plague had a great effect on the design of funerary architecture as it claimed the lives of craftsmen; tombs became much plainer in detail.

The development of humanism during the Renaissance greatly altered burial customs and granted the individual a permanent resting place. Churches and churchyards were thronged with corpses.

The concept of separate burial grounds originated not in Europe, but in southern colonial America and India--primarily for health considerations. As conditions in churchyards grew worse, concern for the health of the living became a prime consideration. Cities grew rapidly after the Industrial Revolution. Large cholera and yellow fever epidemics and consequent miasmatic movements early in the nineteenth century resulted in the organization of committees and the production of numerous reports addressing the disgraceful conditions of church burial grounds. The loss of 16,000 lives to yellow fever in New York City in 1822 prompted one observer to comment

What better contrivance to generate yellow fever, for instance, was ever set up than what was permitted to exist unmolested last year in the city of New York?

Take for the focus of this infection the graveyard of Trinity Church, saturated with dissolved semi-liquid human flesh, oozing from every pore, and the incumbent atmosphere filled with noxious effluvia, concurring with the air of the city, contaminated by unexampled quantities of smoking filth, of fermenting, offensive animal and vegetable substances. The event was what might have been predicted; it was indeed foreseen with frightful apprehension, which were but too fully realized.

Change came slowly, hindered by a reluctant clergy, who stood to lose significant revenues garnered through burial fees. By the middle of the nineteenth century, however, extramural burial became common, and large cemeteries were established on the outskirts of most major European and American cities.

Burial customs in America closely mirrored those of eighteenth century Europe. Grim symbolism garnished the crude stones marking individual plots on farms or in the churchyards and commons of towns. Graves were considered unattractive necessities to be avoided by the living. Individual family plots were lost and forgotten as lands changed hands and cities encroached on once private lands.

American attitudes toward death and burial also began to change. The word cemetery, meaning to put to sleep, replaced graveyard and burial ground, conveying the sense of the body being laid to rest rather than simply planted in the earth. As Washington Irving declared in his *Sketchbook*, "Why should we thus seek to clothe death with unnecessary terrors. . .The grave should be surrounded by everything that might inspire tenderness and veneration for the dead, or that might win the living to virtue." This statement was representative of the changing conception of death and burial in America.

Just as the development of the rural cemetery was influenced by many factors, so did its establishment in turn have an effect on society. Burial customs changed, and the rural cemetery was in large part responsible for the evolution of municipal parks, such as New York City's Central Park in 1856.

The landscape gardening movement was a minor consideration in the planning of rural cemeteries. Moral, social, and medical issues were of primary importance. The cemetery was intended to instruct and inculcate morality. Monuments were designed to provide a sense of historical continuity to the young country; their forms and symbols took on a patriotic flavor commensurate with the ideals of a republic. Greek revival monuments appropriately expressed these ideas.

As cemeteries developed, funerary architecture became quite eclectic. Christian symbols, such as the cross, began to appear in Protestant cemeteries. Urns were popular through the 1840s, and the period prior to the Civil War saw an Egyptian revival. Sphinxes, lotus flowers, winged globes, banded cylinders, reversed torches, and serpents devouring their tails were all Egyptian symbols of death commonly found on gateways and gravestones.

As monuments became increasingly artistic, they had a greater influence on the development of sculpture in America. The winged female figure is common to rural cemeteries, as is the use of lambs and statues of children to mark the graves of the young. Yet another characteristic was the fencing of family plots--generally with ornamental ironwork--revealing the possessive nature of Americans. The excessive use of fencing gave rise to the lawn cemetery after the Civil War, altering the concept of the rural cemetery forever.

Albany was a prosperous, rapidly expanding city of 35,000 when the Albany Rural Cemetery was established in 1844. Burial conditions in the city were as overcrowded and impermanent as anywhere else. As Phelps states, "The living were doing well enough; it was time to think of the dead. . .For 150 years the city's dead had no abiding rest." Mortuary reform in both Europe and America influenced the decision to create a rural cemetery for the Albany region. Mount Auburn in Cambridge, Massachusetts was, specifically cited as an example for the planning of the Albany Rural Cemetery. Many sites were considered; a proper location was to be "so elevated as to afford a bold and enlivening prospect. . .and presenting the facilities that will enable Art to remedy whatever Nature may have left defective." Curiously, the elevated land east of Greenbush was considered, but politics intervened and the great Albany-Troy bridge fight discouraged its selection.

On 7 October 1844 the grounds for the Albany Rural Cemetery were consecrated. A large procession made its way from North Pearl Street to the cemetery. As the *Albany Argus* reported, "The solemn, dirge-like music. . .the gorgeous foliage, which at this season distinguishes our rural scenery--the romantic wildness of the place itself--and the large concourse assembled--all conspired to give to the scene an impressive and sublime character."

The address given by Daniel Barnard was in the typically florid language of the day. The speech stressed the Christian belief in the resurrection of the body and the growing concern that the dead be provided with a place of eternal repose.

> A serious obligation and duty rest on the living. . .It is not their own convenience merely that they are to consult in regard to the proper disposal of the dead. There is a duty to the dead to be considered, and the interests of humanity, the interests of religion, and the interests of immortality seem to be involved in it. . .The grounds. . .have been selected for a cemetery. . .with a special view to their natural beauty, and their capability of improvement after the manner of landscape gardening. . .What pleasant hills and knolls--what bushy dells-- what trees and groves--what silvery, soft-toned, gentle, living waters, are here--and what expressive silence-- what religious repose!

It was further stressed that whenever necessary, art would take a hand in shaping nature, an attitude characteristic of the pervading Romanticism of the time.

The cemetery was declared open to all classes and races; it was to be placed where all enmities would be left behind. The picturesque landscape would be a refuge to the sorrowful, a consolation to the living. "The gloom which usually surrounds and settles over the grave will be here dissipated, and the sacred spot where the remains of the loved and lost are deposited will be associated only with objects and accompaniments the most attractive and beautiful."

The Albany Rural Cemetery is distinguished by its numerous sculptures, many of which are of extremely high quality. The familiar "Angel of the Sepulchre" is only one of Erastus Dow Palmer's fine sculptures to be found in the cemetery. The cemetery contains many rich examples of Victorian funerary art, which serve as "records in stone of the feelings and attitudes about death."

Typically, the cemetery was intended to instruct. "We may expect this place to become a great moral teacher; and many valuable lessons there are, that may be learned here--lessons of humility, of moderation, of charity, of contentment, of mercy, of peace--lessons touching nearly all that concerns life, touching death, and touching immortality." The sermons in the stones, the emblematic sculptures were to help guide the living in their toil, and keep them mindful of their own mortality.

Just as public opinion concerning burial came full circle from the attention paid it by the ancients to the powerful reformations of the nineteenth century, so the neglect characteristic of the seventeenth and eighteenth centuries has returned to present day attitudes. The cemetery in the nineteenth century had a great effect upon society's disposition toward death. Etlin states, "A society fashions its physical world to support and sustain its most cherished conviction and deepest feelings. . .The cemetery. . .did not simply mirror a society's understanding about death. The architecture of its landscape played a role in crystalizing nascent emotions and ideas." So perhaps may we allow the beautiful landscape and art of the Albany Rural Cemetery to reshape our current indifference and denial of death.

This holy ground beneath our feet,
These gently sloping hills above,
These silent glades and valleys sweet
Shall be the home of those we love.

-Hymn sung at the consecration
of the Albany Rural Cemetery

Suzanne Roberson, librarian at Capital Newspapers, was art librarian at the Albany Institute of History and Art. With degrees in art history and library science, she has used her background in many projects on the cultural environs of Albany.

Works Cited and Further Readings

Aries, Philippe. *The Hour of Our Death*. New York: Alfred A. Knopf, 1981.

Churchill, H.W. *Churchill's Guide Through the Albany Rural Cemetery*. Albany: Henry W. Churchill, 1857.

Coffin, Margaret M. *Death in Early America*. Nashville: Thomas Nelson, Inc., 1976.

Curl, James S. *A Celebration of Death*. New York: Charles Scribner's Sons, 1980.

The Victorian Celebration of Death. Detroit: The Partridge Press, 1972.

Etlin, Richard A. *The Architecture of Death*. Cambridge, Massachusetts: The Massachusetts Institute of Technology, 1984.

Fitzgerald, Edward. *A Hand Book for the Albany Rural Cemetery*. Albany: VanBenthuysen Printing House, 1871.

French, Stanley. "The Cemetery as Cultural Institution: The Establishment of Mount Auburn and the 'Rural Cemetery' Movement," *Death in America*. Philadelphia: University of Pennsylvania Press, 1974.

Jacobs, G. Walker. *Stranger Stop and Cast an Eye: A Guide to Gravestones and Gravestone Rubbing*. Brattleboro, Vermont: The Stephen Greene Press, 1973.

Ludwig, Allan I. *Graven Images: New England Stonecarving and its Symbols, 1650-1815*. Middletown, Connecticut: Wesleyan University Press, 1966.

Marion, John F. *Famous and Curious Cemeteries*. New York: Crown Publishers, 1977.

Morley, John. *Death, Heaven and the Victorians*. Pittsburgh: University of Pittsburgh Press, 1971.

Phelps, Henry P. *The Albany Rural Cemetery*. Albany: Phelps and Kellogg, 1893.

Rotundo, Barbara. "The Rural Cemetery Movement." *Essex Institute Historical Collections* 109 (July 1973): 231-240.

Wakin, B. Bertha. *To Rub or Not to Rub*. Woodstock, New York: B. Bertha Wakin, 1976.

Wasserman, Emily. *Gravestone Designs*. New York: Dover Publications, 1972

Palmer's Angel of the Sepulchre, Albany Rural Cemetery.

Anthropologists and archaeologists use data from cemeteries in collaboration with data taken from census records and other historical documents. They are now beginning to compare data they find in cemeteries with data gleaned from other sources. Data sources are often lost or destroyed, leaving little historic documentation. Cemeteries, with their carefully inscribed stones, provide valid information--barring acid rain, destruction, and vandalism.

Social scientists use cemeteries for demographic data for the study of life spans, ethnic settlements, and epidemics. Anthropologists use gravestone inscriptions to find facts on mortality, fertility, social and economic status, and all the topics mentioned above. Burial rites and customs are also topics that are of interest to the anthropologist and cemeteries demonstrate how families throughout the centuries treated their dead.

GONE HOME: CEMETERY INSCRIPTIONS

Richard Wilkinson

Burying grounds. Final resting places. Boot Hill. Whatever they are called, the places where we inter our loved ones, relatives, acquaintances, enemies, or others are special places for humans. I emphasize humans here, for we are in fact the only extant species on earth having cemeteries. Cemeteries had their beginnings in the remote past; perhaps as early as 50,000 years ago a group of people in the Dordogne Valley of France bade farewell to their loved ones, interring them in the floor of the cave where they had been living, accompanied by meager, yet presumably important, objects. These Neanderthals invented one of our most uniquely human activities. If the mere mention of burial rituals or mortuary behavior were not enough to remind you of anthropologists, certainly reference to the Neanderthals should. Anthropology is indeed concerned with both.

Historic demography is an area of research populated mainly by historians, particularly a relatively new breed known as social historians. But historic demography is much more than this; it is a meeting ground for a broad spectrum of people with varied interests. A visit to local libraries reveals a surprising number of people intently searching for ancestors. These people, unwittingly perhaps, are engaged in historic demography.

The involvement of historians in historic demography is relatively easy to understand. The social historian's interest in economic change, migration, family size, population size, premarital pregnancy, views on death, and almost limitless other topics flows naturally into the data base provided by historic demography. Now, I am not a historian; I am an anthropologist, and as such, I would like to represent anthropology's claim to a piece of the historic demography pie. I will discuss a variety of uses of mortality data within anthropology and provide some concrete examples of the utility of cemetery data for the reconstruction of demographic aspects of past populations. Before doing so, it is necessary to set the stage and to provide some definitions.

Because misconceptions are common, a definition of anthropology is a good starting point. Anthropology is essentially the study of human biological and cultural variation, pursued in both time and space. Anthropologists do not simply study rocks, strange people and fossils, despite the media's best efforts to portray us that way. In truth, anthropologists study an amazing variety of phenomena: the behavior of lemurs on Madagascar; the physiology of Tibetan mountain people, and of volunteer firemen in New York; and, of course, the make-up of rocks, strange people, and fossils. The cynical view might be that anthropology is whatever anthropologists do, when actually there is a method in the apparent madness. Essentially, we want to establish the differences among groups of people, viewed across space or through time, and the reasons for these differences. Some anthropologists are interested primarily in biological phenomena, others in cultural; the unifying thread seems to be a curiosity about the what, why, and how of being human, the ideal approach being the combination of biological and cultural data with inferences.

Since anthropology is usually defined ambitiously as the study of humankind, then mortuary behavior, being uniquely human, is clearly one of anthropology's oysters. The secular and sacred behaviors surrounding the death of a member of society are of intense interest to anthropologists, for these behaviors provide invaluable information about the society. Archaeologists, for example, analyze mortuary behavior to provide inferences about the social class system of a now extinct group. The basic assumption is that elements of mortuary behavior reflect the social persona of the deceased. Compare, for example, the apparent social status of a prehistoric Mexican who was buried accompanied by a plain pottery bowl, in a shallow grave under the floor of a house, with that of another individual in this society, interred in an underground tomb with pounds of gold and jade jewelry. Both the quantity and quality of the goods placed in the grave and the elaboration of the burying place inform us about the existence and magnitude of social stratification.

The discovery of a life-sized terra cotta army near Xi'an, China, serves as another example of an archaeological cornucopia in the realm of mortuary behavior. The army, consisting of hundreds of soldiers, horses, and chariots, and thousands of weapons, commemorates the death of China's first emperor. On the basis of this evidence alone, we can infer that the person honored by this burial ceremonialism occupied a social position far above that of those who built the army or modeled for it. We can also infer a great deal about the society itself. The archaeologist has a wide array of variables to use in his or her analysis, most of which are indicative of symbolic behavior, or are themselves symbolic. The orientation and position of the body, the quantity and quality of burial goods, the existence of special structures, the method of disposition of the mortal remains; all of these activities and many more are used by archaeologists to reconstruct aspects of a past society.

In much the same way, cultural anthropologists have utilized mortuary behavior among contemporary cultures, often concentrating on aspects of symbolic behavior. That cemeteries are indeed rich in symbolism is perhaps too obvious to deserve mention; they are, after all, symbolic of our concern with death. Better, they are symbolic of our concern with life after death. Perhaps nowhere is this made more obvious than in the simple declaration engraved on many tombstones from the years around 1900: Gone Home. I have included the two words in the title of this paper because it seems to be the most economical, concise, and pleasingly simple way of symbolizing one aspect of cemeteries. In a sense, "Gone Home" is a somewhat surprising epitaph for the culture that used it. The early Edwardians and holdover Victorians are best known for their fondness of flourish, whether in architecture, dress, or literature, and the simple declaration "Gone Home" is a counterpoint, at least. It would seem almost a sigh of relief, but one must be wary of allowing biases about the culture of the time to color interpretations. Before the "Gone Home" craze captured the imaginations of Capital District residents, another symbol, saying much the same thing, was popular. In the middle of the nineteenth century, obelisks began to appear in cemeteries in the Northeast and on the Atlantic Seaboard.

Obelisks provide us with excellent examples of the use of symbolism in cemeteries and of the reasons anthropologists are interested in cemeteries. In its form, the obelisk provides a clear indication of the direction of the afterworld. Its broad, clear surfaces provide ample space for more symbolic referents--words. Words explain the direction of the departed as he or she makes way toward the desired afterworld; words exhort the living to lead a life most likely to produce the desired end results; and words are designed to symbolize the life of the recently departed. This last aspect is important, as anthropologists are perhaps more concerned with the living than with the dead.

Design motifs on tombstones of the eighteenth century tell us more about the societies that selected them. Several years ago, two anthropologists, James Deetz and Ted Dethlefsen, completed a study of the changes which occurred with the use of death's heads as a design motif on tombstones. These changes were documented through time and space, providing a neat example of the movement of ideas from one group to another. In the case of death's heads, Deetz and Dethlefsen were able to trace the movement of ideas through New England and document the evolution of the motif itself. The change in the motif, from stark representations of skulls to angelic cherubs, provides a symbolic clue to the concomitant changes in the way death has been viewed.

What is perhaps less obvious in the study of changing design motifs is that movement of people is also documented by the tombstones. Migration is a process which has a major impact on the size, distribution, and composition of populations. As such it is a core element of demography. The tombstone study of Deetz and Dethlefsen is, therefore, of considerable interest to historic demographers.

The field of historic demography is populated by historians of several stripes (social historians, economic historians, local/regional historians), anthropologists of equally diverse leanings (ethnologists, archaeologists, biological anthropologists), specialists from other disciplines, and an army of "roots-seekers." Each of these camps is interested in different questions, and can therefore make use of different types of data. One of the lures of historic data for anthropologists is related to the types of human groups we prefer to study. These groups are often called anthropological populations, thereby confusing everyone save a few anthropologists. An anthropological population is a small group of people which is and has been relatively isolated from other groups, especially other groups with dramatically differing technologies, ideologies, and social organization. Because of their small size and isolation, such populations are simpler to study and more representative of human populations throughout most of our history than are the huge national populations of today. Hence, the stereotypical anthropologist studies some remote and seemingly irrelevant group of people; hence also the anthropological interest in historic populations, which tended to be small and isolated, at least by today's standards. By examining such isolated populations, we can attempt to understand their dynamics without the confounding effect of noise from larger, more complex societies. It could be argued that without understanding the simpler human societies, we have little hope of understanding today's highly complex societies.

Returning to the cemetery, tombstones can provide information about the movement of people, their attitudes towards death, and a great deal more. Since demography is the quantitative study of the processes affecting the size, growth, distribution, and composition of populations, and since the most important of these processes are fertility, mortality, and migration, the anthropologist looks to tombstones for information on these processes in past populations. It may be obvious that tombstones can provide information on mortality, and perhaps only slightly less obvious that information on fertility is furnished as well. As is usually the case, however, what is obvious may not be completely true. Certainly tombstones record mortality; hence the old saw, "How many dead people are there in this cemetery? All of them." Having spent quite a few hours working in cemeteries, I can attest to the fact that even old saws can miss the mark.

Conceding that a tombstone bears some relationship to death, a little thought might reveal that some tombstones do more than that. There are tombstones for people who have not yet died and for people who have died elsewhere; some tombstones serve several people; some people die without the benefit of tombstones; and some people are only minimally recognized by a tombstone (e.g., "His Wife"). Demographers, historic and otherwise, are interested in rates as well as the event or process itself. Therefore we need to be able to determine how many people died relative to how many people were living at some time. If we know, for instance, that 15 people were buried in a cemetery in 1866, it makes a great deal of difference whether there were 100 or 1000 people living in the area at the time. In one case, we have an epidemic; in the other, normal mortality in a reasonably healthy population.

Demographers also want to establish who is dying; here the major concern is the age and sex of the deceased. Age and sex specific mortality rates reveal much more about populations and their environments than do simple mortality rates. In the example above, it makes a great deal of difference whether the 15 deaths occurred among children, young adults or the elderly, and the gender of those dying is also informative. Historic demographers have documented relatively high mortality among women in the 20-30 age group in various locations in nineteenth century America. This in turn means that overall mortality among 20-30 year olds was high. If we did not know that it was the increase in female mortality that was causing the bulge in the death rate of this age group, we could never hope to understand the causes, which were related to women's work and were only indirectly influenced by problems associated with childbirth.

To get to causes for observed demographic events, we must have data sources far more accurate and plentiful than those provided by cemetery inscriptions. Very occasionally the tombstone itself gives some indication of the cause of mortality. Such tombstone evidence tends to be restricted to unusual deaths, such as drowning, or sometimes is a reflection of the idiosyncracies of the survivors. Such is the case of a tombstone in the cemetery in Deerfield, Massachusetts, marking the grave of a woman who died in childbirth. In addition to this statement of fact on the tombstone, there is also a bas-relief carving at the top of the stone, depicting a woman and a newborn baby in a coffin. Again, this is rare; the vast majority of deaths are of unknown cause, until we go beyond the cemetery data and into vital statistics.

Why bother with cemetery data at all, if written records are going to provide much better information? The answer, it turns out, depends on the time, place, and questions being asked of the data. Fifteen years ago, Ted Dethlefsen published a paper comparing data from late seventeenth and early eighteenth century tombstones in Massachusetts with corresponding written records relating to mortality. His analysis showed that the cemetery data was in fact superior to the written records in accurately representing the mortality experienced by this early American population. In this case, the key element is time; in the late seventeenth and early eighteenth centuries, record-keeping was haphazard at best, and people were much more likely to insure that their loved ones were commemorated in stone than they were to be visited by a literate record-keeper.

By the middle of the eighteenth century, death, birth, and marriage records in Massachusetts were kept with sufficient care that they surpass tombstones for accuracy and completeness. Massachusetts is, in fact, an historic demographer's nirvana because of the high quality of these vital records in all sections of the commonwealth. The situation in New York is not so propitious. Vital records are essentially nonexistent, and we are left with state and federal census figures, church records, and sporadic attempts to maintain vital statistics. It was just this paucity of written records and the existence of a seemingly ideal cemetery in this area which led me, if somewhat superficially, into the field of historic demography about five years ago.

I had two major questions which I hoped could be answered by cemetery data. One methodological question was essentially, To what extent is an historic cemetery representative of the mortality experienced by the population which had access to the cemetery? The second question is more theoretical: can cemetery data provide an indication of a major demographic change brought about by technological innovation? This question grows out of the concept of the demographic transition which postulates that the Industrial Revolution eventuated in a reduction in mortality, due to improved sanitation and education, without a concomitant reduction in fertility. The result was a substantial increase in population. The implied relationship among demographic processes and cultural processes--a biocultural interaction--is obvious, and thus there is anthropological interest in the phenomenon.

An event took place in the Capital District which seemed an ideal technological breakthrough of the type we might expect to have an effect on demographic processes. It occurred during the early to mid-nineteenth century at a time when the local population should have been experiencing relatively high mortality and fertility, and slight to moderate migration. That event was the opening of the Erie Canal and there is a fine rural cemetery used by the people most directly affected by the event, the Waterford Rural Cemetery. The Waterford area should have experienced a considerable increase in immigration from about 1820 onward, as workers would have been needed to build and later maintain the canal. We anticipated some reflection of this migration in the cemetery data, with tombstones indicating a distant birthplace, or an ethnic identity which would be strong, if there was circumstantial evidence that the person was not a Waterford native. In the Waterford Rural Cemetery, a small group of tomb-

stones of natives of Ireland fulfills this prediction.

The work on the historic demography of the Waterford area was done largely by Dr. Richard Norelli, whose doctoral dissertation addresses this issue: Norelli was unable to document the expected demographic transition in the Waterford area, at least in terms of decreasing mortality. If anything, mortality increased somewhat with the construction of the canal and related economic changes. It appears that the population was growing, due both to increased fertility and the effects of migration. Resultant crowding and poor sanitation gave rise to an increase in mortality. Norelli was able to locate an interesting reference to the increasing problems with sanitation in the form of an ordinance prohibiting the dumping of dead pigs in the canal. One presumes the ordinance arose from experience and not from general caution.

Unfortunately, the cemetery data create more questions than they answer. Was the rise in mortality, for example a real increase in deaths or just an increase in burial in that cemetery? If the increase is real, are the causes truly related to sanitation problems? Here we would need death certificates, records or some form of additional information beyond that available in the cemetery. As mentioned above, tombstones are notoriously silent about the cause of death unless something rather spectacular, unusual, or perhaps fitting happened to the victim.

At this point, it is not unreasonable to ask, why bother? I assume that most historians and sociologists would in fact avoid becoming ensnared in a situation with such dangerously loose data. Anthropologists, however, are more likely to rush right in, chastising the historian for his or her unending search for the perfect number, and the sociologist, for the infinite number. The anthropologist's apparent lack of caution in pursuing answers in the face of imperfect data can probably be explained in terms of a preference for anthropological populations, as discussed above. Furthermore, anthropology has a long and quite respectable history of dealing with the human fossil record.

In this pursuit, anthropologists make rather grand inferences on the basis of very little data. While the inferences change with the data, the profession shows no sign of quitting this affair with fossils; to quit asking questions and suggesting answers is unthinkable to most anthropologists interested in human evolution. It is this background which explains our willingness to attempt historical reconstruction with less than perfect data.

All of this is not to say that anthropologists are blissfully ignorant of the limitations of some of our data bases. On the contrary, some studies are ideal for the investigation of the nature of anthropological data itself. In a science which, because of the nature of its interest with the distant past, finds itself plagued with incomplete information, it is only natural to be interested in the quality of our data as well. The essential questions are, How representative are the data? How closely do they match whatever event was occurring in the past? In the case of tombstones, there are many areas where the data may be unrepresentative. How likely is it that all members of a society--say, Waterford in 1852--were equally likely to (1) die in that year, (2) be interred in the rural cemetery, (3) have a carved stone mark their graves, (4) have minimal biographical information recorded on the stone, (5) have the stone and carving of sufficient quality to withstand weathering for 133 years, and (6) have the stone escape vandalism?

This concern with data brings us back to the first of the earlier posed two questions, How representative are cemetery data of the population in question? The answer, as might be expected, depends on the cemetery, which in turn bears a relationship with the community. Some cemeteries are much more likely to represent accurately the mortality experienced by the population than are others. The establishment of rural, public cemeteries in the mid-nineteenth century would increase representativeness to the extent that people were less likely to be buried in private cemeteries, where they might avoid detection by historic demographers. Cemeteries in communities which were less affected by migration are likely to be more representative than those of communities in a state of flux. The economic conditions bear directly on the chance of preservation of mortality data: as poverty increases, the likelihood that a family will opt for the expense of a durable tombstone decreases.

Although such variables have certainly had an effect on the representativeness of cemetery data, it is difficult to quantify the actual loss of data. In choosing the Waterford Rural Cemetery, we were quite unknowingly presented with an opportunity to determine with some accuracy the scope of data loss of an important type, from vandalism and natural destruction. It was instantly apparent that there were more people interred in the Waterford Rural Cemetery than stones commemorating them. Large open spaces separate the stones in many places, and only the bases of stones remain standing in others. Many of the older stones are still standing, but time and the elements have erased all information from their faces. This all represents data loss, and it is important to know to what extent these lost data are representative of the data which can still be found in the cemetery.

To determine that which no longer exists is no simple task, and it was only good fortune which made it possible in the case of the Waterford data. With the help of my students, over the course of two summers, every tombstone marking a death prior to 1880 was recorded. This same task was undertaken, unbeknownst to me, in 1876 and 1877 by Cornelius Durkee and his associates. The Waterford cemetery was just one of many visited and recorded by Durkee and his friends. In the late 1870s, all of the inscriptions extant in all of the major cemeteries in Saratoga County were recorded by Durkee. These data, when combined with ours, allowed us to determine just how much data (and of what kind) were lost in a period of 100 years.

Summarizing the results of this comparison, the data most frequently lost were those relating to infants and children. By breaking down the inscriptions into various subdivisions, including age, sex, decade of interment, and type of stone, it was possible to identify unusually high or low frequencies of disparity. That children are the subgroup most likely to be underrepresented in comtemporary data is both interesting and relevant. Anthropologists are interested in reconstructing the demographic profiles of prehistoric as well as historic populations, and the issue of infant and child under-enumeration is a recurrent one. In the Waterford study, we can document the quantity of under-enumeration that occurred in just 100 years. We know the causes of this data loss are ultimately cultural. Because of their age, children were given smaller, less permanent markers, which in turn do not withstand time and vandalism as well as the larger, more expensively carved stones of adults. In essence, data on children have been filtered out of the cemetery by a combination of cultural and natural factors. A cultural filter also operates to dilute the data retrieved by archaeologists from prehistoric cemeteries, with the results being essentially the same: children are under-represented because they do not enjoy the same status as adults. They are treated differently in death, as in life.

Another interesting result of the comparison of the two data sets is that the loss of information is not simply a function of time. It is not true that we lose more data as we go back further in time; most of the missing data is from the 1860s and 1870s. It was at about this time that marble began to replace the more durable stones in cemeteries, and the subsequent weathering, abetted by acid rain, accounts for much of the data loss. Vandalism is the other major factor. We unearthed several stones which were totally buried under 6 or more inches of soil, noted the bases of many stones without bodies, and believe that many stones are gone altogether. The magnitude of the loss is staggering. Cornelius Durkee recorded information on 784 individuals for whom we could find none, amounting to 37 per cent of all the stones extant in 1877.

The Waterford Rural Cemetery may be somewhat unique in the magnitude of data loss, but we cannot verify this because we lack sufficient comparative studies. One of my more diligent students, Janet Snyder, recorded all of the inscriptions in the Vischer Ferry cemetery, which was also visited by Durkee in the 1870s. In the Vischer Ferry cemetery, 36 individuals have become lost, representing 16 per cent of the total. Vandalism is again the most likely explanation for the losses. As for the difference in magnitude when compared with the data loss from Waterford, this is most likely due to differences in the accessibility of the cemeteries and the socio-cultural stability of Vischer Ferry as compared to Waterford.

The two studies outlined above are only samples of what can be done with cemetery data. I would like to end this essay with a few additional ideas, and perhaps they can generate more. From a professional standpoint, it is clear to me that cemetery data will never replace written documents as basic data for historic demography. Cemetery inscriptions can be an important adjunct to research in historic demography and perhaps can be invaluable in family reconstitution, but they are not as complete as written records, in all but the most unusual situations. Cemetery data have great heuristic value, however, and should be utilized more frequently for those purposes. As mentioned earlier, mortuary rituals establish or mirror the social persona of the deceased on an individual level, and reflect the status differential within a society on a higher level. Our historic cemeteries are gold mines of information on social and economic stratification. The size, shape, and quality of the stones differ, but do these differences correlate with aspects of class? Some cemeteries have family plots, but does plot size or location correlate with other indicators of status? These family plots, incidentally, are excellent for genealogical exercises. Do gender differences appear in the cemetery, and if so, how? Most of us are aware of changes in the ethnic makeup of communities through time, but can these changes be documented in the cemetery?

Are any of these differences evident among as well as within cemeteries?

Essentially, the questions of interest to me pertain to comparisons: In what ways do people differ, and what explanations do we have for these differences? This essential question brings me back to my starting point in defining what it is that anthropologists find interesting. Despite its limitations, the cemetery offers a vast fund of information relevant to questions about differences. In the cemetery, these questions can be pursued at one's own pace, without fear of intruding on the lives of others, and in an environment which, if nothing else, is conducive to contemplation.

Richard Wilkinson, associate professor at SUNY Albany, is a biological anthropologist whose specializations include the analysis of prehistoric biological relationships and historic demography. He received his B.A., M.A., and Ph.D. degrees from the University of Michigan (1963, 1966, and 1970, respectively). He is the author of a book and several articles dealing with the analysis of human skeletal material from prehistoric sites in North America and Mexico. In the area of historic demography, Wilkinson has conducted field schools in the Albany area, resulting in the collection of cemetery data.

Further Readings

Bendana, Effie. *Death Customs: An Analytical Study of Burial Rites.* New York: Alfred A. Knopf, 1930.

Huntington, Richard. *Celebrations of Death: An Anthropology of Mortuary Rituals.* New York: Cambridge University Press, 1979.

O'Shea, John M. *Mortuary Variability: An Archaeological Investigation.* Orlando, Florida: Academic Press, 1984.

Rosenblah, Paul C. *Grief and Mourning in Cross-Cultural Perspective.* New Haven, Connecticut: HRAF Press, 1976.

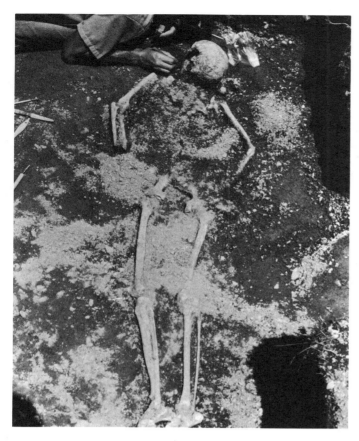

Excavating skeletal bones, an incomplete artifact.

GEORGE W. CALDWELL

Engineer

U.S. Navy

died July 3, 1893

Æ. 63 Yrs

Restoring lettering to stones.

225

Further Word on Albany

A great number of books in the New York State Library relate to the topics in this volume. Using the subject--keyword search capability of the New York State Library computerized catalog, a list of relevant publications was generated. The results were created by taking a general topic such as ART and then related topic words under which to search. Each specific topic word was linked to the word Albany. For example, the New York State Library had 1,177 entries about Indians of North America but none when linked with Albany, 370 entries on Shakers but only one when linked with Albany, 216 on baseball but none when linked with Albany. Linking art with Albany, though, yielded 18 listings.

The search strategy looks like this:

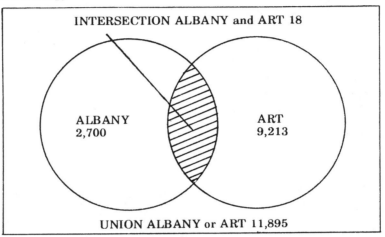

The resulting search is available at no charge from the Rockefeller Institute. It includes 255 listings in 34 topical areas. They include:

TOPIC	NUMBER OF LISTINGS
<u>ART</u>	
ALBANY--ART	5
ALBANY--PORTRAITS	4
HUDSON RIVER SCHOOL	8
TIFFANY WINDOWS	1
<u>DESCRIPTION AND HOUSING</u>	
ALBANY--ARCHITECTURE	5
ALBANY BUILDINGS	19
ALBANY--DESCRIPTION	31
ALBANY--DWELLINGS	1
ALBANY--HOUSING	6
<u>BUSINESS</u>	
ALBANY--BUSINESS AND COMMERCE	12
ALBANY--ECONOMIC CONDITIONS	2
ALBANY--INDUSTRY	4

We are indebted to Bill DeAlleaume and Robert Vines of the New York State Library for their help with this search.

For a free printout of this list, write:
Albany Search
Publications Department
Rockefeller Institute of Government
411 State Street
Albany, New York 12203

Judith Wing was raised in Albany and is a librarian at SUNY, Albany. She majored in history at Russell Sage College and has long been interested in the history of the Albany area. She was active in producing the historical documents on the charter of Albany County and has worked on other local history projects.